GLOBAL COSMOPOLITANS

INSEAD Business Press Series

Roland Berger, Soumitra Dutta, Tobias Raffel & Geoffrey Samuels
INNOVATING AT THE TOP
How Global CEOs Drive Innovation for Growth and Profit

J. Stewart Black & Allen J. Morrison
SUNSET IN THE LAND OF THE RISING SUN
Why Japanese Multinational Corporations Will Struggle in the Global Future

Linda Brimm
GLOBAL COSMOPOLITANS
The Creative Edge of Difference

J. Frank Brown
THE GLOBAL BUSINESS LEADER
Practical Advice for Success in a Transcultural Marketplace

Lourdes Casanova
GLOBAL LATINAS
Latin America's Emerging Multinationals

David Fubini, Colin Price & Maurizio Zollo
MERGERS
Leadership, Performance and Corporate Health

Manfred Kets de Vries, Konstantin Korotov & Elizabeth Florent Treacy
COACH AND COUCH
The Psychology of Making Better Leaders

Manfred Kets de Vries
SEX, MONEY, HAPPINESS & DEATH
The Quest for Authenticity

Michael McGannon & Juliette McGannon
THE BUSINESS LEADER'S HEALTH MANUAL
Tips and Strategies for Getting to the Top and Staying There

Renato J. Orsato
SUSTAINABILITY STRATEGIES
When Does It Pay to Be Green?

James Teboul
SERVICE IS FRONT STAGE
Positioning Services for Value Advantage

Jean-Claude Thoenig & Charles Waldman
THE MARKING ENTERPRISE
Business Success and Societal Embedding

Rolando Tomasini & Luk Van Wassenhove
HUMANITARIAN LOGISTICS

GLOBAL COSMOPOLITANS

The Creative Edge of Difference

Linda Brimm

Professor Emeritus of Organizational Behavior, INSEAD, France

palgrave
macmillan

First published 2010 by
PALGRAVE MACMILLAN

Palgrave Macmillan in the UK is an imprint of Macmillan Publishers Limited,
registered in England, company number 785998, of Houndmills, Basingstoke,
Hampshire RG21 6XS.

Palgrave Macmillan in the US is a division of St Martin's Press LLC,
175 Fifth Avenue, New York, NY 10010.

Palgrave Macmillan is the global academic imprint of the above companies
and has companies and representatives throughout the world.

Palgrave® and Macmillan® are registered trademarks in the United States,
the United Kingdom, Europe and other countries.

ISBN: 978–0–230–23078–1

This book is printed on paper suitable for recycling and made from fully
managed and sustained forest sources. Logging, pulping and manufacturing
processes are expected to conform to the environmental regulations of the
country of origin.

A catalogue record for this book is available from the British Library.

A catalog record for this book is available from the Library of Congress.

10 9 8 7 6 5 4 3 2
19 18 17 16 15 14 13 12 11

Printed and bound in the United States of America

CONTENTS

CONTENTS

PREFACE

THE PATHWAY TO MY LIFE'S WORK

Benjamin grew up in France. But both his parents are American, so he considered himself a typical American kid.

To prove the point, he learned everything he could about the sport that's called the Great American Pastime: baseball.

He was determined to know every rule, every statistic, every player. He was a baseball expert, a walking baseball trivia machine.

At age eight, he went to summer camp in the United States. The children put together a baseball game and asked him to play.

At first, he said no. But the children persuaded the baseball expert to join them on the playing field.

When Benjamin's turn came to hit the ball, he stood at the plate in the traditional position with the bat over his shoulder. And then the first pitch came in his direction.

"Swing!" the crowd shouted. "Hit the ball!"

He hit the ball hard, and it was sailing, heading for a home run. But Benjamin just stood there.

He didn't know what to do. People were cheering and yelling "Run," but he knew that he did not know what to do.

Because he'd learned everything there was to know about baseball except the one thing an American kid would know: how to play.

Benjamin is my son.

When I left Cambridge, Massachusetts, in 1973 for a six-month adventure in the south of France, I never imagined where this decision would take me. Nor did I envision how that decision would affect my identity. Leaving the United States would become a critical moment, a major turning point in my life.

My clinical and academic interest in understanding the impact of living internationally has its roots in my personal journey. Living and working outside the United States, along with my husband and children, and traveling to many corners of the world for work and study have given me the opportunity to develop a global perspective and to observe and interact with other people traveling a similar road.

Although my life story, what I call in this book a personal narrative, is rooted in the stories I heard from and about my immigrant grandparents, the pieces of my life puzzle since 1973 have allowed me to experience and observe what it means to become what I have called in this book a Global Cosmopolitan.

My personal narrative includes many opportunities for confronting the challenges and reaping the benefits of international mobility. The story begins in the United States, where I remained through university and my initial professional activities. Later chapters of my story include life in a farming village in the south of France; studying, counseling and consulting in Jerusalem; then continued studying, teaching and working in Fontainebleau and Paris. To this has been added two months a year working in Singapore, as well as creating a summer home in Wellfleet, Massachusetts, and innumerable travels internationally for work and leisure.

The invisibility of aspects of my journey has been one of the key motivators for my research. The external facts give one story, while my internal journey has been a relatively silent story. It is the subtle, but important, differences between the two that I would like to address in this book. Along with the wonderful experiences, which I never could have imagined as a child, I have accumulated painful moments of feeling alone and misunderstood by the people I know from my different worlds.

As a clinical psychologist, I have been trained to be aware of my own experience and life perspective and its impact on my relationships; this awareness has become an integral part of my life. As a professor and as a researcher, I try to understand what lessons one can learn from the stories that my students tell about their lives, as well as to reflect upon how my evolving point of view and analysis change the way I listen and learn.

This book is a mixture of the stories, ideas and pedagogical approaches that have helped me understand, teach and work with people I call Global Cosmopolitans. It is my goal to help Global Cosmopolitans verbalize their personal stories, their identities, and contribute to bringing the silence of the uniqueness that they experience into a satisfying dialogue with themselves and others.

However, my interest is broader. Global Cosmopolitans are a cutting-edge population with a great deal to contribute to the global landscape and our understanding of it. The challenges they face, the unique perspectives they develop and the skills they learn can be particularly important in a world that is becoming increasingly global. My second goal is to give voice to the internal, silent story of Global Cosmopolitans, so that the people who live and work with them understand the richness of their conflicts, their challenges and, most importantly, their capabilities.

An increasing number of people resonate with an identity as a Global Cosmopolitan. The starting points are almost as varied as the people are. Some followed the global pathway as a result of their parents' mixed backgrounds and lifestyle choices, while others either initiated a global lifestyle or are now considering the pathway for themselves or their children.

The lack of shared memory or shared culture can leave a Global Cosmopolitan feeling very alone in reconstructing the intricacies of memory that carry the threads of identity. There is not one culture or one language that adequately clarifies or defines the identity of people who carry different pieces of the world inside them.

On the plus side, global mobility provides ample opportunities for experimentation and reinvention. But over time, questions often arise about identity. Who am I really? How can I describe who I am? What constant sides of my personality can I describe, and what is still in the process of change or evolution? Which pieces of my identity are core to my identity and travel everywhere with me, and which pieces appear only as situations and relationships and pull me forward?

Stories are core to telling the tale of Global Cosmopolitans and revealing their invisibility. The anecdotes in this book are based on life stories written by Global Cosmopolitans using a technique called the personal narrative. These stories were collected in classes, interviews and therapeutic contexts where individuals had the opportunity to write or recount their life stories and, in doing so, to give shape to their identities. The insights they gain allow them to articulate to themselves and others the value of their challenging yet fascinating journey. Almost everyone who appears in these pages is real, the quotes often word for word from personal narratives they prepared in my class or from interviews. But to maintain privacy, I have often changed names and either obscured or changed details.

This book looks at identities as personal constructions that are made up of the way we put together our partial identities into a single personal story or narrative. Along one's developmental road, situations and relationships might require different identities or roles; at certain times people need to know that I am a professor at INSEAD or that I am a clinical psychologist, while in other situations I might decide to share that I worked as a ceramicist in the south of France. I might talk about the challenges of being a working mother raising children in different countries. I might feel more like an American in the United States and more like a Global Cosmopolitan in Paris or in Singapore.

At the same time, I need to know the story that I carry with me, the core that then allows me to share parts of who I am with others. Learning to become aware of the story and learning to articulate it are significant skills that will be discussed in this book.

The Global Cosmopolitan Workbook at the end of the book is designed to help readers understand and develop their own life stories. Although designed for Global Cosmopolitans, the workbook can be equally useful to all individuals who wish to recognize key elements of their own unique identities and then use this understanding to strengthen important work and personal relationships.

Enjoy the journey.

Linda Brimm
Paris, France

ACKNOWLEDGMENTS

The road to writing this book, much like the journey of the Global Cosmopolitans, has been populated with a number of fellow travelers who have provided support and guidance along the way. Most significant are the Global Cosmopolitans whose stories inspired me and are the basis of this book. Their willingness to share these stories has allowed me to understand and communicate their unique experience.

INSEAD has provided an exceptional context to study Global Cosmopolitans. It draws a unique population of individuals with life experiences that deny description in a single nationality or a summary identity. Throughout my teaching experience at INSEAD on our campuses in Fontainebleau, France or Singapore, I have learned through the stories of students, faculty, staff and alumni. The idea of the Global Cosmopolitan emerged from that learning opportunity. I especially want to thank each and every student who has written their life story in my course, Career Development and Self-Assessment, over the past thirty years. This has provided an exceptional vantage point to learn about how this unique group of people see their identity developing over time.

While many of the stories cited in this book have been altered to respect individual privacy, others could not be adequately disguised without losing their essential quality. Thanks to all of you for letting me share your stories in one form or another to communicate your special experience. I hope that the journey this book has taken has afforded you another opportunity for furthering your insight and development.

In my complementary role as a clinical psychologist, I have learned extensively from my clients as they weave together and give meaning to their life stories. My colleagues from the International Counseling Service and the Relational Theory Group, as well as the many peer supervision groups in which I have participated over the years, have helped me to learn from my clinical experience and to improve my ability in helping clients. While there are many colleagues that have contributed to my learning along the way, special thanks go to Judith Fleiss and Jane Plimsoll, who have been so supportive during the actual writing of this book.

My academic sabbaticals have been significant in the development and framing of the ideas in this book. Many of my views that challenged accepted frameworks in psychology found support and elaboration in a sabbatical with the late Jean Baker Miller and her colleagues at the Stone Center, Wellesley College. A particular thank-you to Jean and Judy Jordan, who contributed to the development of my ideas about relational psychology.

My research group at Wellesley provided a basis for looking at both the narrative study of lives and relational theory. Working with Mei-Mei Ellerman, Nancer Ballard, Birute Regine, Janie Ward, Beth Casey and Karma Kitja, I started to identify the importance of the topic that became Global Cosmopolitans, as well as to validate the use of a narrative approach to understand this phenomenon.

My sabbatical at the Women's Studies Research Center at Brandeis University helped me clarify and solidify this interest. The director and founder, Shulamit Reinharz, has created a research environment for and about women which provided an opportunity for me to question and nourish my voice as a writer. A special thanks to each and every scholar I had an opportunity to work with. My memoir group was particularly valuable in helping me understand the power of storytelling and learn how to tell the story of these Global Cosmopolitans.

During both sabbaticals, Mary Harvey, cofounder of the Victims of Violence Center at Cambridge City Hospital, provided the opportunity to work with her team and her doctoral program on narrative analysis. This gave me a chance to work with Elliot Mishler as well as other scholars studying the use of narrative analysis to understand the impact of trauma or significant life events over time.

My discussions with Catherine Reissman about the narrative study of lives started in Cambridge and continued on Cape Cod, as well as when our life paths crossed in Paris or London. Ed Schein's interest and gentle encouragement came in the form of asking about the book and through his genuine curiosity about the topic.

The supportive and stimulating context of the American women's group that I helped initiate in Paris has been an on-going source of reflection on the experience of living and working across cultures.

When I turned to writing, my friends and colleagues came forward offering to help, to read my work, to give me feedback or to give my life some balance. I hope that I have communicated, at least to some extent, the value I attribute to your encouragement and friendship.

Family support has been the foundation of my work. My children, Tracy and Benjamin, have been my teachers throughout their lives. They have challenged my theories and nourished my curiosity. The have frameworks of this book developed as they guided me through their experience of the challenges and benefits of being Global Cosmopolitans.

There will never be enough room for me to thank Michael Brimm. With my first draft in hand, I asked Michael for feedback, knowing he was my strongest supporter but would also be my most honest critic. His help was invaluable. He pushed me to develop my ideas when necessary and drop the unnecessary or irrelevant pieces. He forced me to be articulate and to keep reviewing, even when I was ready to move on.

Barb Cornell deserves a very special thanks for her writing and editing assistance. She paced me. "I need it next week, Linda" would drive me crazy but drive me forward. My appreciation for her writing guidance and editing runs very deep.

My editors and publisher at Palgrave Macmillan, first Stephen Rutt and then Eleanor Davey-Corrigan, have allowed this to pass from a personal reflection to a published work. Their help and confidence have been invaluable.

While I take great satisfaction in having finished this volume, I also take full credit for any errors in the text. Completing the book has been a learning opportunity in itself as I recognize the vast network of support that has helped me to achieve this milestone in my own personal journey. But in recognizing this, I apologize to any of the array of people that helped but have not been sufficiently recognized in these acknowledgments.

OUTLINE

Part I, Global Cosmopolitans: Meeting the Masters of Complexity, introduces the Global Cosmopolitan phenomenon and its value to the business world.

Chapter 1, Introducing Global Cosmopolitans, presents global leaders and discusses the importance of understanding Global Cosmopolitans in a new and deeper way.

Chapter 2, Inside the New Global Cosmopolitan Generation, introduces members of the emerging Global Cosmopolitan generation. It describes how Global Cosmopolitans have different starting points for their journeys and provides examples of the complexities they face.

Chapter 3, Learning from a Global Life: Developing the Creative Edge of Difference, introduces a set of crucial strengths that are often overlooked or not associated with international mobility.

Part II, The Invisible Journey: The Roots of Strength and Resilience, looks at how Global Cosmopolitans develop their valuable strengths through the complex challenges they face.

Chapter 4, Life Challenges and the Road to Identity, describes a set of challenges that Global Cosmopolitans frequently encounter because of the constant change and uncommon complexity of internationally mobile lives.

Chapter 5, Relationship Challenges: Invisible Rules, Silent Voices, describes how the past is prologue to the present and the future and how the past can be a source of tangled knots or fresh insights. It also examines relationship challenges that emerge from the broader cultural and social context of Global Cosmopolitans and describes how family and cultural stories influence the Global Cosmopolitan identity.

Chapter 6, Relationship Challenges: Connection and Disconnection, focuses on relational challenges in the context of work and personal life.

Part III, The Invisible Journey: New Pathways to Growth, looks at why challenges don't necessarily lead to creativity and positive change and provides insights about removing these obstacles.

Chapter 7, Paradoxical Needs: Finding the Roots of Challenges, explores what I call "paradoxical needs," internal forces that underlie Global Cosmopolitan challenges.

Chapter 8, Two-Edged Swords of Mobility: When Strengths Create New Challenges, looks at how Global Cosmopolitan strengths can have downsides, what I call "two-edged swords of mobility."

Part IV, Moving Forward: Bringing the Invisible Journey out of the Dark, explores how Global Cosmopolitans can give new value to their international experiences when they step back and look at their lives from a new perspective.

Chapter 9, Moving Forward: A Portrait of Two Crucial Decades, assembles the pieces of the internal portrait of Global Cosmopolitans as they consider how to move forward at different stages in their lives.

Chapter 10, Global Cosmopolitans: Unlocking the Power of Stories, describes how the lessons presented in this book can be applied to all Global Cosmopolitans to help them reach their full potential. The chapter addresses not just Global Cosmopolitans themselves but also people in the workplace, family and friends. This chapter ends with The Seven C's of Change and Development.

The Global Cosmopolitan Workbook is for readers who want to relate their own lives to the Global Cosmopolitan stories described in this book. It provides the tools for readers to bring their silent, unconscious inner journey to a conscious level.

PART I

GLOBAL COSMOPOLITANS: MEETING THE MASTERS OF COMPLEXITY

"My parents played a primary role of raising my siblings and me with the perspective that we are world citizens. Specifically, this meant that we were taught to be aware of the world, to be curious about the world and to be considerate of the world. My parents exemplified the ideal of connectedness to the world by giving us exposure to international causes but also by honoring our identification with the Arab world."

1

INTRODUCING GLOBAL COSMOPOLITANS

To see Zoran the successful global businessman is to know nothing of the life that made him that way. He is married with two healthy daughters who have never heard gunshots and explosions outside their windows.

The consulting firm he started in South Africa is more than 5,000 miles from Sarajevo, where he won many mathematics prizes as a boy. In between, his life has taken him to the United States to study and work, and to France for his graduate business degree.

However, the inner journey he took to travel that distance is the key to understanding the entrepreneur that Zoran has become. This, according to Zoran, is where his business background began:

I can trace my attitudes towards responsibility and failure to my experience during the Bosnian war.

I was running the household, since my parents and older brother were absent most of the time, and I took care of my younger sister and wounded grandfather. I never thought of responsibility as being a burden for me. It was simply a reflection of being fair and just to those who loved me and cared for me my whole life. If my parents and older brother were pulling their weight in the war, then I had to pull mine.

During the war, I developed a fatalistic approach to life and the attitude that worrying doesn't help. I learned not to worry about my parents and brother not returning every time I heard a grenade or a sniper shot. I would strive to do the best I could on the things I can change, and I did not worry about what actually happened. I realized that I could control my intentions and actions, but not the results. The consequence was that I learned not to fear the failure.

Zoran has carefully set aside enough money to protect his family from any potential business setbacks.

My attitude towards failure is a helpful one for entrepreneurial undertakings. While I realize that the chances of success are small, drawing on my war experience, I will worry about my intentions and actions but not the consequences.

Zoran has lived through a war but does not see himself as a war refugee. He can return to Sarajevo, and he might someday, but no nation, city or place is central to his identity. Instead, Zoran identifies himself as part of an emerging elite global workforce.

I call them Global Cosmopolitans.

They are a talented population of highly educated, multilingual people that have lived, worked and studied for extensive periods in different cultures. While their international identities have diverse starting points and experiences, their views of the world and themselves are profoundly affected by both the realities of living in different cultures and their manner of coping with the challenges that emerge.

Zoran believes that the combination of challenges in his youth and opportunities of living and studying internationally has given him the competence he needs to accomplish his goals. He knows how to experiment with new ideas and learn about new avenues for growth. He feels prepared for the potential risks associated with starting his own business. He knows that one of the keys to his success has been the people who know him and believe in him. They have given him the chance to explore new entrepreneurial possibilities. From family to professors to colleagues in consulting, he has found opportunities to stretch his mind and his potential.

Diversity and change, two of the watchwords of the modern world, are a fact of life for Global Cosmopolitans. They know what it is like to come to a new country, a new school or a new job and feel that sudden loss of identity. They become experts at re-creating themselves in light of new cultural conventions and relationships. They know how to adapt, to reinvent and to bring about change.

Most people develop a filter throughout their lives through which to understand the world around them. Global Cosmopolitans develop a prism, a multifaceted view forged by their experiences with conflict, alternate belief systems and new ways of understanding and behaving around people very different from themselves. Their view *is* a worldview with a complexity so deep that even they can have trouble articulating it.

This book is designed to help readers understand this complex, fastgrowing and influential group. Full of stories from around the world, the chapters in the book explain how Global Cosmopolitans develop the skills and knowledge that make them so effective. It highlights the breadth and depth of their inner complexity. It provides a concrete way to uncover the hidden value of the Global Cosmopolitan experience so that organizations, families, friends and Global Cosmopolitans themselves can make the most of it.

Understanding Global Cosmopolitans requires looking beyond the résumé that typically serves to define an individual's worth and identity. The missing variable in the equation is paying careful attention to their silent, inner journey, to the strengths they have developed because of the challenges they have confronted over time.

GLOBAL COSMOPOLITANS MAKING A DIFFERENCE

Global Cosmopolitans are already making their mark as global business and political leaders, and their growing numbers suggest they will increase in power and influence. Just two examples are Carlos Ghosn, the Brazilian, French, Lebanese business executive who revived Japan's Nissan Motor Co. Ltd., and U.S. President Barack Obama, an advocate of political change whose biracial, multicultural background intrigued, confounded, sometimes even frightened the U.S. electorate in the 2008 presidential race. They demonstrate the growing importance of Global Cosmopolitans not just in business but also throughout public life.[1]

In the world of business, Ghosn is the classic Global Cosmopolitan.[1] He is the Co-Chairman, President, Financial Director and Chief Executive Officer of Renault, Nissan Motor Co. Ltd. His French citizenship doesn't begin to describe the complexity of his international background. Ghosn speaks four languages fluently and, not surprisingly given his approach to working internationally, has been learning Japanese.

Ghosn's parents are Lebanese, but he was born in Brazil, where his father worked for an airline. When he was six, he and his mother returned to live in Lebanon, where he continued his education. He then went to Paris for his engineering degrees. After working in France, he returned to Brazil to work for Michelin and went to the United States for seven years to run the company's North American operation. From there, he returned to France to work for the troubled Renault. His accomplishments in turning around the French carmaker led to the top job at Nissan. He became the first non-Japanese person to hold the company's symbolic title President and gained such national popularity that he starred in a graphic novel.

Ghosn has developed a trademark style. He brings together teams of workers from different parts of the company and from different countries.

In other words, he allows his workers to share the experience he developed growing up in the complex world of a Global Cosmopolitan. "I've always felt different," says Ghosn. "Because you are different, you try to integrate, and that pushes you to understand the environment in which you find yourself. That tends to develop one's ability to listen, to observe, to compare: qualities that are very useful in managing."

If Ghosn is a visible example of a Global Cosmopolitan, then the other famous example illustrates the opposite: how Global Cosmopolitans can be hidden in plain sight. At first glance, President Obama's international experience pales compared with Ghosn's.[2] The future president was only two years old when his Kenyan father left. He spent just four years as a child in Indonesia and has not lived outside the United States since age ten. As a U.S. Senator, he did serve on the Foreign Relations Committee, but Obama did not follow an international career path. In fact, he spent a number of years in jobs where foreign experience had no direct relation to his work at all. In many Americans' eyes, he says, he was "a black man with a funny name."

Just as Ghosn's French citizenship doesn't explain his cultural complexity, Obama's seemingly limited exposure to foreign living masks how much of a Global Cosmopolitan he is. For starters, Obama's parents were not just black and white. They met at the University of Hawaii, taking a class no typical American or Kenyan would use: a Russian language course. Obama's Kenyan grandfather, the first person in his community to wear Western clothes, had worked for white colonialists in Kenya and Tanganyika and spent three years in World War II traveling to Burma, Ceylon, Arabia and Europe as a cook to a British captain. The heart of Obama's autobiography, *Dreams from My Father*, describes his "personal, interior journey" to understand how these three generations of men struggled silently to re-create themselves as outsiders to their own cultures.

Obama's mother, who earned a PhD in anthropology, surrounded her half-Kenyan son with foreign influences, such as a children's book with creation stories from around the world. But it was when she broadened his world by moving him from Hawaii to Indonesia that Obama's life took a dazzlingly complex turn. At age six, Obama stepped off the plane in Djakarta and found himself in a land of rice fields and water buffalo, with a neighbor boy holding a dragonfly on the end of a string. His stepfather welcomed him with a pet ape. He quickly blended into the world's fifth most populous nation. "It had taken me less than six months to learn Indonesia's language, its customs, and its legends," he wrote. "The children of farmers, servants, and low-level bureaucrats had become my best friends." Yet as an outsider, Obama experienced the world differently than his playmates.

Obama and his mother arrived in Indonesia less than a year after a brutal suppression campaign following the coup that ousted Sukarno, the country's first president. His stepfather, like all foreign students, had been ordered home and sent with the army to New Guinea; Obama saw the scars on his stepfather's legs from digging out leeches with a hot knife. As a boy, Obama had to reconcile fundamental contradictions, like the "needlepoint virtues" preached by his mother—honesty, straight talk, fairness, independent judgment—with the "undisguised, indiscriminate, naked" power he saw in his everyday life. He saw beggars with their "gallery of ills," some missing limbs or pulling their broken bodies around on carts. His mother told him to help the poor; his stepfather told him to look out for himself so that he wouldn't end up being like them. Then one day, looking through pictures in *Life* magazine, the nine-year-old Obama discovered an article about black Americans who had disfigured themselves trying to whiten their skin. With a knot in his stomach, this child of an American and a Kenyan crossed yet another border, this time into the complex black-and-white worlds he had inside himself.

Given Obama's historic role as America's first black president, his life story is rightly seen through the prism of race. It is impossible to determine scientifically how Obama might be different if he had simply been a smart, involved, politically talented biracial American with no foreign ties. However, Obama does have foreign ties, and they have given him a complex global identity that helped him win the 2009 Nobel Peace Prize.[3] In awarding the prize, the Norwegian Nobel Committee noted: "His diplomacy is founded in the concept that those who are to lead the world must do so on the basis of values and attitudes that are shared by the majority of the world's population."

Both Obama and Ghosn illustrate the insight that comes from being a Global Cosmopolitan. Ghosn's trademark leadership style emphasizes the value of difference. Obama's trademark "Yes We Can" style reflects the single greatest trait that Global Cosmopolitans have in common: the capacity for re-creation, reinvention and change. Only history can ultimately judge the value of both men's leadership decisions, but the value of their leadership approach is already clear. With change and diversity at the center of today's management agenda, the time has come to understand the growing phenomenon of Global Cosmopolitans.

Global Cosmopolitans are an elite talent pool that businesses and governments are using to operate in every corner of the world. In addition, as Global Cosmopolitans assume greater leadership power, they build management teams that include other Global Cosmopolitans. Carlos Ghosn, for example, urges managers to "love the country and love the culture... you are in... and make sure that all the people you are transferring with you are of the same opinion." The same tendency is true of Barack Obama. Obama's inner circle includes White House advisor Valerie Jarrett, who was born in Iran and lived in England; Treasury Secretary Timothy Geithner, who grew up in India, Thailand and Zimbabwe; and National Security Advisor General James Jones, who grew up in Paris.[4]

The emerging generation of Global Cosmopolitans also want to make a difference in the business and social spheres, at home and across the world. This book will present their voices and demonstrate how their international mobility has provided learning opportunities that have given them key skills for success. They have developed these capacities through the maze of complex challenges that they have encountered by crossing cultures.

MAXIMIZING VALUE: THE NEED FOR BETTER DIALOGUE

Many organizations have made it clear that they need people who have the languages and cultural know-how to move effortlessly across borders. Ambitious people, eager for adventure, responsibility and advancement, have responded in record numbers. The trend toward borderless business management is unstoppable as highly trained people gravitate toward the best job opportunities around the world. Global Cosmopolitans have the potential for creating and leading this new generation of organizations. These individuals are not solely the creation or province of global business. Global Cosmopolitans inhabit communities and social organizations as well as acquiring vast personal networks during their lives. Medical teams, academic research projects and network organizations continue to develop worldwide. It is not unusual to hear groups referred to as doctors or reporters or donors without borders.

Nevertheless, there is massive work to be done to maximize the value that Global Cosmopolitans can contribute. Many organizations do not fully understand the assets they have created by investing in their global workforce. Global Cosmopolitans themselves feel that even the people who know them well too often undervalue the richness of their experience; what began as an experience to expand both horizons and opportunities can end up in frustration.

Thierry put it this way:

I have been working in Asia for the last five years. My friends and family have never understood how much I miss them. My work has given me a unique opportunity to learn and grow as a person and as a manager. I am ambivalent about returning to France. My friends miss me and want me back, but they never seem interested in what I have been doing in Asia or what I have learned. They want the old me to return. Looking for a position has been challenging, since the interviewers seem more interested in what I did in France rather than what I have done here. I have to help them understand the value of a global experience.

The gap appears in Toshi's experience as well:

I started getting bored and stressed at work in Japan. Also, I do not have much patience, and I saw a long hierarchical road ahead of me. I decided to work and study abroad, which I have loved. I have loved blending the different perspectives I have gained from living and working in different cultures. Now I would love to return to Japan. Although I am more mature and feel the responsibility of my wife and child and my parents, I am hesitant to go back to my company and my country. I have learned about different perspectives, perspectives that would allow me to add a fresh approach to the problems that I will encounter, but the situation is such that I will have to wait years before I am allowed to bring my ideas forward and count on having an impact. I still do not have the patience to wait.

Global Cosmopolitans like Toshi and Thierry see value in the universal perspective they have gained on their international pathways. The inability of companies to retain international professionals suggests their frustration is not unique to Japan or France. Many Global Cosmopolitans who decide to return to what they consider their home country fear that their special talent will be wasted. They are often concerned about being given assignments that will not allow them to learn and develop as fast as they have in their foreign jobs. Returning from their international experience, Global Cosmopolitans feel the emphasis is often placed on what they have missed by being away from the head office rather than on what they have learned that can bring new light to challenging work issues.

Given the experience that Global Cosmopolitans have with difficult transitions, they often know how to find new rules and creative ways to put the pieces of a life together. They can think flexibly and creatively to find workable solutions for career decisions and family life which might not be obvious to people making critical career decisions for them. Yet they have trouble making their voices heard. The challenge they experience is getting recognition for what they have learned and being given opportunities commensurate with their level of experience and knowledge.

Even when Global Cosmopolitans are encouraged to tell employers the value of their international experience, the dialogue remains too narrow to open up appropriate possibilities. Human Resources, for example, might know that a Global Cosmopolitan speaks English and French but completely miss that he is also fluent in Spanish, is quite articulate in German and could easily start speaking Russian again. Commuting from New York might be an option for a woman managing a new venture in Argentina, but the company never learns about the extensive network of contacts she developed when she went to high school there. The solutions for new working designs require communicating the right information to find the best creative solutions. Unfortunately, important details are often lost because of the incredible complexity many Global Cosmopolitans face when they try to articulate how their experiences have shaped them.

Uncommon complexity is a common theme for Global Cosmopolitans. Concepts that are simple for most people can be troublesome for some Global Cosmopolitans to define. The notion of home is a classic example. While many people can take a home for granted, Global Cosmopolitans often struggle with the idea. "I wish that people would stop asking me about my definition of home. It makes me nervous. Right now, home is where my parents are; however, they now live in Taiwan, and I have never been there."

The emerging Global Cosmopolitan generation, for lifelong engaging work, need to fulfill their potential both locally and internationally as the need arises. Not only do they need to communicate their levels of experience and expertise but they also need to communicate clearly that the universal perspectives they gain internationally apply no matter where they live. Global organizations, for a full return on investment, need to refocus their view of this global generation. They need to acknowledge that the real strength of this emerging phenomenon exists not in its languages and passport stamps but in its willingness and capacity to confront complexity and change.

Since many important lessons of global mobility remain locked at an unconscious level, many Global Cosmopolitans do not understand the extent of their own capacities. Organizations and people who are not on the global voyage can be forgiven for not fully grasping what Global Cosmopolitans cannot articulate for themselves. But the importance of understanding their inner journey is illustrated by Carlos Ghosn's earlier observations about what he learned by being different. It is not his specific knowledge of languages and cultures but rather the insights he developed as an *outsider* to those cultures that gave him great strengths as a manager. His perspectives as a Global Cosmopolitan know no borders.

BENEFITING FROM THE CREATIVE EDGE OF DIFFERENCE

The Power of Stories

Both Barack Obama and Carlos Ghosn know how to tell their stories in an authentic, meaningful and timely way. They have been able to see the developmental links in their stories that allow them to let other people know who they are and what possibilities they see and to have a confidence that they can achieve their goals. Having the personal knowledge combined with the ability to use one's story to motivate and challenge others is often seen as a key ingredient for leadership.

The remainder of this book is devoted to the Obamas and Ghosns of tomorrow. It is about harnessing the collective voice of a new generation so that they, too, can fulfill their potential and motivate others to follow them. The tool they need is within their grasp, but they have to know where to look for it. They'll find it within themselves, in their own experiences and in the stories they create to give meaning and continuity to those experiences.

Stories are used throughout this book to emphasize and communicate the texture of Global Cosmopolitans' lives: their challenges, their aspirations and the lessons that they have learned. Many of the vignettes shared in these pages come from the personal narratives, or versions of identity stories, of Global Cosmopolitans. Whenever possible, the challenges and lessons of Global Cosmopolitans are animated through their stories in their own words.

The ability of Global Cosmopolitans to communicate who they are through the stories they recount reflects a process of empowerment. That process starts with personal self-awareness followed by the ability to articulate those personal discoveries to other people. The powerful dialogue that can result creates a context where Global Cosmopolitans and those around them can benefit from the creative edge of difference that international mobility typically provides.

The power of being able to tell a life story is obvious in the hands of master storytellers, which many global leaders are. But with practice and guidance, anyone can learn to tell his or her own story in an authentic and beneficial way.

A Narrative Perspective

The method I use in this book is rooted in the narrative mode of thought. From a narrative psychology perspective, people create a sense of self, a story that they tell to themselves and others that is the basis for their identity. The background of cultural texts they have lived in impacts on the story that they tell. A person tells many stories, and those stories change over time. Every person has a unique life story, even identical twins. The sharing of stories builds intimacy. Human beings use narratives because human events are often ambiguous. Stories are core to telling the tale of Global Cosmopolitans, whose border-crossing experiences add new layers of ambiguity. Stories, even in a limited form, can communicate the subtleties of who the Global Cosmopolitans are.

Their narratives, or stories, have helped Global Cosmopolitans to connect, make sense of and integrate events into meaningful sequences over time. This ability to connect the past, the present and future possibilities gives people the opportunity to make sense of their lives and see the connections that give events cohesion. While the circumstances of Global Cosmopolitans are rapidly changing, their narratives provide a key sense of continuity and relative predictability.

DECIDING TO TELL THE GLOBAL COSMOPOLITAN STORY

At INSEAD, whose graduate business school program attracts faculty and students from all over the world, my classroom has been a special opportunity to learn from stories. Students from Iran, Lebanon, Cambodia and China, for example, have vividly represented worldwide events in their stories since my earliest INSEAD experiences in the late 1970s and early 1980s, when I first started teaching there.

My experience as a clinical psychologist includes listening to the stories of people who have lived worldwide. Many of these people have shared stresses and traumas of being refugees. While working in Israel, I heard stories from people about the challenges of living through wars in their homelands.

However, the vast majority of the people that I have encountered have chosen to live in different countries, motivated by curiosity or adventure rather than by the impact of war or oppression. My interest in the challenges and opportunities of a mobile life expanded as I listened to and learned from my students, clients and the people surrounding me who had extensive experience with geographic mobility. The external story, their languages, their worldwide experience and their knowledge base were highly impressive, but what most captured my attention was their inner journey to find peace, meaning and stability in their lives. I started to understand the extent to which a new generation of highly mobile people was developing, a generation of young adults with extensive global experience ready to make a difference in the world.

Stories of Global Cosmopolitans

Over the past thirty years, I have asked students and clients to both write and share the stories of their lives as they remember them. They begin this process of personal exploration by writing a personal narrative, one version of a life story that gives the writer an opportunity to see the story that they tell about themselves. Since Global Cosmopolitans have so many transitions and discontinuities in their lives, this writing process is often a powerful step toward discovering the core of their life stories.

By writing their personal narratives, Global Cosmopolitans learn to compose their own life stories and use them as textbooks about themselves. Through the telling of their life stories, in a conscious manner, they finally pull different pieces of their identity story together. They can see their creation and derive meaning from it. By changing places, cultures, languages and relationships, Global Cosmopolitans have unique opportunities to define who they are in relation to others, to their context, to time and to their own personal history.

I, in turn, was able to put all these individual stories together to study the big picture. As a result, I have been able to identify the cluster of challenges that Global Cosmopolitans encounter: how they develop their abilities and what can stand in the way of developing them. These discoveries form the basis for this book.

Articulating the Lessons of a Global Life

Fulfilling the promise of the Global Cosmopolitan phenomenon requires unlocking the secrets of identity, the story we tell ourselves about who we are. Identities are formed using far different milestones from the ones listed on a CV. They are based on the lessons learned, helpful or otherwise, throughout the life journey. Helping people mine the lessons that they have learned at crucial turning points in life is one example. This reflection helps develop a much deeper understanding of who people are and who they want to become.

For example, someone who has never traveled internationally might cite going to the best engineering school as a crucial turning point. A Global Cosmopolitan might have gone to the best engineering school in another country, where the language of instruction, norms and expected academic preparation are completely different. Family and friends are far away and have no real understanding of what the experience is like. For both people, understanding the real lessons of that life event can be extremely valuable, but the Global Cosmopolitan's turning point has a complexity all its own. This book will focus on untangling the complexities of a global life, which can enrich one's experience at work.

Reading their stories and how they interpreted them helped me understand what makes Global Cosmopolitans unique, what might be contributing to their creative edge of difference.

LEARNING FROM STORIES

The stories in a personal narrative are not written to establish the truth of what really happened; rather they provide important truths about the perception of an experience and how it defined a person's identity at one point in time. Perceptions of life can and probably will change as people get older. With changing perceptions come changes in some of the meaning that Global Cosmopolitans give to life events.

The stories provide a portrait of Global Cosmopolitans, cut and pasted pieces that create a current vision of what a composite picture looks like. There is no statistical analysis to test the validity of their assumptions. But that's not the point. The nature of a personal narrative is to unlock just the possibility that ideas ring true, thereby creating an opening for a dialogue of greater understanding.

I have had a unique opportunity to gain deep insights into the emerging Global Cosmopolitan phenomenon. The frameworks that I provide in this book and the stories I use to illustrate them are intended to provoke new ways of thinking about this population. The majority of anecdotes reflect the stories of a cast of characters that are young professionals from all over the world, varying in age from mid-twenties to mid-forties. Many of them were students that I got to know while they were studying for their MBAs at INSEAD.

Not all the members of this new Global Cosmopolitan generation aspire to the leadership positions of Obama or Ghosn, but most of them want to make a difference and many of them are or will be in significant leadership roles.

THE IMPORTANCE OF SHARING STORIES

Being able to tell a life story in an appropriate and meaningful manner is a skill that can be developed. Sharing stories is a crucial piece of the learning process, not just for the storyteller but also for the listener, who can understand how meaning is pieced together. Global Cosmopolitans often feel different from the people around them, so sharing pieces of their life journey in a classroom setting reinforces the importance of being able to connect to people with similar experiences. It gives them an ability to be understood, to get feedback and to see how other people put together the personal pieces of their stories in very different manners. They develop a new perspective and sometimes see other ways to interpret or build on their own experiences.

For many people considering serious life decisions, the ability to tell an effective life story—what have I done and what would I like to do—has landed them interesting professional opportunities.

This book can demonstrate the potential for leadership and the creative edge of difference that Global Cosmopolitans might possess, but individual Global Cosmopolitans need to develop and share their stories if they are to reap the dividends that this book has to offer. Global Cosmopolitans need to have the combination of appropriate skill building from their life experience, self-awareness and the ability to communicate who they are. In other words, they need to tell their life story in an appropriate and meaningful way to find the right opportunities that use their unique skills. Readers can explore their own lives by reflecting on the descriptions and through the Global Cosmopolitan Workbook at the end of the book.

Through the work of my students, I have been granted a front row seat to hear the voice of the emerging Global Cosmopolitan generation. This book gives you an opportunity to hear them, too.

2

INSIDE THE NEW GLOBAL COSMOPOLITAN GENERATION

Gunter's problem is classic for Global Cosmopolitans, but he had no idea how common his experience was.

He had been studying and working away from Germany for more than ten years. He met his Spanish wife in London, where they both were consultants.

Now they both were working on MBAs in France and deciding whether to return to London when they were done.

But the decision about where to live left Gunter feeling guilty and confused.

Then he started swapping stories with other internationally mobile people like himself. He discovered not just a common bond but also a path toward a solution.

> *What a relief! I am not the only one here who is married to someone who cannot communicate with parents and other family members because of lack of a shared language or cultural background. I have been feeling so guilty. I see myself as a loving husband and loving son, yet getting everyone together is a nightmare. I have even thought about moving to Australia, which is far away from home for me and for my wife, so that the problem of getting everyone together will not arise. This is obviously not a solution. We are Europeans and love living in Europe. Laughing with other people in our situation has actually helped us feel more open to working on ways to build bridges with our parents.*

The students in my classroom are, in many ways, just like the students in any graduate business program. They want to learn and to make the most of their talents. They learn the same business language and competencies as the other MBA classes around the world. They have made a successful start in school or work and want to build on their experience. Like most ambitious people of their age, they wonder about

17

the best career path, about professional opportunities and about making the right connections. Many of them want to position themselves for consulting, banking, entrepreneurial ventures or senior management. And they want to fall in love. Some students already have young families.

But as internationally mobile people, Global Cosmopolitans are in a class by themselves. The similarity of their lessons ends when students like the one described above begin to discuss the complexities they have faced on the journey that led to my classroom. As a result of confronting these added demands, they frequently develop identities with a dimension not shared by their workplace peers. A growing percentage of aspiring young people are living internationally, so they, too, will share the nuances and complexities of the Global Cosmopolitans whom I teach.

Through the work of my students, I have been granted a front row seat to hear the voice of the emerging Global Cosmopolitan generation. I'll open the door so that you can hear them too as they discuss some of their concerns. Over time, challenges such as these help the new Global Cosmopolitan generation become masters of change and complexity.

Like many Global Cosmopolitans, Joana feels that companies she has worked for did not see her the way she sees herself. Working for the first time in Germany, she had a difficult time proving that she was competent. She felt that she was seen as a Latvian, hard working and good at numbers, inarticulate; personality unknown. "I do not need to be a star, but I need to be somebody, somebody who has a promising future."

Jaya feels like a rubber ball bouncing between the work opportunities she found in the United States and the family she has in India. She wants to return to India with the freedom she has experienced being in charge of her life.

Sasmita didn't have to make Jaya's sacrifice. She has her family from India with her in Canada. The problem, she says, is that she settled into Canadian life while her parents wanted her to behave as if the family still lived in India.

Marwan lived through the experience of war in Lebanon. Working in Dubai has been easy, profitable and safe. He should feel secure and content. Instead he wonders how he can develop a sense of purpose and meaning in his life.

Vlad lived in Angola as a child. He still remembers the trauma of having to leave with his family because, as Russians, their lives were in danger.

Married now, and embarking on his own global voyage, he wants to believe in his ability to deal with the responsibility of moving his family. Will he have what it takes to protect them?

John tells the class about how much he moved around the world as a child. And he has remained on the move in his professional life. But now, with a family of his own, he has begun to think about how his career decisions will affect his children. He wants to create a home for them near his family in the United Kingdom.

Kaz, from Japan, wonders about his family, too. Unlike Stephan, Kaz is new to the internationally mobile life. But he shares Stefan's concern about how his career decisions might affect his son's future. Kaz knows his son loves his first experience at an international school in Singapore. But what if they live abroad for a while? Will his son still be Japanese enough?

Miki tells Kaz about her transition from her life as a budding teenager in Italy back to Japan, where she had to go to a transitional school until she could be considered Japanese enough to go to the regular schools. "Could you imagine me with my Italian short shorts and funky hairdo being accepted in Japan? What a shock! Why can't I have both?"

Avi, an Israeli, grew up between Tel Aviv and New York. His parents divorced; his mother returned to Israel, and his father built a new family life in the United States. Avi enjoyed working both in Argentina and in Belgium until his mother's recent death. Without her, he was feeling homeless.

Fernando has always expected that he would one day return to Argentina. His first step on his global adventure was studying in Chicago. His work experience in China and Indonesia has given him big dreams of returning one day to Argentina as an entrepreneur. He hopes to use the perspectives he feels he has developed as a Global Cosmopolitan to make a difference and lead change back home.

Ada's time at INSEAD was her first experience of living outside Greece. She had planned to move to London or Paris. But now that she understands how the move would mean losing all the comforts and loving relationships of home, she is re-evaluating her decision.

Robert, an Australian sitting in the back row of the classroom, laughs at a conversation about the complexities of international dating. "I'm taking notes," he says. "My girlfriend is Chinese and, boy, do I get in trouble with her!"

One of the Chinese students, Jin, sat quietly, listening to the stories of his classmates. He later tried to capture in writing his experience of being a

Global Cosmopolitan and of listening to people sharing their stories:

This opportunity to share stories with people from all over the world proves again that everyone is another world. I am amazed how splendid one's experience and mind can be. Everyone is so unique. We have a story in China: a frog always stays at the bottom of the well and thinks that this is the only world in the universe. One day, by chance, he jumped out on the rim of the well and found that there is a huge yard with square walls around. The frog said to himself, "How great the world is! Now I know that the sky is not round, it is square!" I always ask myself what if the frog walked a few steps further out of the yard.

The magic of being able to tell one's own story and to have the opportunity to learn from the stories of others is central to my work. Experiences like these provide my students with lessons of mobility. Consciously or unconsciously, they will use these lessons to develop their individual identity and the strengths that they need for their work and personal lives.

GLOBAL COSMOPOLITANS: NAMING THE PHENOMENON

I have identified the students discussed above by the countries where they were born, yet most of these Global Cosmopolitans could not be easily classified by nationality, ethnicity or culture. No one culture or language adequately clarifies or defines the identity of people who carry different pieces of the world inside them. Many of them even hear different cultural voices about what it means to have a sense of self.

I have been determined to find the right label to unite these people from around the world into a single, visible entity. I recognized how their lack of shared memory or shared culture can leave them feeling alone in reconstructing the threads of their identity. Many of them have felt different, misunderstood, undervalued and indefinable. I have spent my professional life helping these globally mobile people answer the question "Who am I?" so that they can answer the equally important question "Where am I going?" I needed a name that reflected their shared global experience. I wanted to express that many were not looking for a nationality but rather a way to identify what it means to live in many different cultures. The name needed to reflect *who* they were instead of *where* they were.

Global Cosmopolitans defy the convenient labels most people take for granted. While some people with multiple passports strongly identify with one nationality, others with multiple passports cannot name a single nationality that captures a sense of who they are. And even those with one passport often feel their nationality does not describe them. Some come from countries that no longer exist or whose names have changed. Others are from an ethnic minority not recognized by the national government. For some, "European" or "African" seems to work.

Motivated to give this group an identity, I tried out different names on the group that I have now come to call Global Cosmopolitans. The labels that they rejected speak volumes about who they are and, just as important, who they are not.

I was not trying to categorize them so much as give them a label and a story that they could identify with. Many Global Cosmopolitans are used to avoiding the topic of belonging to an identity group. They are tired of trying to explain who they are to people that seem more intent on pigeonholing them than understanding them. "Oh, you have an American passport. Then you must be American" is a typical insistent claim. For many people who have felt different for so long, they might be hesitant to even respond. Or they simply say the most expedient answer for the situation, regardless of how inaccurate or incomplete it might be.

Finding appropriate and meaningful identity labels can lead to surprising discussions that illustrate how this group is different. I started by using the label Global Citizen, but the reaction from some people reflected that "While I like to see myself as a committed citizen of the world, it doesn't capture that important identity piece." Global Citizens spoke to their global mindset, their concern for the world, but not necessarily to their identity. Multicultural and bicultural identity works for some people, particularly immigrants or children of immigrants. Global Nomads, Third Culture Kids, transnationals, every label had pieces that were meaningful.

Being an expat (an expatriate) or an immigrant might have fit part of their identity, but this group usually did not feel that these labels captured their mindset or their experience. Maybe their parents or grandparents could be summed up that way, they said. But even those who officially qualify because they are residents in foreign countries do not feel comfortable in either category. The difference concerns how their identities are affected by their global lives.

"Immigrant" is an official term applied to foreigners living within a country's borders, but my grandparents illustrate why Global Cosmopolitans typically feel different from immigrants. My grandparents tried hard to adjust to the United States and make a good life for their families. They gave their children American names. They wanted their children to be able to achieve in their adopted homeland. But just as important, they tried hard to keep a tight social network of people like themselves. When my grandparents left Europe as young teenagers, needing to make it on their own, most of the people that they knew were lost to them forever. Their immigrant community became their new family.

"Expatriate" is a term broadly applied to people living outside their passport countries. Although some Global Cosmopolitans carry multiple passports, many others do fit this definition. Yet they do not feel comfortable with the label expatriate. For them, expatriates leave their country, but they never leave their *home*. Some are looking for the right school credentials or unusual experiences that will make them special back home. Like my grandparents, expatriates often associate with people like themselves and re-create their memories of home. They can live in a world of *we* and *they*, continually measuring the difference between how things are done and how they *ought* to be done.

From the Global Cosmopolitan perspective, immigrants and expatriates keep their identity static and, to the extent that they can, adapt to the world around them. Global Cosmopolitans, by contrast, adapt their *identities* to the changing world. They do not live in a world where *we* and *they* divide along national or cultural boundaries. They are not trying to re-create or transplant their past in foreign soil. Even if they return to the country where they were born or decide to settle in a foreign country, they continue to adapt their identity to the new and changing world around them. Their strengths often result from this perpetual outsider's perspective.

Like immigrants and expatriates, this emerging generation is moving globally to expand their opportunities. But unlike them, Global Cosmopolitans are also expecting to expand themselves. Their ability to connect, to look beyond *we* and *they*, is fundamental at a time when business leaders are developing globally integrated enterprises.

If immigrant and expatriate, two frequently used labels, don't apply to internationally mobile people, then they had no adequate means of expressing their collective identity.

"Cosmopolitan" captured the group's sophisticated worldview. It describes their open, nonjudgmental stance to information that enables them to acquire information from many sources without regard to national or cultural origin. But this label still did not describe this generation for whom change is everywhere.

"Global Cosmopolitan" worked. Given the different connotations of each word, the combined emphasis on global and cosmopolitan described both their experience and perspective. Their ways of understanding and approaching a question involved worldwide perspective.

I started to use Global Cosmopolitan, and the response was immediate. Luis responded, "I am a Global Cosmopolitan. There is no concept that I have come across that I have identified with as strongly as this one. It is an eternal battle of tradeoffs, tough questions and life concepts which are so hard to pin down." The Global Cosmopolitan phenomenon was born.

Nabeel's story explains why people like him identify with the name:

Nabeel's parents had a dream that became a blessing and a burden.

They left behind position and prestige in Pakistan to give their children a better future in England. Nabeel was born there and became a successful young globe-trotting executive.

But when he tried to answer the question "Who am I?" all he could find was who he was not.

He was not like his parents, and English schoolboys quickly let him know that he wasn't like them, either. But he wasn't like the Pakistani boys who tried to be like them. He felt more Pakistani when his technology career took him to Dubai, but he wasn't like the people who'd moved there from Pakistan. To his surprise, he fell in love with a woman his parents arranged for him to meet in Pakistan. But when he got a job there, he was neither a local nor a foreigner.

So, who was he?

A huge smile spread across his face when he heard the term Global Cosmopolitan.

"That's right!" he said. "That's me!"

So does Sabine's story about becoming a Global Cosmopolitan:

As a child, Sabine never wondered who she was.

She was born in Argentina.

Her father was born in Argentina, and her mother moved there with her parents and sister from Germany when she was four years old.

By any measure, especially her own, she was 100 percent Argentine.

But her grandparents had emigrated from Germany to Argentina and had wanted to keep their roots. Her parents felt the same way.

So Sabine, like her parents, went to German schools. She studied with other children similar to her. She played with them. She grew up with them.

Then, one day, she graduated with them.

And suddenly the ground shifted beneath her feet.

At university, Sabine discovered a different Argentina, a world apart from her family's small circle. She started to realize that she felt less Argentine and more German.

She knew that she had a different mindset than the average population.

She decided to study in Argentina. She worked for an international company in Argentina and then got transferred to France. There she fell in love with another South American, a Venezuelan.

They married and soon after moved to Singapore, where they now live.

Now a parent, Sabine is wondering what pieces of her identity she is communicating to their baby son.

The starting points for a global life fall into two broad categories: family choice and personal choice. The family experience sometimes begins before birth because both parents are from different countries. It might start with a global move by parents or, as in Sabine's case, even grandparents. Families might move once or many times. As for becoming global because of personal choice, some people are attracted by educational opportunities, economic advantages or a nagging desire for adventure. Sometimes they fall in love. Sometimes the "choice" is not a choice at all: they are forced by violence, oppression, war or extreme poverty to start their life all over again. Some people start with a strong personal identity, while others struggle from the start to balance elements like nationality, religion or gender.

Moving as a child is significantly different from moving as an adult. Children's experience of the world, their way of learning languages, their level of understanding and their way of remembering differ greatly from their parents'. Their perceptions change with age and brain development. Moving a child at three can have significantly different impact than moving a child at fourteen. No two children react the same, but researchers have looked for patterns, particularly when moves involve new languages and big cultural changes. The number of moves, the circle of people the child can turn to for support and how the family feels about the move all contribute to how a child develops through an international move. As Sabine's story shows, children are also affected by how much a family decides to assimilate or to actively maintain ties with their country of origin.

Education is a significant factor for children, too. Some children attend only international schools, with little parental effort to help them integrate into the local context. Some parents stay within the expatriate environment, sending their children to national schools when they are available. Childhood memories of school experiences are often rich examples of how Global Cosmopolitans develop talent that can be applied in the business world.

U.S. President Barack Obama's life story illustrates how family attitudes and family decisions about education have a major impact on the development of an international child. His mother woke him up at four a.m. every school day to supplement his regular schooling with a U.S. correspondence course. When those lessons were no longer challenging enough, Obama, then aged ten, moved to Hawaii to live with his grandparents.[1]

Other children move with their families to different countries but follow a single international curriculum. "Global Nomads" or "Third Culture Kids" are two popular terms used to describe children who have attended international schools around the world. They grow up surrounded by classmates from many countries, ideally developing skills and ease with people and ideas that are different from their own. Some of these children continue an internationally mobile life as adults; others choose a single home country. Sometimes children study in two cultures at the same time, an example being Chinese immigrant children in the United States attending both Chinese and American schools. Some of these children will grow up to see themselves as bicultural or even multicultural; others cannot identify with these labels at all. The subtleties of being different can have multiple implications. Some childhood memories remain vivid; some are lost to the unconscious world. The labels that they choose to identify with, however, speak to a combination of their experiences and how they feel about them, as well as how they like to be seen.

The journey often starts for Global Cosmopolitans when they decide to study or work in another country. Many teenagers or young adults do not make the decision to live far away from home, but they continue to live out that decision as they advance into adulthood. Rather than just returning home, they embark on a longer voyage. What starts out as an experience for a relatively limited period of time becomes a life journey.

Adults continue to live globally for various reasons. They love the adventure, or they are looking for a different or better future, or they get accustomed to the quality of a Global Cosmopolitan lifestyle, or they just do not see the way back to what they used to call home. At times the choices are quietly influenced by voices from the past. They might have grown up with stories about adventurous or accomplished ancestors. They might have spent their lives listening to their parents' dreams of international adventure or opportunity. Sometimes they have a clear sense of purpose, an idea of their role in the larger world, but sometimes an international experience just "seemed like a good idea at the time."

The story of Toby shows how he was able to transform a vague dream of an exciting life and a desire to make a difference through his experiences in Asia and Africa.

Toby grew up in Britain with the comforts of privilege and a fine education. Even if he had never left home, he would have had many opportunities for a high-flying career.

But Toby wanted something extra that he could not find at home.

He went to Africa to work for an international aid organization before returning to Britain for what he thought was his dream job in international business.

But the more he worked back in Britain, the more restless he became. Something was missing. He increasingly felt a need to use his expertise to help less fortunate people.

Then Toby needed help. He contracted an illness that was eventually diagnosed as Lyme disease. The hours he spent recuperating gave him time to think about the meaning and future direction of his life.

He found his answer in the headlines on December 26, 2004. A tsunami swept through the Indian Ocean half a world away.

Toby volunteered, and by helping to rebuild the devastated region, he helped himself build the foundation for his future.

He met a French woman who was also working with tsunami victims. She became his wife, and together they decided to build careers at non-governmental organizations, careers which would give them significant global experience.

Toby now works for the United Nations.

Toby understood that for him, his life had more meaning when he acted on his values.

Whether Global Cosmopolitans choose to live international lives or someone else chooses for them, they share invisible connections that form this shared identity.

HOW ARE TODAY'S GLOBAL COSMOPOLITANS DIFFERENT?

Throughout history there have been "citizens of the world." There have been stunning stories of survival, lessons about overcoming obstacles and great leaders influenced by years spent in foreign lands.

There have always been important people whose lives transcend national borders; the Hapsburg Emperor Charles V is said to have remarked, "I speak Spanish to God, Italian to women, French to men and German to my horse." The global demands of the modern world have changed not just the face but also the age, work and social class of people living internationally. The result has been a recent and massive generational shift in the highly educated, globally mobile workforce.

This emerging Global Cosmopolitan phenomenon differs primarily along generational lines. The technological revolution has made it not just possible but even routine for people to establish roots and maintain ties across great distances. When I first lived in the south of France in 1973, laptops and internet cafes were concepts that had yet to be invented. My calls to the United States from the post office were hardly private and very expensive. I wrote letters and made audio-tapes, but contact with family, friends and previous work colleagues was minimal.

Today's generation, by contrast, is all about connection. Cut-rate or free worldwide phone service, low-budget airlines and internet booking, news and social-networking sites, mother-tongue DVDs and iPod music in virtually every language are just a few possibilities that were science fiction to earlier generations. At work, the new Global Cosmopolitan generation can be reached almost anywhere with a BlackBerry; video conferencing and virtual teams are a daily feature of work. Cultural fusion has brought an explosion of flavors to world cuisine, sounds to world music and body decorations to fashion. But it's not just fashionable to be global. Many people see their own future connected to the world around them.

Global Cosmopolitans can often identify family members who traveled the world generations before they were born. While they might see a connection to their own stories, they believe that modern technology and their current position in the world give them a very different experience and perspective.

EXPLORING THE IDENTITY OF GLOBAL COSMOPOLITANS

Maria is a young Global Cosmopolitan with great potential to develop into a global leader. But the same life that has given her such promise has presented her with a labyrinth of complications.

I am twenty-six years old. I speak five languages fluently as a result of living and learning in five different countries before I was seventeen.

I have had to pick up and move all my life. My parents placed a high value on education and on meeting people from all over the world.

I graduated from a 'grande ecole' in France, which has given me excellent credentials for working in the public sector. While I was able to have some work experience in France, it was limited due to problems I had with working papers. I hope that the situation will change once I get my MBA this year.

My father was born in Argentina. My mother is from Colombia, which still feels like my home base. I go back there on vacations. I have family there, and I feel Colombian. But I cannot go back there and work because of the current political situation.

My parents are divorced and both of them are working in different countries where I do not have the right to work.

More than once in my life, I had problems with having a passport. As much as I cannot identify with one country, I felt lost when I thought I did not have one. I do not feel like a person without a country. Now, I have a passport from Argentina but no real connections there.

I know that I am good at learning new languages and fitting into diverse cultures. I know how to engage with people and projects. I have been called a natural leader wherever I have lived.

I know that these skills have served me well and have protected me from feeling alone.

I want to stay in France, where my friends have become my family. If I have to leave Paris because I cannot find an interesting job here, I will be leaving the family, the home and the place where I am excited about the possible pathways I see for making a difference in the lives of others.

Maria's success in life will depend largely on how she meets complex challenges like these and the lessons she learns from the experience. This ongoing process is what transforms the external facts of Maria's life into her internal, often invisible, identity story.

This book at its core is about identity stories.[2] Strengths and skills are gained from the successful resolution of the challenges we face that confront a sense of who we are. The stories we create about ourselves are often rooted in the life challenges we have encountered, how we resolved them and what we learned. The narrative studies of lives depict identity narratives as stories people create about their lives, that they tell to themselves and to other people, and use as a lens for interpreting life experience. Global Cosmopolitans like Maria, whose story introduces this section, have different life stories, but their international mobility gives their identity a particular shared dimension.

There is no formula for identifying Global Cosmopolitans. People respond to different aspects of the journey that I describe. While individuals react to different perspectives of the Global Cosmopolitan experience, what make this identity group distinctive are the challenges that they have encountered and the opportunities for learning they have experienced. They are a distinct category of people with a unique outlook on life. It is certainly true that they gain rich perspectives from different cultures and languages, but this traditional passport-based view misses the greater expertise that Maria's generation is developing as Global Cosmopolitans.

FIVE GLOBAL COSMOPOLITAN CHARACTERISTICS THAT TRANSCEND LANGUAGE AND CULTURE

Studying the phenomenon of Global Cosmopolitans, I have identified a set of five important characteristics that frequently develop as a result of the complexity of a Global Cosmopolitan lifestyle. These characteristics are often overlooked in favor of the more visible signs of global experience, such as cultural mastery and language ability. Significantly, *none* of the qualities described below requires an international context in which to use it. And *all* are essential to meeting the management challenges faced by today's global leaders: transition, change, difference and adaptation. What's more, Global Cosmopolitans develop these qualities so subtly and naturally that many don't even know they have them. These five characteristics combine to yield a Global Cosmopolitan identity.

1. *Global Cosmopolitans see change as normal.*
2. *As outsiders to fixed cultural rules, they rely on creative thinking.*
3. *They reinvent themselves and experiment with new identities.*
4. *They are expert at the subtle and emotional aspects of transition.*
5. *They easily learn and use new ways of thinking.*

Global Cosmopolitans develop these characteristics not just because they live in different countries but also because they, like Maria, live in a world of uncommon complexity. This book will explore these elements, considering both the challenges encountered and the possibilities for developing lifelong skills.

People growing up in a single culture develop a filter through which to understand the world around them; their life story has a fixed center of shared wisdom and learned responses on which to build their identity. But Global Cosmopolitans develop a prism that yields kaleidoscopic perspectives. Their center is a multifaceted collection of contradictions, often undefined. Much of their identity is built around their experiences with conflict, alternate belief systems and new ways of behaving around people very different from themselves. Through their stories this book provides a window into their complex world.

IDENTITY STORIES

Growing up is a complex process for everyone. But the following three examples illustrate the complex personal puzzle that many Global Cosmopolitans must put together. They balance multiple passports, parents from different cultures, schooling in various languages and relationships with people very different from themselves.

Marc writes: "What word should I use to describe my background? I was born in France to an Italian mother and a Spanish father. I grew up in Singapore, Hong Kong and Argentina, where I was raised and educated in local schools until I went to university in the UK. I worked in Paris for five years, finished my MBA and am prepared to change careers and countries. I plan on moving to Madrid for a position as a management consultant with my girlfriend, who is English. I know that the move will be exciting for me, but she has never moved before. Will she be happy being so far away from the familiar?"

Mei's parents are of Chinese origin, although her father grew up in Malaysia and her mother in Indonesia. She spent her first five years in Malaysia, then moved to Thailand, where she went to an English day school, before moving to the United States to finish high school and university. Before getting her MBA, she had already worked in the United States, Japan and Singapore. Fitting in was never normal for Mei. She had comfortably found her way to be different, certainly at work. Creativity was at the core of her identity and her power at work. She was ready to start her own enterprise. Everything was ready except for knowing where she wanted to base her operations. Where would she feel at home?

Carla was born in Geneva to a German mother and an American father. Her parents met in Paris and returned to Geneva when Carla was six. But in the interim, they left Geneva for Antwerp, Belgium, where Carla went to a French-speaking school. The move to France allowed her to continue studying French, but in an international school. The family summered in Spain, where she learned Spanish. Vacations were also in Germany and Italy. All of this was enjoyable and easy for Carla, and she continued on to Yale University for her undergraduate studies, worldwide travel, publishing work in Berlin and then back to France to study politics. The challenges of so much international mobility appeared while she was working in publishing and at an entrepreneurial venture. By the time she came to INSEAD for her MBA, she began facing tough questions about commitment to place and to a relationship. She was already a Global Cosmopolitan, but did she need to keep traveling to keep her identity?

Even much simpler circumstances can still create a complex puzzle for Global Cosmopolitans.

Take Michael. His parents are American, but he was born in France, giving him the right to two passports and a lot of choice in the future. At age fifteen, he identified himself as an American. Being an American in France gave him a role, a way to be different. His parents sent him to boarding school in the United States, where he assumed that he would fit in. He was American, right? Wrong. Instead he assumed his French identity. Putting both halves of his identity together took time. Going to university in Paris helped. He found a circle of international friends that helped him find his own unique place.

"Identity is the ultimate act of creativity—it is what we make of ourselves," says Ruthellen Josselson. "Identity represents who we are in the context of all that we might be." For Global Cosmopolitans, the creative challenge of identity-building is particularly strong because they must pull together their different cultural selves. They become adept experimenters. They typically are not bogged down by the extent of the questions and challenges they face. By necessity, they develop an extraordinary capacity to learn. But Josselson cautions that crisis in identity can be spurred by inner change or social dislocation, two commonplace occurrences for internationally mobile people. For Global Cosmopolitans to build what Josselson calls "a bridge between who we feel ourselves to be internally and who we are recognized by in our social world," they face both challenges and opportunities. Through it all, they must create a continuity that continues to have meaning over both time and place.[3]

What could I learn from their identity stories? My curiosity about the challenges and opportunities of a mobile life grew as I listened and learned from my students, clients and the international milieu of people surrounding me. The external story, their languages, their worldwide experience and their knowledge base were very impressive, but so was the way that this journey had shaped them as people. What happens to people leading highly mobile lives, whose identity stories cross cultural and linguistic boundaries? What do we know about people in the middle of social change? How do they give up their old ways and take up new ones? What are the challenges they face, the ways they adapt and the potential expertise they can contribute to the management of transnational organizations?

My research sheds light on what kinds of challenges and skills develop through managing life transitions, intensified by changing cultures and relationships. I have helped clients and students learn to compose their own life stories and use them as textbooks about their lives. By changing places, cultures, languages and relationships, Global Cosmopolitans have unique opportunities to define who they are in relation to others, to their context, to time and to their own personal history. Through this definition process, they learn to define their strengths and their path to the future.

LEARNING THROUGH STORIES OF RESILIENCE

Farid was just a typical middle-class ten-year-old boy with no clue how closely his fate was tied to a man who lived in a palace.

But in January 1979, Shah Mohammed Reza Pahlavi fled Teheran and Farid's comfortable childhood ended abruptly. He and his eleven-year-old brother suddenly found themselves in Turkey, struggling to set up a new life.

Farid's brother was lucky. He got a student visa to Canada. But Farid, all alone, had to find a different solution.

He managed to reach a homeless shelter in Belgium, where he struggled to feed himself and work. At the same time, he kept moving ahead with his education, and the force of that determination eventually pulled him out of poverty.

Farid took a test for a language course at an elite engineering school. He did so well that the prestigious school let him enter the program rather than just take language classes. His classes there were a first step on his way to a highly successful career in management.

He never did return to Iran. But Farid is back in touch with his parents and his brother. He was also able to trust, fall in love and build a new family for himself in Belgium.

Because of Farid's resilience, his own children have the childhood he never knew.

His decision to pursue an MBA led him to INSEAD to tell his story to me.

Farid's story has two important implications for Global Cosmopolitans. On one hand, it reflects the extreme challenges that some people have faced. On the other, it displays the resilience that contributed to his ability to build an interesting and secure life for himself and his family.

Farid exemplifies the ability to respond to life challenges and continue making a difference: in his case for his family and in his profession. He is an expert at adaptation. In the face of what seem like overwhelming odds, he has been able to hold onto the core of what was important to him. He knew who he was and what he could be, all the while navigating the process of survival and personal change.

Most Global Cosmopolitans do not have such dramatic events in their lives, but their stories give clues about their unusual ability to adapt. They, like Farid, exhibit resilience. Although their circumstances might be seen as reasons to develop defenses or disconnections, they are able to successfully confront the transitions and discontinuities that characterize their lives. They seem to enjoy the complex and ever-changing challenges that others might shy away from. They continue to test their possibilities.

Through the ability to tell their stories in a coherent and authentic way, Global Cosmopolitans like Farid give voice to their experience and to their sense of self. They begin to see their personal resilience and its sources. They begin to picture their strengths and weaknesses, their values and ideals, history and goals. They start to understand how they cushion the changes that they go through to make the most out of their global experience.

What is resilience? Simply put, resilience can be defined as the capacity to rebound from adversity by becoming strengthened and more resourceful. It is an active process of endurance. It involves self-righting and growth in response to crisis and challenge. The quality of resilience enables people to heal, take charge of their lives and go on.

Brooks and Goldstein describe the factors that are central to resilience. These comprise one's ability to feel in control of one's life; know how to fortify one's hardiness in the face of stress; display effective communication and interpersonal capabilities; establish realistic goals and expectations; learn from both success and failure; and feel special, but not self-centered, while helping others to feel the same.[4]

Even for someone who demonstrates key elements of resilience as a child, such as strong self-esteem and self-efficacy, what contributes to the continued development of resilience over time? How do they continue to move extensively and experience loss on multiple levels? This book will explore the centrality of the role of positive relationships in helping someone remain resilient.

Farid pulled together the pieces of his story for the first time when he wrote his life story, what I call his personal narrative. Picking up his story and rereading it changed his life. For the first time, he had drawn a picture of his life that he could understand. He could see who he was and describe himself to other people. He could see the challenges he had faced and what he had learned. He had a sense of his identity.

He started to talk about himself. It was not any story that he was telling. It was authentically his story. He could get enough distance from his experiences that he could look at them with an analytic eye. He also realized that the more he told his story, the more he became liberated from the pain and the more he felt open to the opportunities that his life had provided for him.

What had he learned? How did he adapt? What gave him the power to keep starting over? For the first time, Farid started acknowledging the power of the values that he had been given and that he kept close to his core. For him, the poetry that he had learned linked him to his culture and his history. He started to see that the same strengths that helped him keep moving forward in extreme adversity could be used very effectively in other, more positive, settings.

He also saw that key to his resilience were the people in his life. With all of the loss that he had experienced, strong relationships had helped help him feel strong in times of challenge. His life had developed in a very different way than his parents'. While he had gone through angry times, feeling deserted and betrayed, he now began to reconnect with his family. Now in love and about to be married, he got his MBA and returned to his company with a new vigor and view of his future possibilities.

Certainly not afraid of hard work, Farid, in his early thirties, took the time and effort to have a reflected life. The result was that his hard work could pay more meaningful dividends.

3

LEARNING FROM A GLOBAL LIFE: DEVELOPING THE CREATIVE EDGE OF DIFFERENCE

Liv learned not to make assumptions about other people, because other people always made wrong assumptions about her.

She can "pass," as she calls it, for a Moroccan, Indian, or even for a member of the Shawnee Native American tribe. And with mastery of four languages, she fits seamlessly into many cultures.

But in fact, she is a blend of a Swedish father and a mother who is Indian but grew up in Kenya. Liv was born in Sweden and then moved to Ethiopia for a couple of years. She returned to Sweden; then, at age seven, she moved to Somalia for a couple of years. At age nine, she moved to Sweden, where she lived until before she finished high school.

"I never assume," she says. "I make sure that I try to understand to learn about people."

Having studied hotel management in the United States and worked in Switzerland, New York City, Sweden, Myanmar, Bora Bora, Wyoming, Thailand and Morocco, she now lives on the Indonesian island of Bali, where she is general manager of a top luxury hotel.

It would be easy but wrong to assume that Liv's languages and cross-cultural knowledge explain her success in the tourism industry.

Certainly they play a role. But Liv's art is that of understanding people.

She has a deep and genuine curiosity and soft, approachable style that have gained her respect and trust across the globe. Her knowledge comes from an ability to both observe and relate to the world around her.

Opening a hotel resort in Morocco, for example, Liv had to cross borders that are not marked on any map, understanding everything from the needs of the architect to the expectations of future guests to the doubts of the maids, who needed to clean facilities they had never seen before but that guests took for granted.

"As a young child, I had access to understanding different paths," says Liv, "which helped me feel connected to the human experience."

Liv was seven when her father, who worked for the Red Cross, moved the family to East Africa. She remembers traveling frequently to see relatives on her mother's side in Kenya. During an uprising while she was with family in Kenya, she vividly remembers spending most of each day hidden in the cellar.

Some of her strongest childhood memories are about refugee camps that she visited when her family was stationed in Mogadishu. She wanted to do something to help. She wanted to take a child home. In a way she has come full circle: she just adopted a child from India.

She also brings caring and a sense of community to work, traits she attributes to her Swedish values. The children from her village, for example, take Balinese dancing and music lessons in the afternoons at the hotel.

As a teenager, Liv worked in Stockholm as a luxury hotel maid and in Geneva as a waitress at a hospital restaurant. She worked alongside Chilean political refugees who had been professionals, such as doctors and teachers, back home. She saw what it is like to stay motivated when doing the same job day after day.

Now she always asks her staff how they plan to grow with the work they are doing. "What's important to me," she says, "is that you challenge yourself and stretch yourself."

Over the years, Liv has had many learning opportunities to refine the skills she uses to understand the people she meets. She also has had many chances to rethink her identity, learn about herself and give meaning to her life.

"I have opened a number of resorts. Each is an opportunity to create windows," says Liv. "I love what I do with my company. I can bring what is important to me to work: my values and the work ethic and, of course, who I am."

Liv's broad experiences are unique, but she exemplifies the competence and potential that Global Cosmopolitans bring to a business world in need of innovative, globally sensitive solutions.

And she foresees the emergence of more people like herself.

"I am a reflection of one part of the future of the world," says Liv. "This is where we are headed."

LIFE IN A WORLD OF POSSIBILITIES

Liv knows how to adapt to new situations and get things done. She is a product of complexity, diversity and change. She is an excellent manager with a unique style and set of capabilities. She sees life as an opportunity to learn, to love and to make the world a better place.

Her ability for self-reflection contributes to her strength. She is aware of what she knows; she is open to admitting what she does not know but needs to find out. She can see her strengths as well as her limits, although she believes that no problem is too complex to try to solve.

She also has the gift of being able to communicate her knowledge. She is a wonderful storyteller. Her personal stories are laced with meaning and emotion.

So even though changing family needs are leading her toward a major lifestyle transition, Liv feels excitement about the possibilities, not fear. She has been rational and meticulous in preparing for the new realities she will face. She knows that she can no longer have the same adventure and opportunity that she found in remote environments. But she is also aware of finding new possibilities and new adventures in her next home.

She understands the challenges of a Global Cosmopolitan life as well as its opportunities for personal and professional development. Her ability to learn, reflect and communicate underlies the ability to use the skills she has developed.

A BACKDROP OF UNCOMMON COMPLEXITY AND CHANGE

In a sense, Global Cosmopolitans are just like everyone else. They want to earn a living. They want to fall in love. They face the same challenges as other people in their everyday lives. But they do so against a backdrop of uncommon complexity and change. As a result, they develop capacities that modern managers need to make sense of their surroundings. The cluster of strengths that can emerge from globally mobile lives is the subject of this chapter.

Global Cosmopolitans learn to interpret and respond to their surroundings, to find meaning in what they do and to imagine possibilities when other people are stuck. They develop the ability to constantly shake up perceptions, to question assumptions, to construct, deconstruct and reconstruct reality in personal and creative ways. Research is only beginning to shed light on the complexities of how global mobility affects Global Cosmopolitans' minds and how they approach their professional and personal lives.

Other people besides Global Cosmopolitans can possess the strengths outlined here. And there are, of course, factors besides the complexity of global mobility that might explain where these strengths come from. Genetics could play a role, as well as experiences in early childhood. Howard Gardner has described different kinds of intelligences that might contribute to understanding Liv's curiosity and her extraordinary relational sensitivity with people.[1] But the strengths presented below emerge in my dealings with Global Cosmopolitans who combine their knowledge base with their competences to work in a changing world with creativity and style.

The strengths and skills developed by a Global Cosmopolitan lifestyle can, if identified and used correctly, provide a significant competitive advantage in any marketplace.

LEARNING FROM THE EXPERIENCES OF THE GLOBAL JOURNEY

Reality Pales in the Face of Perception

What becomes our own personal reality depends on how we filter the world around us. Global Cosmopolitans, who must grow and thrive in an environment of extreme complexity and ambiguity, develop filters that are unlike those of many of their peers at work. The critical skills that Global Cosmopolitans develop to filter their personal reality give them a creative edge of difference.

Global Cosmopolitans are experts at being different. They develop the ability to look at issues from an outsider's perspective. Their experience across cultures gives them multiple lenses and perspectives for seeing and understanding the world around them. The demands of successful adaptation might thrust them into roles such as the family negotiator or translator, which can become the basis for future professional success. They can develop chameleon-like behavior to fit quickly into new environments and learn a range of flexible thinking skills to cope with the demands of change.

As these skills sharpen over time, Global Cosmopolitans begin to master transition and change. They develop a capacity to draw on all their resources and bounce back from the challenges they face. The result is a resilience that allows Global Cosmopolitans to find new pathways for adaptation and development.

The Perception of Change as Opportunity

For most Global Cosmopolitans, change is normal.

This new project will require that I alternate between Singapore and Paris. I know how to live in different countries at the same time. It takes some

organizing and making sure that I stay in touch, but it does not seem to be
strange or difficult to me. That is just how life has been for me.

Many Global Cosmopolitans talk about the pleasure and motivation
they receive from change. They frequently go so far as to describe an
addiction to change. "I get bored if I don't have it," they say. Trying
new solutions is often a source of excitement, a reinforcement of their
belief that they can make a difference.

Navigating through changing geographical contexts can feel more
normal than staying in one place. Global Cosmopolitans know how
to do it. They know what they need to make a change work. With the
repeated experience of change as an opportunity for learning and trying out creative solutions, Global Cosmopolitans often develop a very
open attitude.

But this attitude does not mean that change is always easy. Many
Global Cosmopolitans express ambivalence about losing what they
have worked hard to build. They remember what it was like to be
taken care of. They miss their friends. They sometimes struggle to
meet basic needs such as food and shelter. With initial success and
practice over time at finding creative and innovative solutions, Global
Cosmopolitans can learn to overcome these challenges. And when
they do, change becomes a powerful path to growth.

Global Cosmopolitans perceive change in a powerful and dynamic
way. Where others might see certain changes as a disruption, an obsta-
cle in the middle of their life road, Global Cosmopolitans often see the
same changes as opportunities, a source of learning about themselves
and the world. Because these starting perceptions are different, Global
Cosmopolitans experience the period of transition and uncertainty
completely differently.

A rigid approach that resists change requires outside help to provide
the motivation and necessary steps for change to succeed. Change is
passive, something that happens *to* you. But a fluid approach that wel-
comes change calls up powerful internal forces from a person's own
values, background and depth of experience. Change is active, something that happens *for* you. The result of the change process is that
Global Cosmopolitans seek out more opportunities to continue on
this path to development and success.

For many Global Cosmopolitans, the positive perception of change
begins when they choose to go to a foreign country for school. A classic story of early growth from change comes from Ariana, a young
woman from Albania.

Studying in America was a marking event of my life. For the first time I lived away from home in Albania. I was fully independent and responsible for myself, and these were traits that I had not had the opportunity to explore to great depths until then. Besides the obvious cultural shock, it was an enriching experience in terms of personal relations with people. Not knowing anyone on the campus the day I arrived, I had to make efforts to socialize and be proactive. In a social context, I would normally be quite passive and wait for someone to come up to me for fear of appearing needy. In the United States, I had to break this pattern and go up to people myself. I noticed that I was good at doing it when I had no other choice, basically when I was put on the spot.

These initial personal changes help Global Cosmopolitans adapt to their new circumstances, but the significance runs deeper than that. The experience defines the Global Cosmopolitan's pathway: it links living with cultural difference to the possibility of opening doors and opportunities.

Nitan described the steep learning curve that led him to make this link:

I could not wait to go to the United States. I never thought about what it would mean to be on my own. I do not eat meat. Being in India, that was never a problem. Moving to Middle America, all I could see were McDonalds. I also realized my budget would never finance my modest eating habits. Guess what? I went to work. Suddenly I went from a child that had been protected by a village to a grown-up that could more than take care of myself. This change changed the rest of my life. While I had been a confident student, I never saw myself as being capable of being self-sufficient or even skillful in the business environment. This was the crucial step that led me on the path of entrepreneurial adventures that allowed me to confidently and successfully start my own company.

Alexi's fond memories of change continue to motivate his dreams and his attitude that change is normal and stimulating.

I had a wonderful life growing up in three different countries in Africa. There were five of us and our little family unit moved easily from one country to another. At least that was my experience. The emphasis in my family was on the new adventure and the new possibilities. Returning to France was much more challenging for all of us. Suddenly we were swept away from our dream life into the responsibilities of school and going our separate ways. I could not wait to grow up and start my own life adventure. I think that I will always see change as both normal and as an opportunity to do something new and different. I realize that I am hooked on change. I do not have to continue changing cultures, but I have to work in a dynamic environment where change is not just possible, but preferred. I am at my best when I can see my way to bringing about something new and different.

Alexi knows that his experience has given him the confidence that comes with knowing how to navigate change. He knows what to do, and he knows what his sources of resilience are. This knowledge gives him the confidence he needs to take risks in new and changing environments.

Given their experience and perception of change, complexity and difference both as normal and as enriching opportunities, what is the nature of the skills often seen in this group? What do they learn that allows them to thrive in an atmosphere of uncertainty and change and to contribute their creative edge of difference?

Adaptive Capacity

Moving to a new culture requires adaptation to new values, attitudes and behaviors. Learning in a new context is more than the experience, knowledge and skills that can define one's cultural competence. The adaptive capacity needed for meeting the challenges of a global life with resilience is the key. When Global Cosmopolitans talk about new situations, they often adapt so seamlessly that they do not have the words to describe how it happened.

Global Cosmopolitans develop characteristics resembling what social psychologists and psychologists refer to as high adaptive capacity.[2] Social ecologists say systems have high adaptive capacity when they are able to keep going without any essential difficulties at the same time that they are reinventing themselves. They go beyond just knowing how to learn in uncertain environments and combining knowledge in creative ways; they actually create opportunities for reinvention so that they can thrive in their new circumstances.

Miki was born in Japan but moved to Italy at age thirteen. "It was a tough process," she wrote, "as I had to get rid of most of my confidence and pride in order to build my new confidence to live comfortably in the new country from scratch." The more she moved, the more experienced she became at integrating into her new environment and its culture. "Now," Miki writes, "adapting to a new location to me is almost like a sport that I play by reflex rather than by thoughtful processes."

This adaptive capacity of absorbing a new culture requires extraordinary perceptual skills and awareness of nuance. To understand this strength, consider Miki's description of a recent family vacation.

I am Japanese, a Global Cosmopolitan Japanese. A short trip to Kyoto we did this summer gave me an epiphany. It was a three-day trip, and I've barely been to Kyoto before. Kyoto is known to have a very particular culture completely different from the rest of Japan, including Tokyo. They're different in all perspectives, from language, attitude, to the way they walk. On the second day of our trip, my husband looked perplexed every time I spoke. After a certain period, he spurted out, "You changed. You're speaking in this Kyoto dialect and acting like Kyoto people. What are you doing? Why are you doing this?" I had no idea I was doing any of that. But within a day, I was speaking in a nearly perfect Kyoto dialect and acting like the Kyoto people, and local people actually didn't realize that I was from out of town, Tokyo. Then I realized that when I arrive in a new place, I observe and absorb the norms automatically, intensively and speedily. I think I learned this skill with a sense of survival through experiences of living in different places all the time. I could say that I'm a very experienced copy machine.

Global Cosmopolitans are often seen as people who know the rules and behaviors expected of them in different cultures. But their competence is actually richer, requiring such a high degree of self-awareness and sensitivity that they can be referred to as Cultural Chameleons. Miki describes the experience of being Japanese but not brought up in Japan and working in Japan as a Japanese employee for a German company with an American manager. She was able to display her ability to read the subtleties of difference that each situation and relationship called for, even when dealing with people from countries she had never visited:

My first job was to set up a Tokyo office of a German company. I did that with an American General Manager who just moved from New York and knew only a few words in Japanese. When we went to meet our Japanese clients, I was expected to play Japanese. When I reported the content of the meeting with the clients to people in the German headquarter office, I was expected to play the bicultured Japanese. Sometimes the two identities were expected in the same office at the same time. For instance, as the office grew, the GM hired quite a few managers who were all Japanese. When I had something to say to one of the managers, I had to first knock on their door, and when I was asked to come in, I had to act as if I was still too shy to open the door. If I acted the same way with my American GM, he either would get angry or would ask me what I did wrong. So the switching of the identities becomes quite tricky and complicated in Japan when you work for a global company.

Taking the Risks That Lead to Self-Efficacy

Desiree's parents wanted to give her a birthday present the day she was born: United States citizenship. They gave birth to her in New York City before heading back to Lebanon. After years of turbulence, Desiree decided to return to the United States when she was eighteen. She had her U.S. passport. But she still had a problem. She had enough money only for airfare. So Desiree left the protection of her family and took a risk. At first, she stayed with relatives. But she quickly learned that she would need a job and money for university studies. She did it all. And she did it all on her own, finding independence and confidence in the process. She attacked her career in San Ricardo the same way and with great success. She learned how to take calculated risks, a strength that she will carry with her no matter where she goes.

Because of the complexity in their lives, Global Cosmopolitans excel at taking calculated risks. Throughout my years of working with Global Cosmopolitans, I have seen hundreds of variations on Desiree's life story. Forced by political, economic or family circumstances to fight for their dreams, they develop a sense that they can handle whatever the future throws at them. They learn that seemingly impossible situations turn possible and even rewarding. They learn that the rewards of living with uncertainty can be far greater than the risks. They learn to believe that if they set goals, they can reach them. They feel like masters of their own fate. This is called self-efficacy.[3]

Tomasz described his experiences this way:

Why should you go to the United States to some small, unknown school without knowing English when you can go to an excellent university at home? I couldn't answer that question, yet I knew that I had to try. My mother had gone to the United States before me, and I needed to follow the impossible path behind her. She could not help me; she was really only a cleaning woman and she had married a very inadequate man. At some level I wanted to understand her experience, but I did not know that until much later. So I went on my own, and I struggled, and I won a U.S. degree in engineering and a position in an American company that was not that exciting but gave me the opportunity to open doors that I would never have seen from my limited vantage point at home in Eastern Europe. I probably will never understand my mother's experience, but I have learned how to dream about the impossible and make it possible. I have a track record now. It was not what I thought that I would learn at age sixteen, but it is what I have learned.

Relational Awareness and Competence

Survival for Global Cosmopolitans requires developing the competence to forge successful relationships with all kinds of people. Given their experience with and sensitivity to difference, Global Cosmopolitans understand the importance of withholding judgment, sharing respect and trust, and finding common ground.

The complexity of their lives offers new relational challenges as they mature. They have to learn how to make quick connections and to avoid social isolation and frustration. They need the ability to deal with multiple and diverse clients and huge social networks that have become particularly diverse through globalization. The Global Cosmopolitans' experience of successfully managing complex, worldwide relational networks is a significant area of expertise.

Understanding Difference

Clearly diversity has been a core value in how I have lived my life: in the friends I have sought, in the profession I chose, even in the food I eat. I seek diversity in whatever I do. It is perhaps the one value where I risk judging others. When I find someone who values routine over diversity, I am truly puzzled and have a difficult time relating.

Global Cosmopolitans understand difference at many levels. Even the surface skills they typically are known for display a complex knowledge of the world around them. They have long been valued in the workplace for their ability to interpret, literally and figuratively, the needs of both home office and foreign operations. They know whom to talk to and how to get answers. They know the fine points of doing business. They are people who get things done no matter where they are in the world, people such as Eduardo:

My parents moved a lot when I was a child. I learned by immersing myself in the new cultures, becoming one of them. Now when I move to a new country to open a site for my company, I do the same things and I expect my team-mates to do the same. When I create teams to immerse into a new culture, as I just did in India, I look for people with potential skill in this area, and then I share what I can to show them how to be successful. So far, it has worked beautifully.

Since isolation can undermine adaptation, survival requires Global Cosmopolitans to listen, learn and understand people in a new culture. Resilience requires the ability to build relational bridges. Children learn the rules quickly, adapting like chameleons; their ability to adapt and communicate across difference is a lifelong skill. Miki describes how her strengths gave her a direct advantage in the international work world:

I am able to translate not only languages but also cultures and nuances to people. I'm able to work with both Japanese and Western people without any translators in between. With this strength I have, I was able to gain many valuable experiences. I remember my first job at a German advertising company; one Japanese woman who was working in the company's branch office told me, "You know, having the job content and the responsibility you have at your age is extremely uncommon." I somehow knew, but her remark reminded me how fortunate I was. Without the bicultural characteristic I have, I would definitely not have gotten that job.

Just knowing that rules change from place to place in subtle and surprising ways already gives Global Cosmopolitans a head start in a new environment. They know to step back and observe, to take the time to learn about these important differences.

Managing difference for themselves and their family can help Global Cosmopolitans develop lifelong relational skills. Many Global Cosmopolitans developed family roles as children such as being the family diplomat, negotiator or translator. They develop these early skills and use them effectively as they continue to bridge differences between people.

When George's family had to leave Lebanon, he was only eight, but he quickly found himself in the role of family negotiator. His parents left a life of luxury to live in an immigrant neighborhood. As they struggled to rebuild a life, he learned how to take care of himself. He won scholarships to the best schools and quickly developed a network of friends. After school, he became the family negotiator, starting with helping his mother shop for essentials and moving to finding emergency medical care. The skills he learned during that period have traveled with him. Now, he describes that ability as instinctive, without effort he can find a place to negotiate.

45

Observational Capacity

Global Cosmopolitans develop observational skills that allow them to perceive with focus and intensity. They use these skills to figure out whom to trust and whom to respect and to determine appropriate interactions in their new surroundings. This careful and skillful observation allows people to see the world from another person's perspective, and then suspend judgment in order to understand people on their own terms.

Juan was sent to live with extended family in the United States. The first months were excruciating for him as he struggled to learn English and find a friend. Very shy as a child, he watched everyone and everything. While frustrated by his inability to learn how to communicate in English, he learned other ways to connect to other children by observing how they played during recess. He even started sharing the pictures he drew of life at school with others. His ability to learn language has improved in his adult life, but his key skill is being able to communicate what he sees around him.

Different Ways of Knowing

Global Cosmopolitans find themselves in situations where they are unable to rely on past experience. Without language, without rules, they invent their own ways to learn and connect. Global Cosmopolitans develop the perceptual skills they need for highly complex thinking.

SOME OF THE STRENGTHS THAT GLOBAL COSMOPOLITANS DEVELOP THAT UNDERLIE GLOBAL COSMOPOLITAN PERCEPTUAL SKILLS

Knowing, Not Knowing and Knowing How to Find Out

To accomplish integration into a foreign country, Global Cosmopolitans need to be keenly aware not just of what they know but also of what they don't know. Their cultural competence is really a blend of cultural knowledge and skills with this highly developed self-awareness.

Going to a doctor can be a nightmare without the correct words and cultural references. An American, for example, might describe a pain as a backache. That same American speaking to a doctor in France would benefit from being able to describe his kidney.

Feeling comfortable with the uncertainty of knowing that they don't know allows Global Cosmopolitans to excel at finding out what they need to know. This capacity is a fundamental business skill, a crucial asset to companies seeking opportunities in times of uncertainty.

Cognitive Complexity

Because their perception is open and flexible, Global Cosmopolitans have what psychologists call high cognitive complexity.[4] People with less cognitive complexity can be taught to see the many complex details in a situation. But someone with high cognitive complexity can perceive new, complex details on their own, even in completely new situations. They have much higher ability to detect subtleties.

When confronted with a situation or event, Global Cosmopolitans not only are capable of identifying more distinct elements to analyze, but are also capable of perceiving more ways in which these elements can be tied together. The result is a wider range of potential solutions and greater likelihood of success.

This analytical capability gives Global Cosmopolitans much strength in the complex work world. They are more likely to find information from unconventional sources, to put their observations together in a creative way and to form a more complete picture as a result. They are more flexible in finding alternatives and can consider a broader range of possible outcomes for them. They can change their minds more easily than people with less cognitive complexity.

Especially important to businesses seeking to encourage new ideas, Global Cosmopolitans are less likely to see issues in *we/they* terms; they also feel comfortable around all kinds of people rather than tending to seek out people like themselves. Not surprisingly, given that people with high cognitive complexity generate more original ideas outside the mainstream, many Global Cosmopolitans are drawn to entrepreneurship.

Meena provides an example of how the ability to handle uncommonly complex problems transfers from personal life to work.

Meena comes from a family in Katmandu that could never imagine sending her to university to study engineering. But she was determined to study engineering in a foreign country. And she did.

She earned a degree and continued her studies at the prestigious Massachusetts Institute of Technology. She risked losing much of what was important to her—family and friends—to pursue her dream, yet was excited at exploring a different world. But she wanted to work for a better world, a dream she has made reality with her job at the World Bank. The uncertainties and complexities of her moves have not been easy. They have meant managing relationships from afar, getting work documents, making sure she has enough money and paying off loans, making her new life feel like home while at the same time staying in touch with the values she learned growing up.

She has often felt alone, because no one else could understand the complexities of her world and the challenges of her life. But, as a result, Meena has learned how to manage complex problems. She has had to attack each personal decision with a perspective on the different, often conflicting aspects of her life. And the lessons from those experiences allow her to deal with complex problem-solving issues at work.

Global Cosmopolitans know how to find out information because they become experts at learning in an unstructured environment. Researchers call this phenomenon cognitive flexibility. In this form of learning, people construct their own knowledge from multiple conceptual building blocks rather than by simply being fed one concept at a time.

Global Cosmopolitans like Meena are able to build new systems that make sense of their world rather than simply retrieving an old system with fixed ideas. Old systems can create bias or prevent new learning. Cognitive flexibility, on the other hand, allows people to complete complex knowledge puzzles in a creative way, based on their own perception of how the pieces fit together. Their minds are less tied down by what they have learned before. Because of their greater flexibility, Global Cosmopolitans who think this way can reinvent themselves in light of new conventions and relationships. They can recreate a sense of home in new surroundings and reestablish a sense of meaning in their lives.

Kaleidoscope Thinking

Global Cosmopolitans are flexible and original thinkers in part because they have a highly creative ability to join information together. Kaleidoscopes give a different image of how creativity and different perspectives can occur. Rosabeth Moss Kanter calls this competence "kaleidoscope-thinking skills."[5] A kaleidoscope can produce startlingly different patterns when the same colored bits inside are shaken up. The same image, she says, applies to perception: "Often it's not reality that's fixed; it's our perspective of reality. Creativity and innovation come when we can shake up our thinking and challenge conventional patterns." As the patterns and concerns of their lives change, Global Cosmopolitans can rotate different aspects of their experiences to arrange their roles and relationships in new ways. Liv, whose story introduced this chapter, shows how kaleidoscope thinking can redefine the perfect place to live in light of changes in work and family needs.

Liv's current situation in Bali is aligned. She has a fantastic job, great child-care and stunning natural surroundings. She has time for family, yet she also can do work that is socially responsible and involved. She feels comfortable with the possibility of moving while the children are still young if she wants to make a change. She believes that children are still adaptable until age ten or twelve, and then it is important to be in one place for their schooling. At that time, she will have to think about providing appropriate schools for her children. She is confident that no matter where she moves, she will find an environment that will help her learn and grow. Whatever new perspectives she gains will help her see the pieces of her life differently. She looks back at her life that way: a kaleidoscope with different patterns and adventures. With each stage of her life and with each move, she knows that she must give the kaleidoscope a turn so that she can see her life from a different perspective and look at the pieces of her life from a different angle.

MULTIPLE LENSES AND PERSPECTIVES FOR UNDERSTANDING THE WORLD

Their mobile lives teach Global Cosmopolitans about the different ways cultures experience and understand the world. The deeper the contrasts in the cultures, the more lenses and perspectives for seeing the world around them Global Cosmopolitans develop.

Peripheral Vision

Many Global Cosmopolitans have a highly developed capacity for what Mary Catherine Bateson calls "peripheral vision."[6] This strength allows Global Cosmopolitans to expand their awareness beyond the narrow vision that other people see by drawing connections from their intuition and different life experiences. They can focus on the periphery of the picture and give new meaning to the foreground. They can see a situation from different angles.

Bateson identified this phenomenon because she wanted to describe the limits of traditional learning environments. But her observation applies to Global Cosmopolitans, who are experts at finding meaning and patterns in the unknown. Bateson understands this capacity for peripheral vision first hand. She is a Global Cosmopolitan, having lived in Iran, the Philippines, Israel and the United States.

Truth Is Not Absolute

Global Cosmopolitans can also maintain the openness and flexibility required for highly complex cognition because they understand that truth is not an absolute; it changes depending on the cultural context. This is Sanjay's experience:

The most valuable lessons I learned about work were during the last five and a half years at a major American multinational. Among those lessons, the most important one was ethics. Being from India, ethics had a very different meaning to me. Bribing someone was not unethical. If you do not bribe the government official then it will be almost impossible to get the work done; even if it will get done, it will take ten times longer. The state I am from is especially infamous for corruption. The kids used to dream to become a civil engineer so they can find a government job in the public works department and earn huge amounts of bribes.

Critical Consciousness

Multiple lenses and perspectives for understanding the world allow Global Cosmopolitans to be both an insider and an outsider at the same time. This strength is what Brazilian Paolo Freire called "Critical Consciousness."[7] Along with the analytical benefits that come from this dual perspective, Global Cosmopolitans are also aware of what costs they pay for moving between the two.

The challenge that Global Cosmopolitans face by being different will be explored in depth in the next part of this book. But the strength that can emerge from this challenge gives Global Cosmopolitans a powerful ability to bring about change.

Business literature has examined successful international managers and formulated the essential elements of a Global Mindset.[8] Beyond a Global Mindset, Global Cosmopolitans have a Global Skill Set. These favorable traits describe many of the strengths of someone like Liv, the luxury resort general manager. Her openness and awareness, her curiosity and desire to mix with all kinds of people, her focus and ability to process information all contribute to the professional success of Global Cosmopolitans like her.

This chapter has now presented the key components that are essential for the development of a Global Skill Set. The adaptive capacity, relational awareness, different ways of knowing and multiple lenses and perspectives of Global Cosmopolitans provide an ability to understand, recognize and integrate across complex global dynamics.

Even when a job is more local than international, Global Cosmopolitans can draw on their advanced relational and problem-solving skills. They can also use these skills to resolve the complex dynamics of their own lives.

Taken together, these strengths explain why Global Cosmopolitans become masters of complexity and change. But where can Global Cosmopolitans best apply their strengths? How can someone who is so different find a place that fits?

THE CREATIVE EDGE OF DIFFERENCE

The creativity, understanding and sensitivity that come from being different can give a Global Cosmopolitan a creative edge. It can also allow them to help others see, develop and use their difference.

Many illustrations of how Global Cosmopolitans can use their creative edge of difference are woven throughout this book. Different experiences, different individuals yield many creative solutions to life challenges and opportunities at work.

Global Cosmopolitans know about different ways to do things. Rules in one country disappear or transform in another. Experiencing this first hand leaves an openness to exploring new roles or new ideas or new rules. Global Cosmopolitans often talk about learning how to be creative in the margins or the places in between. Business ideas emerge from ideas that have been developed in one part of the world that could be valued and valuable in another.

Global Cosmopolitans can often be heard discussing ideas for new ventures. "Remember that fabulous 'green hotel' that we stayed at in Chile? Why don't we develop the concept here?" or "I found a way to redesign the shoes I wore in Ecuador so that they could be used here. They could be sold for ten times as much, and I could help sustain a number of villages on that income."

Learning how to deal with change over a lifetime and understanding what it takes to move from a stage of loss to a stage of transformation form an experience base that Global Cosmopolitans can adapt to manage change in organizations.

Mei could not relate to identity based on nationality. She believed that the label confused people trying to get to know her. She could not really identify what her nationality felt like. Her parents are Chinese, although her father grew up in Malaysia, and her mother in Indonesia. She was born and spent her first five years in Malaysia, after which the family went to Thailand, where she went to school, although in English. University was mixed; it even included a sojourn in Canada and the United States. After school, she went to Japan, where she loved her work and felt very much at home. Getting her MBA in Europe was a step out. After graduation, she decided to return to Japan, maybe starting an entrepreneurial venture with her brother. This felt like a first step toward creating a home base.

In her assessment of her life so far, Mei, like many of the women trying to compose an international life, expressed a concern about her friendship base. People were all over the world, never understanding her different selves. Creating a place where she could feel at home in her relationships and at home in her work seems like a good step to creating connecting threads for her story. Since an essential life thread for her is being creative, using her creativity to weave her life story also felt like a meaningful way to begin the continuation of her life voyage.

She acknowledged her extensive experience with the many facets of being different. She started to see the pattern of her attraction to and comfort with difference. Her professional interests in Japan used her creative thinking, which she believed were linked to her life of mobility and change. She could design and see aspects of situations that others had more trouble visualizing. She entered a creative universe that was another world that she could experience and contribute to.

Mei had experienced so many different ways of being and living. Since she was never on the inside of any cultural experience, she learned how to live on a creative edge, choosing activities that allowed her to integrate while being different. Seeing this as a positive adaptation to her mobility helped her to see its potential for her professional plans.

Rajiv currently lives in Singapore, where he has used his diverse experience in industry and in the world to create a digital media company.

Rajiv was born in Kerala in the South of India. He speaks many languages. He decided to go to the United States to study, where he was given a scholarship to get a masters degree in computer science. Changing countries gave him an opportunity to learn in different ways. He learned through work, through school and through life. He saw possibilities that he had never envisioned at home.

Very soon he found himself working for a Fortune 500 tech company. Rajiv moved to California. While he excelled at work in the computer industry, he realized that his passion was in media and the performing arts. He made short movies that were featured in international film festivals and experimented with theater, successfully. He also started to learn about possibilities of combining media with computers. He discovered that he could realize his passion in work. Skills in hand, he decided to get an MBA to pull his diverse strengths into a company where he could follow his passion.

A consultant, Stephen knew how to give people what they needed. His analysis would always be right on target. He was definitely a high flyer. With reflection, he started seeing the unique perspective that he had being an outsider.

Stephen grew up in Hong Kong and in Britain. His parents, of Armenian origin, gave him a strong value base. He developed a desire and ability to adapt, to achieve and to excel. He quickly learned what he needed to do to succeed, and succeed he did. He learned early on to be the best at doing what is expected of him; to be number one, whether it was academic or athletic. He became a consultant after university. He enjoyed and excelled at understanding new situations and helping people see what steps they need to take. Quietly, he became an expert at working the margins, at finding the interface between very different perspectives and ways of being. This was the beginning of the development of his creative edge of difference. As someone that learned how to adapt to the needs of a new situation when he was growing up, Stephen used the same strategy when he started working as a consultant. Successful, his next step was to bring his Asian experience to his work in London.

Having introduced the growing Global Cosmopolitan phenomenon, its identity and strengths, this book has now moved beyond the traditional limited view of the globally mobile workforce. But key pieces of the puzzle are still missing. The next part of this book will show where the strengths of Global Cosmopolitans come from.

PART II

THE INVISIBLE JOURNEY: THE ROOTS OF STRENGTH AND RESILIENCE

"My lack of national identity has left me with precious few external factors on which to base my identity. However, the world is an ever-changing place: external factors such as professions, friends, and countries are in a constant state of change. I believe that if I continue to search outside of myself, my reference point will always be changing. My search has finally led me to the conclusion that the only viable, long-term anchor of my identity must be somewhere in myself, inside of me."

4

LIFE CHALLENGES AND THE ROAD TO IDENTITY

At school, she was the star pupil; at home she was the perfect daughter; in her love relationships, she tried to be the perfect partner. At work, she could be a good listener, a comedian or an aggressive trader. With all of her success, there was a part of her that felt more and more uncomfortable. She knew that she could adapt; now she wanted to know whether she could let others know what she wanted.

Here is what Fiona has to say about herself:

My family immigrated to Vancouver from Hong Kong when I was eight years old. Although I had gone to bilingual schools since kindergarten and spoke British English, I thought in Chinese when I first arrived in Canada. I came from a biracial background so it was difficult for my classmates to categorize me. To my inexperienced ears, my teachers and classmates spoke so quickly that I was not able to understand them. I felt unable to communicate all that I had to say. There was only one other Chinese child in my class. When I saw him, without thinking, I would speak in Cantonese to him automatically. He spoke a different dialect of Chinese and did not understand me at all, not to mention the fact that he was utterly embarrassed that I spoke to him in Chinese at all. When you are eight years old, you just do not want to be different or stand out. I cried almost every night.

Fiona felt like she was slipping academically, too. She had been top at her demanding school in Hong Kong and expected the same from herself in her new country. "I was completely stressed out by school and I was only eight!" she writes. "Academically and socially, I felt like I did not belong."

She soon dropped her British accent and picked up a Canadian one. She entered a program for gifted students and graduated early at the top of her high school class. She went on to the University of British Colombia and then the London School of Economics. This led to her choice of working in London as an investment banker.

But no matter how high Fiona climbs, a part of her is always eight years old and standing in the schoolyard.

My feelings of alienation in my elementary schoolyard resulted in my drive to integrate early on and as an adult. Most people would say that I could fit in almost anywhere. I would also say the same about myself when asked. Yet I know that I have become an excellent actress, playing the roles so well that I am the only one that experiences the weight of the role. Being dislocated from a familiar environment as a child has an enormous impact on me as an adult: I have a deep desire to fit in or belong and to please; with that desire come the inherent insecurities of not fitting in and not belonging.

Taking time out, Fiona knows that she has to find the right environment and the right people to allow her to bring her own personality to her life, while still using her ability to adapt. Now she has a chance to discover who she really wants to be.

Not everyone who lives in East Africa is a world-class runner, and not every world-class runner is East African. But to find a talent pool of world-class runners, East Africa is an obvious place to look. The same logic can be applied to Global Cosmopolitans. Just as the challenges of traveling long distance on foot at high altitude contribute to the extraordinary competence of East African runners, the challenges of living, studying and working across cultures contribute to the crucial cognitive, adaptive and perceptual skills of Global Cosmopolitans.

This chapter explores the role that challenges play in shaping Global Cosmopolitans. The uncommon complexity of these challenges gives the Global Cosmopolitan identity its particular shared dimension. Global Cosmopolitans need a great deal of creativity to compose their identities. Their ability to make sense of their complex lives helps explain the creativity that Global Cosmopolitans display to make sense of the fast-changing business world.

Most people enjoy relative stability. Their lives change with time, but their nationality, surroundings, friends and loved ones provide a backdrop of continuity. Global Cosmopolitans, on the other hand, must construct their own continuity in the midst of multiple transitions and change. "Do you ever get that dizzy sensation when you wake up somewhere and think to yourself, how the hell did I get here?" writes Nancy, an American student. "The room is spinning, the place doesn't smell like home, and you have that familiar queasy yet strangely elated feeling. That feeling is the story of my life."

The richness of the Global Cosmopolitan life story lies in understanding the special nature of the demands placed on them. The reason many Global Cosmopolitans cannot articulate the breadth and depth of their inner complexity is that the hard work they do to meet these demands is often hidden in the commotion of everyday life. They have to deal with the loss of the worlds they left behind, with changing who they are to fit their new circumstances, with being different and with the rootlessness of having no real home. They have to find meaning in the complex and changing mosaic of their experiences. Internal challenges such as these provide learning opportunities through which Global Cosmopolitans become masters of transition and change.

THE INNER JOURNEY: THE UNCOMMON CHALLENGES

In my case, growing up without a national identity has undoubtedly contributed to my unease about who I am. I cannot say that I am a Belgian or an American, even though that is written on my passports. Neither can I claim to be a German or a Hungarian, despite those countries being the roots of my origins.

My lack of national identity has left me with precious few eternal factors on which to base my identity. However, the world is an ever-changing place: external factors such as professions, friends and countries are in a constant state of change. I believe that if I continue to search outside of myself, my reference point will always be changing. My search has finally led me to the conclusion that the only viable, long-term anchor of my identity must be somewhere in myself, inside of me.

Inside ourselves, we are constantly composing the story that explains to others and ourselves how we have become who we are. The construction of that story is deeply intertwined with the culture and people who surround us. Our ongoing personal narrative connects who we are today with who we were yesterday, a year ago, in childhood, and with who we imagine we will one day become. The fragmented external factors described above suggest how complex the process of composing an identity story is for Global Cosmopolitans. Without the master narratives of a single culture to provide the templates by which to create an identity, Global Cosmopolitans must create their own internal identity core that anchors them. Often, they do not even have a single language to unite their memories.

What was strange was looking at what I could remember about my life without using the language of that time period. I had to write my story in three languages. Unfortunately, the language of my youth is not particularly articulate. I wonder what has been forgotten because of words that do not exist for me.

Most people who look for the roots of Global Cosmopolitan strength and resilience are drawn to Global Cosmopolitans' outer journey. But the real roots lie in their inner journey and the uncommon challenges they encounter there. The exploration of the Global Cosmopolitan inner journey begins with this chapter.

A growing body of evidence suggests that narratives are a fundamental technique that our mind uses to find personal meaning and to make sense of our lives. We don't just remember facts. We select parts of our experience and imaginatively blend them into our coherent picture of ourselves. We are not telling ourselves lies. Through these personal stories, each of us discovers what is true and what is meaningful within the context of our own life.

We learn who we are from the challenges we face. Through a process that is often invisible, we convert challenges along our developmental pathways into learning opportunities to find our strengths and change our perceptions of what we are capable of in the future. Reversing the process can allow us to shed light on the invisible developmental pathway we have followed.

Sometimes there are powerful moments in life—positive or painful ones—that significantly change our understanding of who we are. These moments can be a single experience, a longer episode or even a sudden flash of memory. Sometimes the significance becomes apparent only later in life. I call these moments "turning points." A time of discontinuity, variability or change, they open the possibility of personal redefinition.

For Shamir, moving from Pakistan to study and work in Europe was a redefining moment:

One of the major turning points in my life so far, that had the most impact on me, took place when I left my home country of Pakistan to pursue my dream of living, traveling, studying and working in the heart of Europe. The journey was full of setbacks and mishaps, heartbreaks and misfortunes, but one that allowed me to live my dream and develop as an individual in a way I would have never done had I continued to live in Pakistan. I believe I have come a long way since my migration to Europe. I have become more sensitive toward and tolerant of people from different nationalities, cultures and social backgrounds. I have become much better at acknowledging differing points of views, adapting to new environments and at the same time respecting my roots and cultural heritage. I have learned to view, understand, value and cherish my family back home in a different light. In a sense, I would like to believe that I have become more humble and sensitive as a human being than I was before. Nevertheless, life will never be the same again.

It is difficult to quantify the confidence gained from learning new languages and navigating in different cultures. But my research has identified a cluster of common challenges that provides a window into the world of Global Cosmopolitans. Their ability to see opportunity in difficult times and to take risks with confidence parallels the work they have done to construct their own identities in the face of uncommon complexity and constant change. By systematically looking at the challenges in their lives, Global Cosmopolitans can give voice to their experiences and strengths. They can see how the lessons of past experiences can be applied to new situations.

Challenge: Transition and Change

Although learning a new language and cultural skills are important for adapting across cultures, underlying challenges shape the Global Cosmopolitan experience. The first of these is the challenge of constant transition and change.

Change management expert William Bridges draws a distinction between change and transition.[1] "Change," he says, "is a situational shift. Transition is the process of letting go of the way things used to be and then taking on the way they subsequently become." In his words, transition is the way that we all come to terms with change. But there are stages of transition that we have to go through—letting go, the neutral state and the new beginning—all, in retrospect, opportunities to learn and develop.

Transitions can also be defined simply as passages from one state, stage and subject or place to another. They are so much a part of life that cultures have ceremonies to mark or celebrate them. The Balinese, for example, have tooth-filing ceremonies for adolescence. But transition in the context of a Global Cosmopolitan's life is experienced without ceremony; it is the internal shock and dislocation of seeing a familiar world turned upside down.

Sometimes the dislocation is welcome.

I was fat, short and unpopular. I was miserable. My parents decided over the summer to move from France to the United States. I grew! And I grew. By the time I got to the United States, I was seen as a beau mec (a handsome guy). Life changed for me.

But the Global Cosmopolitan challenge of change and transition does not always resolve itself so naturally.

Too many key transitions at once can be highly stressful, yet Global Cosmopolitans routinely face multiple changes at the same time. Geographic transitions often coincide with other life transitions. Getting married, having children, changing schools or jobs while changing cultures is stressful even if it is welcome. It's not surprising, then, that many Global Cosmopolitans feel competent and yet ambivalent about change.

Mastery of change is a familiar feeling, but it can also be painful, like reopening a wound each time. The work of psychologists often involves helping people move through different stages of transition. Ambivalence about letting go or moving forward can leave someone trapped. Global Cosmopolitans can feel pulled in two directions by the needs of their new situation and one they left behind. Many feel pressured to move back to their families. Despite living in many countries, they can feel pressured to marry someone from what their family considers home. The ambivalence created by these pressures makes it difficult for many people to make a commitment to a relationship or even to a career track.

The fundamental challenge of transition and change is loss. The theme of loss presents itself in many ways.

Adults can suddenly find that

They have lost the ability to relate to people and to motivate them.

They have lost the power they need to get things done.

They feel a loss of control, a loss of security, a loss of feeling anchored.

They feel responsible for the losses their families experience because of the move.

They feel the loss of knowing the most mundane things, such as where to go shopping or where to find a good doctor.

Then there is the loss associated with command of the language and its cultural meaning. Even if they are comfortable with the language, they still can experience isolation because of a loss of humor. Puns or funny gestures do not communicate across the culture barrier. One of the important skills of living internationally, Global Cosmopolitans say, is the ability to bridge the humor gap. They can become particularly sensitive to finding humor even where there is no language link.

For children, loss can mean going from being one of the best in the class to suddenly finding they are the worst. It might be not knowing how to ask someone to play or different ways of doing math at school. It might be moving from a city that is warm, green and safe to one that is cold and too unsafe to do anything on one's own. It might mean living with extended family or with parents struggling to survive.

My parents are American, but I was born and raised in Italy. In my local school, I was the American, but when I went to the United States for high school, I was suddenly Italian. It felt like everything changed. I was big for my age in Italy, but average in the States. In Italy, I was the expert on American movies and American sports, yet in the States, I did not know anything about TV series and I certainly did not know how to play basketball or American football. They did not even know about how good I was in soccer, let alone at school. That first year was a nightmare as I tried to figure out who I was.

Children can feel inadequate or alone, unable to express their losses or unwilling to burden their parents. Many highly successful Global Cosmopolitans have childhood stories about how they overcame extreme transitions caused by political instability or economic hardship despite having parents who were suffering and were inaccessible during those difficult times.

Children can experience loss when they see their parents change without understanding why. This has been the case for many Global Cosmopolitans who started their journey when the family had to move suddenly because of political unrest.

Mina moved to the United States when her family fled from Iran.

For years, Mina's mother could not stop crying because of all the losses she felt after leaving her way of life behind. With her mother so incapacitated by sorrow and her father trying to find any possible source of income, Mina became the adult child in her immediate family. She felt responsible. She became so skilled at being the translator and the protector that she helped even members of her extended family who had been forced to leave.

After graduating from university, she became an assistant to the founder of a small company. Years later she realized that the skill that made her invaluable to her company was the ability to translate the needs of her clients.

Because of the complex changes in their lives, Global Cosmopolitans understand the notion of stages of transition extremely well. They know what new beginnings require. They develop confidence by learning how to resolve seemingly impossible situations. Their moves might be chaotic, with many pieces of their lives out of control and changing at the same time, but out of the chaos they learn valuable skills to manage complex situations. Charles showed what he has learned about positive change: "I need to be doing something when I am part of a major life transition. I am coaching a sports team while working on my MBA. They speak Chinese; I speak French. But it works and I am happy. It pushes me to be very organized."

Challenge: Identity: Who Am I? How Much Can I Change without Losing a Sense of Who I Am?

Sitting in the airport lounge in Hong Kong, absorbed in reading about a man who had lost track of what he wanted and who he was, a character that had lost himself, I realized that I was reading about me. It was almost New Year's. I sat between two years. I sat between different lives. I had just left my family at home in Ireland after a fun Christmas. I had just left my job in New York. I had just broken up again with my long-term boyfriend in Germany. I was on my way to Argentina to be a bridesmaid in my college roommate's wedding. The day after the wedding I was heading to France to start my INSEAD adventure. I felt like a dislocated soul. I was but a plane ride away from the several different lives I had led, from the seemingly contradictory person I had been whilst leading these different lives. I could change flights and go to any of the places I had lived: Ireland, Boston, Paris, New York, San Francisco or London. The same person would have got on these flights, but when I disembarked the plane I would have been a different person based on the memories involved with that place. Through all of these moves, I'd lost track of myself. Who was I?

Adolescence, the awkward time when we try to figure out who we are, is a common theme in literature and films. Developmental theorists describe adolescence as a time when people start creating their identity story as teenagers and young adults. Who am I? Who will I become? Am I attractive? Am I smart? Am I good enough to be on a sports team or be a star in a school play? But Global Cosmopolitans have periods of adolescence where they go through turbulent internal changes in the midst of shifting circumstances and contradictory contexts. "I have lived many lives," says a Global Cosmopolitan who studied and worked on four continents, "but nothing seems to hold them together."

Sometimes Global Cosmopolitans have a straightforward answer to the question "Who am I?"

Going to high school in France, I became a different person. At first, it was not easy and I missed everything about home. My new best friend helped me become more outgoing. I begged my mother to let me stay. I was petrified that I would return to my former, boring, mousey, Canadian self. Luckily, I kept the confidence that I gained and returned home with my new personality. Now I see the challenge of changing cultures as an opportunity to enrich who I am.

But as circumstances grow more tangled and contradictions increase, the answers become more elusive. Two stories illustrate how Global Cosmopolitans struggled to fit into the world around them before they found the identity that they knew was right for them

I was born in Africa and I grew up in Africa. I am Belgian, insofar as my father is Belgian, and I am English by virtue of my mother being English. I carry around a vague sense of being European. Although I come from an old, traditional Belgian family, I grew up in the bush. When I am in Belgium, people think I am a foreigner; when I am in England, I also have Englishmen detect a trace of foreigner in my accent. I have an English education though. My father only half-jokingly introduced my brother and me as "British-educated Belgian savages." I always felt different and increasingly confused about who I was. For years, I wanted to tell people that I was African, but I knew that they would laugh at me. I know that there is a part of me that loves that personality best. Now, I can look at myself and see my different personalities emerge depending on my surroundings. The longer I live in London, surrounded by other Global Cosmopolitans, the more I begin to feel that a mixture of cultural personalities is just me.

When I left Japan to live in Italy, I was the perfect little Japanese girl. It took me a while to learn how to adapt to my new friends in the international school in Rome. I changed my clothes, changed my accent and changed my way of being. Everyone loved me. It was fabulous. I almost looked Italian. I knew exactly what to wear, how to move and how to be. Three years later, my parents moved back to Japan. At first I was miserable. I felt lost. I did not know who I was. I did not belong anywhere. I am adaptable, and before I knew it, I was a perfect little Japanese girl again. At least, that is what people thought. I knew that I had changed, and that I would be someone that would live and learn in different countries. I would be truly international.

Global Cosmopolitans who begin their international journey as young adults often learn that once-competent and articulate persons can be inept, inarticulate and seemingly useless in their new environment. They can suddenly find themselves feeling infantilized and insecure. They can also return to what should be home and find they are again going through a period of personal examination as reentry pushes them to examine who they really are. Sometimes, like Eric, they discover that they have become two people while they were gone.

There is obviously a deep divide between the young French student who went to the United States and the English-speaking professional I have become. I do have two sets of behaviors, two approaches to life, whether I function in French or in English.

The English-speaking Eric is confident and self-assured not only in what he can do but also among others, in society. He has no fear of what others think of him. He has completely assumed his differences, his weaknesses and his strength. I think he is self-aware and quite hard to destabilize.

The French Eric—that sounds a little schizophrenic, but I promise I am not—is less sure of himself, especially in society. He is more on the defensive, more of an introvert, more aggressive also sometimes. He knows what he can do as well and knows his strengths, but his attitude is different. He is quieter, more on the inside.

I think that at least on a personal level the two Erics are getting together more and more, but it is not an easy process, especially with family and old friends.

Dramatic changes in economic situations lead to identity confusion, too. Global Cosmopolitans who have left a home in difficult economic circumstances know that every year and every pay raise take them farther from their roots. Returning can seem impossible. The challenge to identity is particularly strong for people who grew up poor in countries that are remote, where there is extreme poverty and where their parents still live. Motivation to enjoy the advantages of a dominant, economically developed culture can take Global Cosmopolitans a long way, but the memory of childhood lingers.

My family was very well educated, both of my parents being professors. In the one-room apartment that we lived in with my grandparents, we had many books and many wonderful moments together. When I left to do my MBA at age twenty-one, I never imagined how life would change for me. I wanted to earn a good salary, but I never imagined becoming an investment banker in London. By everyone's standards, I am a wealthy woman as result of my success in investment banking. My friends are from all over the world. Unfortunately, nothing replaces the warmth, love and support that I had growing up. I know that I cannot go backwards. I have changed too much. My parents miss me and do not understand my new values. They would trade all of the money to have me closer to home. I feel the tug of the warm togetherness that we had, yet I know that I would be miserable going there, even though I know there are more opportunities in Moscow now.

For Global Cosmopolitans, identity questions also revolve around issues of what passports they carry and want to have their children carry.

The year that I did not have a passport was the worst year in my life. I felt like I didn't belong anywhere and I lost a sense of who I was. My whole sense of self was threatened. I did not expect that reaction. I have grown up in three countries with parents who are from two different countries. I had done a lot of thinking about which passport would be better for me and which one I wanted. I never expected that a bureaucratic mistake would cause me such anxiety. I knew it would work out. I actually hate it when people ask me where I am from. I have a number of answers to give depending on whom I am talking to. I could play with my identity, but I did not want to be seen as a man without a country or roots.

Knowing that passports can also provide security and ease of passage, Liv took the necessary two years and mountains of paperwork to settle the passport issue for her two children. Her daughter is Italian, like her father, and could have an Italian passport, along with her Swedish and Swiss passports. Her son has a Swedish passport like his mother and a passport from India, where he was adopted.

Resolving the challenge of identity gives Global Cosmopolitans confidence in confronting change. Hieu, for example, moved to the United States from Vietnam at age five. The family had to start over, and the initial economic stresses were immense:

I've always been curious for a new perspective. That's not an intangible statement. As a child, I scraped knees and elbows climbing trees and roofs, digging deep holes and shinnying into dark narrow corners to see what everything looked like from a different angle. As a teenager, when the family was sleeping, I'd open the eaves window, side step outside onto the roof and then scuttle to the highest point to look at the stars. My friends and I requisitioned a screwdriver, unlatched the attic door to our school hall and climbed through the old attic to reach the top of the clock tower. In adulthood, I think this has given me the courage three times to arrive in a new city far, far from home and make a new life for myself without knowing anyone. Curiosity to see the world from a different location overrode desire for security and belonging.

Because Global Cosmopolitans must reinvent themselves to fit their changing circumstances, they must also learn not to change too much. The danger of losing oneself emerges in the words of Claire: "I felt like a rootless individual, a person that I do not recognize, a multitude of my selves, fitting in for others but not being myself." The challenge is to find the right balance so Global Cosmopolitans can remain true to who they really are.

Keeping all the elements of identity in balance is "like the different instruments in an orchestra, playing together in a symphony," writes a Global Cosmopolitan whose background encompasses four nations. "The idea is that they are all important for the beauty of the music, but if one of them takes over or becomes too loud, the music ceases to be beautiful. This also raises the issue of the need for a conductor to tame the different instruments, to know when it is their turn to play or to be silent."

Challenge: Being Different and Managing Difference for Other People

Two stories dramatically illustrate what it means for Global Cosmopolitans to be different:

I cannot identify the point in my life when I became uncomfortable with being Chinese, but I suspect it was during my adolescence. When I felt rejected, I began to question whether the source of my problems was my Chinese face. Perhaps my Chinese background explained why no boy asked me out, why I was not invited to a particular party … the list could go on and on. When I was thirteen, my family went on a one-month trip to China, where no one in China ever saw me as purely Chinese. I was solidly American, with my fluorescent clothes and strange accent. My identity confusion only grew when an American Boy Scout spotted me at a train station in Shanghai, mistook me for a native Chinese, and gave me a Boy Scout patch as an American memento. I was too stunned to respond; at that moment, I felt myself falling in a chasm between two cultures, between two countries.

I expected Americans to know about India, at least as much as I know about the United States if not more. But in Nebraska people thought India is similar to the way it was described in an Indiana Jones movie. People asked me about how many elephants I own and why do I not wear a turban. It was a big shock to me; very soon the realization hit me that I am from a Third World country, which most of the people do not even care about. I had very

high esteem of Indian culture and its contribution to the world. But my feel-
ing after coming to the United States for university was that in the Western
World, their history books perhaps did not even mention India. The only
thing average people who I interacted with seemed to know was Gandhi. No
one knew or even cared that there is a religion named Hinduism, which is
followed by nearly a billion people. I prefer to call Hinduism a way of life, not
a religion. I was curious: if someone from Nebraska went to my hometown in
India and met my old grannies, and I told them that she does not know the
name of the God that they worship for hours and hours, what would have
been their reaction? Perhaps a heart attack!

Being different is part of the normal challenge of children and ado-
lescents. Just being short, tall, fat or thin at the wrong time in life can
be devastating. Being different can make people feel alone, like nobody
could possibly understand them. But the examples above illustrate the
added complexity that comes from straddling different cultures. The
challenge is particularly strong for children getting started in new countries, because often their parents cannot help. Not speaking the language
is an obvious barrier, but so is not knowing how to play the most common local sports or not watching the same television programs. Children
quickly learn that they have to overcome their differences on their own.

The turning points Global Cosmopolitans describe often involve
the challenge of being different and the lessons that they learn from
that experience. Sabine's turning point happened when she went from
her German community in Argentina to an Argentine university. She
could see how organized she was, how time focused, how different from
her Argentine friends. But she loved their spontaneity and warmth and
tried to adapt. She found that the more her friends were spontaneous,
the more rigid she became. She realized she needed a different style of
friendship. The experience helped her understand not just how to be
with people who are different but also to understand who she could
become and who she could not be.

Julie felt born to be different. Her mother is an Indian Muslim and
her father is French. Growing up she lived from Mumbai to London.
She lives in Japan with her American husband and their children, and
her mailing address is in the United States.

I was born different or so I wish to believe. In my life, I have gone from
wanting to be the same as others, to looking for others who were unusual, to
clearly flaunting my difference. If you cannot join them, beat them became
my motto. I enjoy being original and yet do not want to reveal all about
myself. I wish to be seen as a citizen of the world.

Both children and adults learn to deal with difference by developing coping styles often related to the way they prefer to learn. While some might prefer to step back and observe or read, others jump in and take a more active approach, experimenting through trial and error. "You know that people do things differently and you have to figure out how to manage that difference," a student writes. "First you have to see it, even if you learn by making mistakes." Ultimately, many Global Cosmopolitans learn to use their difference to get ahead or find ways to turn the disadvantage of difference to their favor. They turn the complexity of learning about a new culture and how to find a place in it into an adventure. Mastery in a new setting becomes a familiar feeling, and they learn important skills from the process.

If I had stayed in Chile all my life, I never would have learned how to deal with people from such different cultures and different ways of working. I was smart and arrogant and thought that I was better off doing things myself. Then I went to school in California. I learned what it is like to feel incompetent and silent because I did not know the language. I learned how to observe and I realized that by watching and listening there was a lot to learn. Then I took a job in Vietnam. Although we all spoke English, I remembered my experience and used it. I am seen as a leader in my company, thanks to those skills.

Children also can find themselves in the position of managing the cultural difference for their parents. Translating language and cultural communication becomes a normal part of daily life. "This is how it is done" or "This is what they mean" are constant refrains as children guide their parents. As the traditional role between parent and child changes, children can find themselves in the role of adults. That challenge is why many Global Cosmopolitans say they become expert negotiators and develop powerful people skills to use in adult life.

Seeing Prashant manage relational tensions in a group, the label "diplomat" comes to mind. His family moved to the United States before he was born. Although they spoke English, they lived with other Indians that had just moved to the United States. Prashant became the interface between his family and life outside of that neighborhood. It became very important for him to achieve in the American system, to be successful academically and socially. He wanted to go to the best schools, which meant that he had to find a way to get accepted and earn scholarships. Ambitious, he wanted to be class president or the football captain. He knew that his best route was through using the diplomatic skills he had learned to protect and help his family.

Challenge: Where Is Home?

I woke up one Sunday morning in Sydney feeling very depressed and empty, although I had plenty of reasons not to be. I had all the material comfort in this world: great living space on the most fashionable city harbor, plenty of money to burn, beautiful weather, streets full of good-looking surfing types who were ready to buy me drinks. After spending three years traveling the world, I managed to accumulate friends in most major cities. I had all the freedom in the world. In short, I was the fashionable woman often spotted in a city café talking on a mobile, seemingly with no worries in the world.

And yet I was unhappy.

Well, years later I am still a globetrotter and am still unhappy. In the past five years, I lived for months at a time in Boston, New York, São Paolo, Hong Kong, Beijing, Singapore and Sydney. This is a traveling itinerary to be envied by many of my friends: so free and worldly. But I feel that for every additional place, I become more detached from all the places I have been. I am sometimes envious of my friends' lifestyle, particularly of their connection to a place, a set of friends and a basic value system. I have not gone home to Boston for three years. I have not seen my parents for eight months and my best girlfriend for six. I cried when I heard the news that the flat I grew up in in Shanghai was torn down. It was old and full of cockroaches and I could not ever live there again. But that beat-up flat was my only attachment to a place. Without it, I am now truly homeless.

People often define who they are by where they live. Home is such an important part of who we are that it is often one of the first questions we ask when meeting a stranger. Yet this simple concept is complex for Global Cosmopolitans. It is even more complex for those who are born into families that transcend national borders. For many of them, the concept of home is so foreign that they become uncomfortable when the topic comes up in conversation. They hate the often-asked question "Where is home?" Many Global Cosmopolitans struggle with the question "Can I find a place where I can belong?" or "Can I find a creative solution that allows me to have more than one home where I feel like I belong?"

The challenge of life without home is almost unthinkable to many people, and it requires a great deal of creativity on the part of Global Cosmopolitans. For them, home becomes a relative concept. It might be a place where their parents live, even if they have never lived there. It might just be an image of home, a kind of impossible dream. Even people who think they have a home are shocked to discover after years of absence that the home they remembered doesn't really exist. Not only have their perspectives changed because of their international experience, but family, friends and social trends have all changed in their absence. Katherine, for example, felt stuck between her feelings about home, real and imagined.

I have lived outside of South Africa now for ten years; most of this has been in the United Kingdom, with one year traveling, one year in the United States and one year in France. The question of where I live has worried me a lot over the past few years. While South Africa is always home, I have been away for a long time, and the crime, violence and uncertain future of the country bother me. My family has been involved in violence there and has been threatened with guns, and many times I have wondered whether, having been away for so long, it makes sense to go back. There is no other place, however, that I feel I could clearly call home. While I have lived in the United Kingdom for a long time, I have for some reason never bought a property there and have always felt it to be a transient place.

Living without home can be liberating, allowing greater room for self-expression and reinvention. But it can become wearying, too, and many Global Cosmopolitans ultimately seek to set down roots either in their country of birth or in a foreign country that provides good possibilities for home and work. Morton describes his challenge of home this way:

Something changes in your soul when you travel a lot. You get a much broader view of the world and tend to start to assimilate parts of many different cultures. This is at least what has started happening to me. It worries me. But at the same time I do not want to go back to Denmark. There are too many things about the Danish society that I am not comfortable with. So I am stuck in the middle and probably destined to become part of the international traveling nomads with no real home anywhere. Wherever I have been, I have seen these traveling business nomads on the constant move. Some of them have scared me. I look at them and think, "Is this how I want to end up?" One of the solutions that I am considering seriously is to buy a small house in the southern part of France where I can make myself a base. No matter where I am in the world, I would always be able to come back to that place.

The decision to find a home can often become a complex balancing act between the needs of the individual, family, extended family and professional opportunities. Joanna met her French husband while they were getting their MBAs in Boston. They both worked in investment banking in New York City for a few years. After the birth of their twins, they thought seriously about where they wanted to raise their children and create a home. Creating a permanent home for their children was very important for both of them. Joanna had grown up in Hong Kong, although her parents moved to London before she finished secondary school. She lived with her grandparents until she went to Cambridge University in England. Guy had grown up in Africa. His parents sent him to boarding school and university in France. Now his parents had retired to France. They both had excellent professional possibilities in Brussels and decided to try living there, raising their twins to appreciate their diverse cultural backgrounds and integrating into the culture they have chosen to make home.

Falling in love with someone from a very different culture means Kim might have to create a new sense of home. She wonders what the change will mean:

I have a hard time identifying where or what home means to me. I say "home" all the time—"I'm going home this Christmas" or "Let's stay at home tonight"—but every time I use it, I am referring to somewhere different or relating a different emotional concept. I have friends all over the world and I thrive on moving around, traveling to new places and meeting new people. I face a constant internal battle of knowing when to stay and when to move on. Do I want to go somewhere new? Is it time I finally put down some roots? Am I ready for that? Do I even want to do that? If I do, what am I giving up? I am constantly questioning whether I want to build a community around me and whether I want to invest in integrating fully into a group of people.

Alex had already lived in Africa, Europe, Asia and South America before he began to figure out what he needed from a home:

I am starting to understand that my home will be with my good friends. I need to find a home base where I can create the relationships that I need. I know that I am overtly very skillful with people, but it is very difficult for me to build and keep close friends. How can I find a place to live where the quality of life is appealing and where I could start to create a home base that would allow greater possibility of relational commitments? I think that I will take the position as a consultant in Australia.

Challenge: A Sense of Meaning

Growing up, being at home was enough for me to find meaning in my life. Everything I did seemed to have a sense and a purpose. Now, I am an investment banker in London. So far, I am very successful by every standard, yet my life feels increasingly empty. I have lost a feeling that my life has meaning. I am searching.

Many people reach a point in their lives where they wonder about the meaning of their existence. For Global Cosmopolitans, the need for meaning is heightened by the loss, rootlessness, sense of difference and identity confusion described above. A strong value system, as pointed out in the previous chapter, plays an essential role in the development of resilience. Creating a sense of meaning from that value system allows Global Cosmopolitans to construct the continuity they need to be resilient in their changing circumstances.

For some young people, international experience begins with volunteer work in other countries. This is their first opportunity to understand life from a global perspective. The experience can have a profound impact on how they understand the world or how they choose to create a life. It can also help them see pathways to meaning through socially responsible activities or professions.

Two stories illustrate how meaningful action can give direction to a global life.

Liv has felt a strong drive to help others ever since childhood, when she accompanied her father on Red Cross humanitarian missions. No matter where she is in the world, she knows that her life is given the richness of meaning through socially responsible activities. There are no geographic boundaries to her perspective on what she can do to make a difference. Whether she helps develop a green school in Bali or donates to an orphanage in India, it is her world.

Deciding to return to Portugal was a difficult decision for Goncalo. While he knew that he would retain his global mindset, he worried about returning home after years of excitement and the challenge of a global life. He knew that he would travel as a consultant, but he wanted to make sure that he always kept his perspective on the world. He needed to feel like he made a difference. This factor was an important piece of giving meaning to his life back in Portugal. Negotiating to work on a humanitarian project in Mozambique as part of his work contract helped him make the transition.

Other Global Cosmopolitans initially find meaning in pursuing careers but paradoxically begin to feel spiritually rootless just when they have reached their professional goals. As a result, like the student at the beginning of this section, they can be outwardly highly successful and yet feel inwardly lost. Just as the other losses that Global Cosmopolitans confront provide opportunities for strength and growth, the challenge to find meaning can help Global Cosmopolitans learn important lessons about themselves. Alfredo, a Chilean, discovered through firefighting that "the entrepreneurial side of me loves to follow a cause."

I think that by being an entrepreneur, I need to identify a cause and follow it. This same process happens to me in the firefighters. What I like a lot is to get organized to do several tasks like fundraising, training and, of course, firefighting. Here I like to be accountable for what I have done and then also get recognition for the accomplished tasks. Probably what I like most about being a firefighter is this social entrepreneurial side that is implicit. When I am passionate about a cause, I really love it.

Shedding light on these five challenges is a first step in helping Global Cosmopolitans to move their invisible journey out of the dark. But they describe only one part of the uncommon complexity of a Global Cosmopolitan life. While changing where they live and how they live, Global Cosmopolitans must also rebalance their relationships with the people around them. The next chapter explores relationship challenges.

5

RELATIONSHIP CHALLENGES: INVISIBLE RULES, SILENT VOICES

Ariana works in financial services in London.

Her life, she says, would have been unimaginable to her parents in Albania, where history, politics and society shaped entirely different attitudes and priorities about work.

Ariana writes:

My first recollection of a profession comes from my parents' relations to work. Under the Communist regime, job predictability and security were among the main characteristics of the job market. Both of my parents had the same job for most of their professional lives. After they finished their degrees, they started working in their professions: my father as an engineer in a factory, my mother in a military institute.

By Albanian standards, they were well paid and the salary was an important consideration of the job. There was no questioning of the validity of the job choice. They had loyalty for the employer and expected the same. For them, starting to work for a particular company meant that their whole professional lives were more or less marked by the boundaries of the company.

I never heard them discuss whether they should move or look for another position somewhere else. There was a certain degree of fatalism in their attitude toward jobs. In addition, there were rarely discussions in the family regarding the intellectual stimulation that the profession gave them. I don't remember my parents discussing whether what they were doing matched their dreams of childhood. What was more important for them was to get recognition for their work performance and feel part of the company.

I grew up with the view that work is something that grown-ups take on to make money and integrate in the society. The personal stimulations that a professional position would generate were not factors.

As I started my professional life, these were some of the values that I brought with me.

My moves to the United States, France and the United Kingdom led to a complete change in the way that I would view my work and my profession. It challenged my views and my assumptions, created a lot of uncertainty and opened the path of considering new options that I would have not thought about if I had remained in Albania.

THE PAST AS PROLOGUE TO THE PRESENT

Identity is a combination of different parts of a person's history. It is a distillation of past and present stories blended with a sense of future possibilities. As Global Cosmopolitans face new challenges, they can reexamine their past to discover fresh insights about who they are. Taken together, the stories that Global Cosmopolitans tell about themselves span many cultures, so the voices that shape their lives are both varied and fascinating. Their vignettes provide a glimpse into the inner complexity of their lives. This chapter describes typical ways in which cultural and family stories combine to help form the Global Cosmopolitan identity story.

Why culture matters is reflected in every aspect of their lives as they face challenges and seek opportunities. Having different cultural messages to adhere to can be confusing, but it also can give Global Cosmopolitans multiple options to respond to. Clarifying areas of flexibility can become important for Global Cosmopolitans, since many cultural rules are learned at a very young age and so are harder to recognize or change. Although the world has become smaller, there are still very different ways of understanding the notion of self, as it is defined in certain cultures.[1] While the self is generally defined as being a separate individual in some cultures, the boundaries between self and others are less clear in other cultures. This alone has a huge impact on how people experience their life issues.

When people narrate their identity stories, they frequently contextualize who they are, even to the point of describing the smells and sounds of childhood. The word "context" comes from the same root as the word "textile" and literally means woven together. Since we spend our lives surrounded by other people, our identities are woven not just by our own thoughts and actions, but also by our relationships with the people around us. As Ariana's story illustrates, even concepts as personal as the meaning of work or the fulfillment of childhood dreams are typically a product of our context. I often ask people trying to understand their personal narratives to close their eyes and picture their lives as a fabric, to imagine the individual threads and the colorful or clashing patterns that emerge. What are the circumstances, stories and people in their past that contribute to the complex picture? What unique challenges are in their dreams and their relationships?

To convey the intricacy of relational issues, consider a scene on the first day of spring in the Luxembourg Gardens in Paris. Classmates from a nearby secondary school had spread out on the grass in groups that seemed easily identifiable by age and behavior. Students about twelve or thirteen years old tussled and giggled, acting silly and playful. In the next age group, classmates a year or so older talked in a circle, some of them smoking. Students in the next age group had mostly split off into couples who were playfully flirting. The group had dissolved entirely for students a year older; they had split into couples off on their own. The oldest group of classmates, aged seventeen or eighteen, had formed a group again, laughing and listening, their interactions laced with cigarettes and wine.

The students spoke French, although some might have been born in other countries or had parents that were from elsewhere. Some children probably felt teenage awkwardness, but these classmates appeared to know each other well and to know the invisible rules of social behavior. Despite the complexities of teenage life, another Parisian child could most likely identify enough similarities with these classmates to understand how to adapt and fit in.

But what if a student had just arrived from Singapore, speaking only Mandarin and English? Language would only be one adaptation challenge. What about sitting on the grass? Or spending school time, which was obviously work time, sitting in a garden with cigarettes and alcohol? How could they identify similarities? How could they adapt and fit in?

The unique relational challenges of Global Cosmopolitans exist in this uncertain atmosphere where suddenly and often repeatedly they need to understand a complex web of unwritten rules seen by cultural insiders as universal behavior. From intimate norms about making eye contact or determining how close to stand to broad social considerations about how to exercise power or interpret historical events, Global Cosmopolitans need to reframe their perceptions. In the process, they need to examine their own unwritten rules and question their own assumptions about what constitutes acceptable behavior.

As a result, crossing the line between cultures opens a whole world of relational challenges. The further Global Cosmopolitans move from the values and cultures of their family and childhood, the more they can feel like they are becoming separated from their past. Some Global Cosmopolitans grew up between cultures, steeped in their parents' cultures and values but expected to move seamlessly between that world and the dominant culture. As adults, many of them will integrate or find friendships with other Global Cosmopolitans or colleagues. Some deliberately move away from their childhood culture, only to discover old, hidden patterns that refuse to let go. History and culture can be deeply ingrained, disappearing and reappearing in different geographical locations or stages in life. The residue of other people's lives, of ancestors or family members whose stories pass through generations, can expand or limit perceptions of opportunities.

To arrive at their sense of what the future holds, Global Cosmopolitans must untangle the knots of the past. While sorting all these threads can be a daunting, sometimes painful task, it can also be fascinating, enjoyable and rewarding. Learning how the pieces of a collective past can affect identity provides Global Cosmopolitans a chance to understand who they are in relationship to others and helps them to improve their relational comfort and competence.

Living, studying, working, forming friendships and falling in love with someone from a different culture all provide Global Cosmopolitans graphic lessons about themselves. They can discover how their individual identity is a product of the culture, history, family and other relationships that surround them. They weave their relational fabric in contrasts, providing multiple opportunities to see different ways to understand life, social roles and manners of relating.

The ability to question universally held assumptions, to pull back and separate themselves from norms of behavior and traditional ways of thinking constitutes the core of their capacity to help businesses adapt to the fast-changing global world. CVs and résumés, the traditional measure of a worker's worth, are all about action. But much of the strength of Global Cosmopolitans at work stems from the challenges posed by interaction.

SOCIAL AND CULTURAL CONTRASTS: THE CHALLENGE OF LIVING BETWEEN WORLDS

Наведена глава, саба не я сече—A bowed head will never be cut off
The nail that sticks out gets hammered down
The tall poppy syndrome

Dimitar describes these old sayings as the core of "Laying Low Syndrome," a social system in which showing neither drive nor initiative is seen as a virtue ensconced deep into the core of the Bulgarian psyche.

> *Basically, people are never respected for making or leading an effort to do something new, different, implementing a change of whatever sort. The moment they are perceived to be changing the status quo, they are doomed to be slandered and ridiculed. The real kicker of course is that it won't even matter if they succeed or fail: the amount of animosity toward them will be the same as long as they dare challenge the status quo.*

Arriving in the United States, Dimitar said, was "a complete shock to my system, my behavior and my way of doing things. Here I was, a Bulgarian who excelled at successfully beating the system, dropped in a culture built on initiative, leadership, and achievement. All the way through college, I struggled with this difference."

Over time, though, Dimitar discovered that the United States had its own social syndromes. "Eventually I understood that it was not as clear-cut as it all appeared to me at first. People would volunteer to do work, but not haphazardly; it was more along the lines of, What can I do that will require the minimum amount of effort but will have the highest visibility and impact in front of my boss?"

His instincts and cultural upbringing conditioned him to work hard for the team. He worked long hours and shared his insights with team members, who would grab the spotlight when they presented the results to management or clients. "Most bosses didn't know about my existence," he writes. "Indeed, this was reflected in my early review, where apparently they would ask themselves, Who is Dimitar?"

Dimitar realized that his firm talked big about the value of teamwork but actually promoted people based on individual success; he had discovered the American psyche's counterpart of Laying Low Syndrome. His break happened when the person who hired him unexpectedly pulled him into a high-profile project and assigned him an essential role. The clients were difficult, but the project was a success.

> *All at once, without doing any more work than I did before, I was considered one of the star analysts in the office, someone who makes a real contribution to projects and can be trusted with complex and difficult pieces of work.*

Identity is deeply connected to a person's values and relational world. Dimitar's story in many ways illustrates how international mobility imposes shifting relationship challenges on Global Cosmopolitans.

Initially unaware that his own outlook on life was not universally shared, he was shocked and disoriented to discover an alternative approach to life. He struggled with his difference and initially interpreted his new surroundings in a superficial way that worked against his professional success. He saw others taking the initiative, so he did the same. Dimitar saw himself as a hard worker and team player. But ultimately his identity did not depend only on how he saw himself. It also depended on how others saw, or didn't see, him and how he saw himself in relation to others.

In Dimitar's case, he emerged from his on-the-job cultural training with a synthesis of old and new invisible rules. He acknowledges that without his lucky break to show him how to move forward, the situation could have easily slipped into a downward spiral. Yet, without changing how hard he worked, he transformed from an anonymous and frustrated team drone to an office star. Building on that experience, he has used both the collectivism of his childhood and the individual initiative of his adopted cultures to arrive at an executive style that transcends borders.

"This experience," he writes, "prompted me to begin to realize the importance of not only taking on responsibility but also of making sure that the manager knew that I did." Yet, he realized that his success was also due to a lucky convergence of circumstances and people. Today, as a senior manager in a large multinational, he believes that good performance is not just about getting the work done but also about leading projects and people to successful ends. "After all," says Dimitar, "I realize that I do gain satisfaction from seeing people happy and knowing that my doing X or Z has contributed to that."

THE CROSS-CURRENTS OF CONTEXT

Prakash sat next to me in class. He belonged to a lower caste. Next to him was Raj, who belonged to an even lower caste. Paradoxically, Raj was from an affluent family, unlike Prakash and me. When one of the test marks was distributed in the class, Prakash passed a snide remark that your ninety is equal to my eighty, which is equal to Raj's seventy. Due to reservation of seats in the university based on caste, I had to score far higher than my classmates from lower castes. I found myself at a disadvantage. The system appeared unfair, the system retaliating for the evil that my ancestors may have perpetrated on lower-caste people. Why should I suffer for the deeds of my great-great-great-grandfather? It does not follow the karma belief that I had developed. On one side, I started analyzing the situation to understand caste issues and the historic causes for overreaction by the public. On the other side, I came to realize that the social system brings me to a state of helplessness. By strangling my opportunities for the future, the community sends a message that I am not wanted. This feeling was popular among many Brahmin classmates. The result of such latent oppression was brain drain from India to the West, a much talked about topic. I chose to escape the clutches of self-centered politicians vilifying me.

When do people move internationally? Why do they decide to move? Why does one member of a family choose to leave while others choose to stay? The explanations, of course, are varied; the same story can even differ depending on who is telling it and what version he is sharing. But Global Cosmopolitans in their personal narratives repeatedly emphasize the role of context. Like Gopi, whose words appear above, their relationship to the world around them has been shaped by broad historical and contextual factors: political, economic, social and religious. In what manner do these four contextual cross-currents affect the life stories of Global Cosmopolitans? How do families transmit their rules and values? How can Global Cosmopolitans start to see the way these cross-currents affect their approach to life and their understanding of themselves?

Political Context

Given time to reflect on who they are, how they relate to others and how they relate to the larger world, Global Cosmopolitans often describe circumstances such as danger and scarcity or privilege and status, which set patterns of adaptation both for themselves and for other important people. Their stories describe how the overthrow of the Shah of Iran, the Russian Revolution, the two World Wars, the conflicts in the Middle East and Apartheid in South Africa are among the historical and political events that have created family upheaval, dislocation, barriers and opportunities for progress and change.

A classic illustration of political context is William. The Communist victory in China, along with Chairman Mao Tse-tung's Cultural Revolution and other social-engineering policies, left indelible marks on his family history and relationships.

My grandfather was working in Hong Kong for a trading company. After the Communist Party liberated the mainland in 1949, he decided to come back to China in 1950, with encouragement from his uncle, who was quite a successful businessman and had faith in the Communists. Due to my grandfather's experience in Hong Kong and connection with capitalists, my family was greatly affected during the Cultural Revolution (1966–1976) in China. People searched my grandparents' house and confiscated almost all their properties. My grandparents had to give away most of their houses and only kept one apartment for a six-member family at that time. My father experienced all these dramatic events, which are still part of his dark memories.

As part of Chairman Mao's initiative of climbing mountains and learning in villages, university graduates during the Cultural Revolution were asked to leave their hometown and go to remote and often underdeveloped areas to put their knowledge and skills into practice. My parents are both university graduates, which is quite rare for people at my age and is absolutely something my parents feel proud of. However, their university education didn't actually open up opportunities for them. Instead, they had to leave Shanghai in 1970 after graduation and were allocated jobs in different places of two faraway provinces. They were dating remotely and eventually got married in Shanghai. My grandparents rather than my parents raised me. In fact, I only met my parents once a year when they came back for annual leave before the age of nine, and I started to live with them at the age of fourteen.

Economic Scarcity

Economic scarcity often plays an important role in shaping the drive of Global Cosmopolitans. Limited educational and job opportunities push them to excel, often with considerable pressure from families who are counting on their success. William's story, above, is typical of Chinese students whose parents were forced into the countryside. Global Cosmopolitans from the former Soviet Union often describe being raised in highly educated families with harsh economic conditions. Many Global Cosmopolitans whose families emigrated or fled oppression faced difficulties on the road to personal and professional success.

For Global Cosmopolitans who succeed, poverty can become like a culture of its own, the biggest source of difference with the people around them. Consider Ricardo:

Ricardo was born in a remote area in Brazil. His parents had no formal education. In school, he proved to be a model student. His older brothers and sisters sacrificed so that he could stay in school instead of work. Ricardo sacrificed, too. The further he progressed in school, the farther he was sent from his family to study. He felt lonely, different, isolated. By the time he'd received advanced academic degrees, he realized he'd have to leave Brazil. The interesting, well-paying work he sought kept pulling him further away.

He won a science scholarship to earn a PhD in the United States. He perfected his English, earned his degree and found a job in Europe with the pharmaceutical industry, where he learned another language and became part of the management team before earning his MBA. As a scientist among managers, he felt different. But that difference was nothing compared with the giant step he has taken away from his hometown and his family.

Social Norms and Expectations

Social norms and expectations can greatly affect Global Cosmopolitans. For example, Global Cosmopolitans often mention the way gender roles impose responsibilities and restrictions. When they live or work in cultures with different norms from those of their parents' generation, the expectations can be multiple and confusing.

Sometimes Global Cosmopolitans have to discover how to translate messages from their past into attitudes that fit their new lifestyles. Men who are brought up to be economically responsible for their families, for example, try to find ways to provide for their family of origin but also struggle to understand how to live in a dual-career couple. Many women describe mothers who stayed out of the workforce to raise them and yet told them to get an education and find work that would allow them economic independence.

Many Global Cosmopolitans describe changes from one generation to the next in their cultures and family circumstances while they were growing up. That was the case with Meena from Nepal.

Meena's high degree of education, ambition and professional success seem to contrast sharply with her humble upbringing, and yet they are tightly linked to the context she grew up in.

> *Being herself uneducated, my mother put a high priority for us to get good education. Especially for daughters, she would always say, "An education is the only option for daughters." My mother cannot read and write. She told us that she left school when she was in elementary school, right after my uncle was born. My uncle was the first male child born to my grandparents. In my society, a male child usually has greater value than a female child. So when my uncle was born, there was a lot of joy, and sending a daughter to school was not a priority. She stopped going to school to take care of my grandmother.*

While Meena was born to a very humble "Newari" family in Kathmandu, her father had a university degree, and so did an uncle and two aunts. Her aunt's changing situation had a huge effect on her:

My aunt, who is a biologist, was the first woman in my entire family who went overseas to pursue a Master's Degree. Back then in 1980, it was very rare for a Nepali woman to go overseas independently for higher education. I always recalled knowing this aunt as a very ambitious woman. To her family, because of her ambitiousness, which was not expected of daughters, she came across as self-centered, which my other aunts and uncle often complained about. To me, she was an inspiration and I dreamt that I would do the same one day.

After living, studying and working on three continents, she decided to get an MBA.

At first, my parents did not understand why I wanted to study for an MBA. Their main concern was my personal life. Like every parent, they wanted to see me find a good partner and settle down. However, they have always been very supportive of my decisions. They fully trusted me as they think they did not know enough to advise me. For them, what really mattered is that I was pursuing a higher education again. No doubt, their first concern was finances. For a normal Nepali, this is simply not affordable. This was my concern too. In my tradition, parents do not feel comfortable asking daughters for financial support. Daughters are the ones to be taken care of. However, I felt responsible to support them financially since I am the most educated. In a way I felt selfish because I could have used my savings to help my siblings rather than spending on myself. But I was also convinced that I could not make anybody happy by compromising my own desire and ambitions.

Living in Singapore, Meena is now focused on building a different kind of life. She wants a way both to realize her professional dreams and to create the relational context where she can grow, love and contribute to the development of other people. Although, by her family's standards, she should have married long ago, she feels she can find happiness in her own way and in her own personal time frame.

Values and Religion

Global Cosmopolitans describe the religious context of their lives as a source of strength, rebellion, values and identity. Nitan felt total shock at discovering that nobody he met in the United States seemed

to know or care about Hinduism, a faith he called "a way of life, not a religion." Deepak, in his comments below, describes his rejection of Hinduism as well as his inability to totally escape it.

Both sets of grandparents were very religious and Hinduism was ubiquitous in my upbringing, from vacation spent on religious pilgrimages to being sent to a school that would train me to be a proper Brahmin (priest). Religious influences were particularly pervasive at home, with a separate prayer room and devoted and ritualistic celebration of every single festival of importance. However, I rebelled from religion at an early stage and did everything possible to avoid being cloistered in the Brahminical world. Pivotal decisions such as going to the United States when I was seventeen were particularly based on my intolerance of Hinduism and its classist approach and my need for freedom from that world. At the same time, whether I like it or not, I have internalized some aspects of my religious upbringing, which have directed other choices. For instance, I believe that my desire to settle down or get married before the age of thirty stems from a stigma in Hinduism about marriage after that age.

Marriage often stirs up issues about religion. Besides Deepak's questions about when to marry, religious upbringing raises questions such as whom a person should marry or even how someone should celebrate a marriage. Even after the marriage ceremony, questions continue to arise concerning religious practice and the raising of children. These questions are often complicated further when the person grows up in a culture that might not understand or accept the family's religious identification.

Even names, which are basic to identity, can be steeped in religious significance. Gopi describes growing up in a Hindu family rich with culture and heritage:

I listened to many fables. The fables form the backbone of my character and beliefs. A lesson from the fable is the basis of the rule with which I perceive the world: karma, beget the fruits of deeds. The many stories told to me as a child reiterate the message. I picked the following story, which exemplifies the basis of the system I feel I am built on: the story of my name.

My father's side dominated in any decision taken in the family. It was an unwritten cultural code of practice. As it was customary to name the first grandchild after the paternal grandfather, my parents dutifully chose Gopinath, a stylized version of Gopinatha Rao. But calling an elder by his name is a sign of disrespect. Since my namesake was an elder in the family, I needed an alternative name. My maternal grandparents had dibs on my unofficial name.

They chose Giri, meaning "hill" in Sanskrit. My maternal grandparents had just returned from a pilgrimage trip to their native temple, located on a hill. Since they went on an around-the-hill trip (pradakshana), Giri was an apt choice. I go by the name Gopinath at school and Giri at home.

The funny clash of identities became a daily routine. My friends from school would call me Gopinath or Gopi, but kids I played cricket with in the neighborhood called me Giri. Gopinath was an obedient, studious, straight faced teacher's pet. Giri was a flamboyant, silly, talkative, funny, chirpy ball of energy. I grew up having to forge two characters, seamlessly blend my two distinct lives and learn to transition from one to the other with ease.

INVISIBLE RULES: FAMILIES AS TRANSMITTERS OF CULTURE AND VALUES

Families, through their traditions and stories, are transmitters of history, culture, pride and honor. These powerful forces help form the filters through which people experience the world. Global Cosmopolitans who grow up in times and places that are different from parental cultural origins have to integrate their messages into their internationally mobile lives.

Nothing is as hard as trying to live with my parents' values and the values I have adopted in the country that my family immigrated to when I was very young. Given the sacrifices that my parents made so that I could be successful, I always felt that I had to succeed in two different worlds. In my case that meant a Chinese world and an American world, and I had to learn how to work hard to succeed in both worlds. The situation was even more complex, since my grandparents came to live with us directly from very different parts of China, which made our household highly complex yet helped me understand so many different worlds.

Now, I am about to marry a non-Chinese man and live in an American city far away from my parents. While we share many values, we have different religions; his family has its roots in Europe. I have had to be very creative to find ways to create adult relationships with my parents and help my husband understand all of the invisible rules that guide my life.

Sometimes, as in Gopi's world, the transmission of rules is obvious and formal. Extended family remains in close contact, coming together for festivals and celebrations of rites of passage. But transmission can also be subtle and informal, quietly embedding values, attitudes and transitions that come to mind years later. Elena, a senior investment manager in the Netherlands, describes visits to her grandparents in Kyrgyzstan:

My grandparents on the mother's side are an important part of my childhood. We would often visit them on the weekend or on holidays or they would come to visit us. Being both teachers and maybe using a privilege of an older generation, they talked a lot to us, their grandchildren, about life's basic values. Every visit would usually finish with a little lecture from grandma or grandpa on one of a variety of topics: respect for parents, importance of health, importance of education, honesty and integrity, etc., etc., etc. At times these lectures seemed awfully boring; however, I can still almost hear some of the things my grandparents were saying, and am once in a while surprised to discover how deep the values they tried to teach us are inside me now.

Voices from the Past: Family Stories as Role Models

In 1947, when British colonial rulers separated the Muslim and Hindu populations in the Asian subcontinent, they also separated Vinod's family from almost all its wealth. The partitioning of India and Pakistan ultimately drove Vinod's grandparents from India, but they carried with them the astute business sense that had built the family's wealth in the first place. Vinod's father carried on the tradition, and within a generation the family had built a substantial business. As a boy, Vinod grew up listening to family stories about the skill and intelligence that led to the family's success. And then the tradition of leadership passed to him. Vinod was an excellent student. It was clear that he carried the same business sense in his blood. But he wrestled with how to carry on the family tradition in today's world.

In between his grandfather's generation and his own was the birth of globalization. To succeed, Vinod needed to find a way to bridge that gap. Like his grandfather, Vinod needed to move to find what he wanted. He studied in Britain and France, seeking to build the skills and intelligence to expand the family's success around the world. As his company grows under his leadership, he is creating new family stories that will pass the tradition of leadership to yet another generation of Vinod's family.

Many Global Cosmopolitans cross into other cultures with a strong sense that determination and success flow in their bloodlines. Like Vinod, they have been nurtured on family stories of powerful ancestors, courage and bravery, and family traditions of leadership. As they encounter obstacles in their own lives, they can draw inspiration from the strength, creativity and cunning of earlier generations.

Storytelling Cultures and Families

Certain cultures are known as storytelling cultures, but individual families have their own means of communicating values and expectations through the stories they tell. Whether they are true or not, whether they are recounted with or without intending to transmit a message, these stories pass through successive generations. Sometimes the stories have such a life of their own that even when they are proven totally false, they are difficult to let go.

Nancy comes from a storytelling family in the southern United States with many generations living in close proximity. Even her great-grandmother was around to tell and embody the family stories. Nancy has inherited the awareness of the power of stories and the wonderful ability to tell them. No matter where the stories were told or who was doing the telling, the messages in her family stories were typically very clear: being a member of her family meant being outstanding. Besides academic excellence, her family stressed service to others, and that value has stuck with her throughout her life.

Nancy continues the tradition, telling the stories that have given her a value structure to travel the world. A quote from her grandmother is one example: " 'Of those to whom much is given, much is expected,' my grandmother used to remind me as we cleaned up trash along the highway on a scorching summer day or spent Christmas playing the piano for elderly patients. For me, selfishness was never an option."

Even in family stories with less-than-pious themes, Nancy can still hear values and expectations about getting the most out of life.

One of my great-grandmothers, whom we called Granny Beth, was a salty cat who had lived in all the Gatsby-esque decadence of the roaring twenties and who still had the look of an aging flapper when she zoomed around madly in the sports car of the day, smoking unfiltered Camels and cursing at anyone and anything in her path.

She had been living on vodka, ice cream and cigarettes for at least fifty years, and since everybody kept thinking that she was bound to die soon, we great-grandkids were encouraged to spend quality time with her as often as possible.

I remember one particular time when I had brought my university transcript to show her, thinking that she might be pleased at my straight A's. When she looked unimpressed, I decided to go with a topic closer to her heart. "I'm also really enjoying the parties," I told her shyly.

Granny Beth took a long drag off her cigarette and then blew some of it vaguely in the direction of my face. "Parties?" she laughed. "You don't know the first thing about parties. When I was your age we would start a party on Thursday night, and I would wake up naked in a bathtub full of gin on Monday morning. Now THAT was a party."

Marta, through the stories she was told growing up, knows the distant voices of grandparents who escaped hardships in Europe to build a new life in Argentina. The political and economic downturns that her family experienced in Argentina provided still more stories about fighting for survival. Her parents then immigrated to the United States, where Marta and her sister were born. The stories communicated the importance of having the courage and know-how to survive, lessons that spurred her to work hard, succeed, be curious and learn about people and the world.

But the challenge for these Global Cosmopolitans is to prove to themselves and their families that they are worthy of the family name. Vinod's family is typical of many families who pass stories about the tradition of leadership from generation to generation. But the considerable obstacles that previous family entrepreneurs have overcome are different from the obstacles that today's leaders face. Across multiple cultures and multiple transitions, Global Cosmopolitans must find their own way forward.

The challenge is also difficult for Global Cosmopolitans whose past contains negative role models. The same dynamic is at work, only in reverse, creating fear of stumbling and plunging themselves and their families into disrepute. The challenge of overcoming stories of family shame and failure can weigh heavily on a Global Cosmopolitan's identity. A senior manager now living in London writes about his family:

What happened? I grew up in the biggest house in the best neighborhood in town. My father was a self-made man, an example for me and for everyone. Given his role in the community, I grew up with an umbrella of respect surrounding my family and me. We were raised with strong moral values and to always make sure that we contributed to the community in which we lived. For me, from one day to the next, we lost everything. My father's business collapsed, and so did he. I still do not understand what happened, but I know that my fear of failure comes from that downturn. After university, I worked as an accountant. I was secure, I thought that I knew what I wanted, yet I was miserable. It turns out that my personality is very similar to my father's. I want and need to do my own thing and I want to start my own business. Given the trauma I lived through as a teenager, I hope that I am prudent enough to be a success but not too prudent to be risk averse. My motivation to be a success is very much linked to his failure. I know it, and I know that is why I am trying to develop my ideas far away from home.

Following Parental Footsteps: Can I Make a Difference As Well?

Having parents actively and publicly committed to social justice can clarify or cloud beliefs about being able to carry on an important family tradition.

Steve's parents' world involved fighting for social justice. They were known for taking the risks necessary to change their home country. He feared that he would never have the fame of other people in his family and questioned his ability to become an outstanding contributor to the world. How could he follow his passion and still feel that he deserved the family name and heritage?

Reema grew up in a turbulent household because of her parents' activism. Her parents were actively committed to fighting for and changing their country. They also transmitted greater goals for a better world at large. But Reema grew up sometimes longing for a better world at home. From one minute to the next she found herself living in another country. While she could be critical of how it affected her, she knew that she too had to follow her beliefs and values, just as her parents had done.

> *My parents played a primary role of raising my siblings and me with the perspective that we are world citizens. Specifically, this meant that we were taught to be aware of the world, to be curious about the world and to be considerate of the world. My parents exemplified the ideal of connectedness to the world not only by giving us exposure to international causes but also by honoring our identification with the Arab world. Even at a very young age, I would attend seminars and conferences with my parents.*
>
> *Growing up with this sense of duty toward my surrounding environment and society, I was always encouraged to use my time for worthwhile issues. That ranged from selling tickets for a fundraising event to rallying for greater freedom for women. Having parents actively involved in government and in efforts to change political systems can lead to a sense of duty to a larger good.*
>
> *My identity is linked to more than the country of my ancestors, where my parents have been actively involved in the political landscape. I am*

committed to a greater Africa. I am an African. Wherever I have lived, wherever I live, whatever I do, I will not forget that.

My career has been molded with great determination to excel and achieve everything that I envision; however, I believe success is measured by the legacy you leave behind and the effect you have on other people's life. My question is therefore "How and when do I make the next big step?"

What If I Cannot Live Out My Parents' Dreams?

Many Global Cosmopolitans talk about parents who were unable to live out their dreams because of political or economic strife. In some cases, it is the children who feel the need to give their parents a gift by fulfilling those personal dreams. Sometimes a particular talent, in music or art, for example, is the strongest thread that ties families when they are moving around the world. It can represent the language or love that they share. But the life of a musician can be tedious; not everyone has the stamina or drive to stay focused. Instead, many Global Cosmopolitans choose to develop careers that allow them personal and financial independence. Their solution is to give their parents everything that money can buy, but deep down they know that the real thread of connection is music.

Lucy's Chinese parents sacrificed everything to bring their talented young daughter to the United States to study. Rebecca traveled the world on her own to study piano, thanks to the sacrifices of her parents. Both women, while they loved their music and loved their parents had to find a way to separate from their parents' dreams in order to find their own.

Should I Repeat My Parents' Global Lifestyle and Raise My Children to Be Global Cosmopolitans?

Arno's life echoed his mother's global childhood. He was born in Nigeria to Dutch parents while his father was working at Shell. His mother, too, grew up in a Shell expatriate family. Arno went to a Spanish-speaking school in Venezuela and an American-Dutch school in Britain. He went to boarding school and university in the Netherlands while his parents moved to Oman. At that point, echoes from his mother's life stopped, but only temporarily.

His second-generation global lifestyle remained dormant until years later, when he moved with his own wife and family to Singapore so that he could complete his MBA. He started reliving the excitement of being a world traveler. He found himself pulled back into the life he knew so well. He decided to share the global childhood with yet a third generation, his two children. Arno took an Asia-based job with the company he'd worked for in the Netherlands. But as he watched his children grow older, he began to question how much moving and traveling he wanted to do. Ultimately, he decided to resist the pull of the familiar. His life might not be as exciting as his parents', but he wanted his children to grow up with family around them in the Netherlands.

There are many ways in which people feel the pull of their parents' lives on their own. Sometimes life decisions reflect cultural messages about a person's proper place in society. Sometimes they reflect familiarity with a certain life path, a respect for a parent's accomplishments and a dream for a similar future. What parents did, what they did not do, failure in marriage and at work all reverberate in people's life stories. It is not unusual to find teachers, doctors or lawyers pursuing the same professions as their parents and grandparents. It's not surprising, then, to find Global Cosmopolitans following their parents' footsteps on a global pathway.

I loved the way I grew up. My father was a very successful consultant. He went to the same business school thirty years before me and became a very successful consultant and a respected leader in the community. While we lived in Belgium, we had a summer home in Italy and traveled extensively in Europe. All of the children in my family speak at least three languages. Like my father, I was a very good student. Although I look just like him, I was a lot more spoiled and a lot more rebellious. Can I be half as successful as he has been?

For Global Cosmopolitans, the relationship challenges posed by the pull of parents' dreams for their children are complicated by global mobility; parents literally and figuratively cannot see the changes in their children's world. Global Cosmopolitans need creativity, skill and agility to find and communicate their own needs to their parents. Many eventually find the balance they need to move forward. "Sure they want me to get married and to live closer to them, but we now have a loving relationship, which is what I needed, and when they come and visit me, I have their undivided attention."

For Global Cosmopolitans, like Arno, whose parents were Global Cosmopolitans, the trade-offs can be stark and the answers difficult.

In both examples quoted above, the fathers had successful careers, and their families had exciting lives. Their excitement about rekindling their global lifestyle reflects positive memories of growing up around the world. But their challenge is to weigh the pull of their parents' life against the reality of their present relationships. In Arno's case, he preferred to give his children the gift of stability that he lacked in his own childhood. The same is true of Liv, whose global childhood and hospitality career have been presented previously. She plans to settle for a extensive period to provide educational stability, but she plans to choose an international city like Geneva. Although Liv will no longer be moving her children around the world then, her plan is to have her children grow up surrounded by other Global Cosmopolitans, in effect bringing the international experience to them.

Looking back at the school groups in the Luxembourg Gardens at the start of this chapter, the young foreigner who is learning to understand his French schoolmates is also learning to understand himself. Working through the challenges created by varying contexts—the sweep of political, social and religious forces; the unwritten rules of cultures and subcultures; the silent voices that transmit values and goals across the generations—Global Cosmopolitans can emerge with a broader sense of how they and other people are shaped by the world around them. This awareness can prove to be a fundamental skill for global leadership.

6

RELATIONSHIP CHALLENGES: CONNECTION AND DISCONNECTION

From the outside, Mourad is the consummate global professional. But inside, he faces complexities and uncertainties in his work, marriage and family relationships. The creativity and communication skills he needs to face these challenges contribute to his strengths as a Global Cosmopolitan.

Mourad has lived and worked as a General Manager for French companies in France, China and Thailand. A Moroccan, he speaks seven languages, including Mandarin, and can quickly understand new cultures. When he doesn't understand, he knows how to ask. His work has given him opportunities to demonstrate his operational and management competence. His cultural sensitivity is nuanced and highly skillful. Having suffered from prejudice and lack of respect, he makes it a point to show respect for people that are different. Yet in learning to respect people around the world, he has somehow lost the feelings he once had for his own country.

After China, I became aware of the Global Cosmopolitan part of my personality. On one side, I feel lucky I have this ability to adapt and appreciate living in different countries. It can open so many possibilities. On the other side, I am somehow bothered by the loss of affection I have for my home country, Morocco. I do feel bad that I am not able to spend more than a few days each time there. Also, however enriching and great the expatriation is, I do realize that I am always a guest in that country. I tend to identify myself to the human race, but this sense of belonging to the global community can be treacherous. Visas, travel restrictions and discrimination always remind me of this. Language also, and sometimes people's stares, do remind me that openness does not guarantee belonging. All these uncertainties lead to the issue of settling down somewhere. I am a family man now, hoping to be a father soon. Do I want my children to be citizens of the world, with all the advantages and inconveniencies of such a life?

Mourad decided to get his MBA in Singapore because his wife, a financial controller, could find a good job there while he was in school. The couple used the year to spend time together and discuss what they wanted next in life. This close communication was a top priority for Mourad, who is determined to base his marriage on everything he has learned about strong relationships. They are both committed to returning to Morocco together, but both want to remain Global Cosmopolitans for now. They will have their first child very soon, but Mourad knows that his wife enjoys her work and would expect it to be part of their international life together. Mourad loved working in China when he was single but questioned what it would be like to be there married and wondered how easily they both could find good jobs.

> *In the long term, I would love to be able to come back to Morocco and give back to the community. In the medium term, however, I still have this craze of devouring what the world has to offer. I think that I will do it as long as I can, and I am already very excited at the idea of finding a job in an area of the world I have never been to. So I guess my decision is made now. I will not go back to Morocco now. I will continue nurturing my curiosity for the next five years or so before thinking about settling down somewhere I would call home. Finding a job in an area of the world I have never been to is very exciting right now. Life is just too short to watch human endeavor on National Geographic. Living it from within, witnessing how different people, cultures and countries live the present and shape the future is not only enlightening, but also nurturing to the soul and mind. So, I guess my decision is made now. I will not go back to Morocco now, the somewhere I would call home. But, will I ever?*

After his MBA, Mourad decided to move to Germany to work for a Swiss pharmaceutical company. It is the tenth city, and the sixth office, he has worked in over the past eleven years. German is the seventh language that he speaks. For him, it was a hectic couple of months settling down with his wife and into his new job, new house and new environment. As he says, "It is always like that: hectic, but enjoyable. It is like a genetic mutation, really, like putting a zebra in the North Pole. The zebra needs time to put on some fat and white fur, and finally become a polar zebra."

Life, however, is hardly settled for Maria. She and her boyfriend, Peter, also face multiple transitions, because they are considering a move to Sweden, where his family lives. They want to build a life together but have no long-term commitments yet. They both are ambitious and highly competent and have excellent positions in London. They really do not know what their relationship will be like if they leave London and go to less neutral territory.

Peter feels very strongly about going back to Sweden. Now is the best time for a professional move, he believes, and he wants to be closer to family and friends. But Maria, who is Spanish, is not so sure. She wonders what will happen if they have to build a life that includes his family and friends. She feels that their relationship is too young, that they have not established a solid enough base of commitment and mutual understanding to leave London for Sweden. She would rather move to New York City and not have to worry about learning Swedish yet. She also knows herself. She needs to have her own work, her open space and independence.

No matter where Maria goes with Peter, their move will involve losses, gains and surprises. Will knowing what she needs from life and knowing that they both have a commitment to making their relationship work be enough to keep them together?

At every age, at every stage in life, people describe challenges that arise because of how their own lives intersect with those of the people around them. Sometimes the challenges involve clashing ideas or ways that people relate to each other. Sometimes people feel like others impose arbitrary, unfair limits on who they are or on who they want to become. Sometimes the challenge involves finding the best way to maintain and enjoy relationships over time and across distance. All these challenges are part of a dynamic relationship puzzle.

Lessons learned in childhood can play an important role in the process of confronting these relationship challenges in adult life. But Global Cosmopolitans, to make their journey easier, also require a broad range of new ways to create bonds with other people. Their lives give them many opportunities to reflect about themselves and to grow from their experiences.

The challenges of multiple transitions, including disconnection from people, places and a sense of self, lie at the heart of the Global Cosmopolitan experience. Yet many psychologists work on the assumption that human *connection*—in other words, the exact opposite of all those challenges—is at the center of healthy psychological growth. For Global Cosmopolitans to develop against this backdrop of constant disconnection, they must become experts at finding flexible and creative ways to understand connection and make it happen. And just as important but not as visible, they also must become experts at making sense of disconnection. Given this experience base, it is not surprising that a central theme in the biographies of many high-profile Global Cosmopolitans is an exceptional degree of relational intelligence.

Broadly speaking, working globally requires an ability to understand a global perspective and yet connect to local concerns. Speaking at the individual level, this ability to connect translates into personal inter-action. Every interaction has an *I* and a *you*, but there is also a *we*. That connection, that *we*, is the relationship. While people associate high self-esteem with success and achievement, a relational perspective suggests that our sense of personal well-being is not linked to feeling special, unique or better than other people. Instead, it is linked to our ability to connect in an authentic way, to being able to bring ourselves fully into a relationship where we are responded to with authenticity and respect.[1] This relational perspective has profound implications for Global Cosmopolitans in their personal and work lives.

Finding acceptance, confronting different values, overcoming limi-tations on self-expression and finding new ways to be active on a team or in a relationship are just a few of the challenges that arise amid cross-cultural connections and disconnections. To understand their feelings of confidence, strength and respect, Global Cosmopolitans must be alert not just to their present context but also to the context in which they have grown up. But to form successful relationships across boundaries, they must take this understanding a step further. Global Cosmopolitans must also be alert to the skills they need to respond to people who grew up in highly different contexts.

CHILDHOOD CONNECTIONS AND DISCONNECTIONS

Moving to the States when I was ten was a mixed blessing. Mixed because I believe that I would have developed differently as an adult had I grown up in Korea. I feel that the dislocating feeling I had from immigrating at a young age had led me to develop defense mechanisms that may not necessarily be healthy in terms of relationships as an adult. My main defense mechanism is to act tougher than I am. I never want to cry, especially in front of other people. I also developed the defense mechanism of not wanting to feel in order not to get hurt. This is because kids at ten can be quite vicious. Wanting to belong and yet not being comfortable with the English language to do so can be quite dislocating for a young girl. This early experience of being an out-sider most definitely impacted me as an adult. I developed the personality trait of a charmer and an entertainer. I am always eager to please. I have also developed the empathy for outsiders as well. I am always on the look-out for people who are not included, in parties, in conversation, at school. Sometimes I feel as if my role in life is to be the guardian angel of the disenfranchised!

What is the relationship between the Global Cosmopolitans' adult relational self and the reactions and adaptations they developed in childhood? Kim is convinced that she would have developed into a different adult if she had stayed in Korea. But the viciousness of her schoolmates changed her in significant ways. Suddenly and painfully aware of being different, of being rejected, Kim needed to find a way out of loneliness. Her childhood experiences became central to her ability to connect with her surroundings. At age ten, she had to become conscious of how she perceived herself, how others perceived her and how she perceived herself in relation to others. Kim adapted by developing the parts of her personality that made her pleasing, charming and entertaining and by masking and ignoring emotions that might interfere with her ability to connect with people. As an adult, she has assumed the role of guardian angel, helping other people to connect. Her choice of the word "disenfranchised" is telling; she is literally restoring to people their right to belong to a group.

Global Cosmopolitans who grew up between cultures describe how changing contexts shaped their resilience, independence, focus and ability to build new communities. But the price they pay to gain those valuable skills can follow them into adulthood. In their relationship stories from childhood, many Global Cosmopolitans say they initially responded to disconnection by disconnecting even more. As they rebuild their relationships in a new context, these disconnections can remain. Phillip, who had grown up in francophone Africa, expected a smooth transition to boarding school in France. "I did everything wrong socially and was terribly rejected by my peers," he writes. He ended up shutting down his feelings and burying himself in his studies. The childhood formula worked well enough to give him "a fabulous CV" with "incredible responsibility at work." But at this stage in his career, he needs more than focus and achievement to succeed; he needs to concentrate on connecting with other people. "Now I need to trust my feelings and pay attention to the feelings of others," he writes. "In order to get ahead at this crucial turning point in my professional life, I have to pay attention to my emotional intelligence."

Some Global Cosmopolitans have the opposite relational challenge. As children, they connect so quickly and completely that they disconnect from themselves. Carol, for example, attributes her adaptability to her need to be accepted. Moving to Spain and Italy as a small child, she was mistaken for a local within weeks, a pattern that continued through her childhood. "Sometimes I adapt too much to what I perceive is what others need and do not bring my different perspectives to a situation. With each new professional move, I can adapt to the needs of the people I work for. Now, with sufficient professional experience,

I want to be able to share my own ideas faster and take the risk of not adapting to the ideas of others."

Harry loves people. His enthusiasm for the people in his life and the work that he does is memorable. He knows what he learned growing up moving and living on his own and he knows how to use those lessons.

Harry was the eldest son in a Chinese family that had a great deal of international experience.

His parents had such faith in his maturity that they moved him from Malaysia to Canada at age fifteen, set him up in his own lodging and sent him to boarding school as a day student.

The experience was excruciating.

Harry felt painfully isolated. Compared with his schoolmates, he was short, dark and different. He did well in school and slowly looked for ways to connect with his peers. He started by listening carefully to everyone, which gave him an important skill for the rest of his life.

His life changed when he moved in with other teenagers. He discovered he could tell great stories and make people laugh.

As his confidence grew, he took on activities where he could demonstrate his leadership ability and increase his new-found social skills to build solid friendships.

By the time he finished school, he felt like one of the crowd.

As an adult, he became a manager in a large multinational. Identified as a high-flier, as a global resource, he was asked to start projects in different countries.

But because of the relational challenges he faced as a teenager, he pays attention to people; he knows how to include them and knows how to build solid relationships. Wherever he goes with his family, he knows how to create a community around him and his family, so every move has been a success.

RELATIONAL CHALLENGES CONTINUING INTO ADULTHOOD

I am from a small village in China, where my grandparents raised me. My parents never show the affection that I know they have for me. In China, we do not need to physically show our affection. I was lucky enough to study in the United States, where I met my husband. I learned how to hug and kiss in public, and I love it. Now I want my mother to understand my need for physical affection. I need a hug from her. It is so hard for me to live so far away from her. She does not understand!

When Global Cosmopolitans talk about moving, they often describe how it affects relationships. Relationship challenges change as people mature and start to have committed relationships, children of their own and aging parents. As they have positions of greater responsibility at work, their relational competence is increasingly significant. Global Cosmopolitans raise important questions about the definition of family, the definition of a good friend and the long-term effects of global mobility. Moving internationally complicates standard features of strong relationships, like keeping in touch, celebrating rites of passage and being supportive when friends and family are in need. At work, recognition for global competence means knowing how to get the job done with people who have significantly different ways of working. The global journey provides opportunities to build strong professional networks but raises the challenge of how to manage them effectively.

This section looks at five categories of relational challenges that are both complicated and potentially enriching for Global Cosmopolitans.

Challenge One: Who Am I in Relation to Others?

Lars's life clearly portrays this challenge that Global Cosmopolitans face as they move through different cultures around the world.

Lars moved twice in Norway before moving to Switzerland. He went to a Norwegian school and then a French school in Switzerland before going to a boarding school in France. He went to university in both France and Britain, where he had many challenging opportunities to develop his relational competence. From his family background, he brought certain relational skills, such as his uncanny ability to read other people's feelings. He also picked up many other strengths along the way, such as risk taking and the ability to see different ways of approaching things. But at a certain point, he started to see a pattern in his relationships that concerned him. Each country represented different sides of him, different parts of his identity that had emerged at different times in his life. He had been developing this way for years and was able to function at a higher level. But he wondered what might happen if he stopped splitting himself and pulled all the pieces together. He wondered what it would feel like to actually be himself, his whole self, in relation to others.

Given that his girlfriend knew him only in Norwegian, he felt that she was missing out on who he was and that he was missing out on being able to share his life completely. He was concerned that she could never understand or adapt to his Global Cosmopolitan identity and way of life. While this concern emerged on an intimate level, it was also a significant factor on the job. Splitting himself in pieces left him feeling disconnected at work, like he wasn't really there. He had trouble knowing what he felt or what he cared about. As an investment banker, he put in long working hours in London, using his excellent skills of risk taking and understanding what he knows and does not know. But with different aspects of his personality cut off from one another, he continued to feel increasingly alienated at work. He started to see that he was losing the part of him that was creative. He needed to find the playful child inside that likes to be different and to use this part of him at work to find different perspectives and ideas.

Challenge Two: Being Relationally Competent at Work

Global Cosmopolitans are widely recognized for their ability to learn the languages they need for foreign assignments, but the deeper ability is that of forging work relationships even in the absence of linguistic fluency. They arrive as outsiders and build bonds from there. While that outside perspective can be useful, it can bring on familiar angst, such as insecurity or fear of rejection. By repeatedly gaining the skill to develop authentic relationships at work, Global Cosmopolitans develop the confidence to meet, even surpass, challenges.

Quotes from two Global Cosmopolitans illustrate the shock of feeling like an outsider on the job:

I am an impatient person. I like to be integrated into a new team right from the start. I know that I am a very competitive person. It is a game to me that I love to play with other competent people. Given my experience as a child moving around, I am very sensitive to issues of inclusion. I like to be chosen to work with others, and I want them to be able to see me as highly competent. When I am feeling insecure, I feel particularly sensitive to this.

It has only been six months since I have been working here, but the subtlety of the power games eludes me. I will never be as expert as some of my colleagues, but my learning curve has been steep. I would feel more confident if I could master the language enough that I could present my ideas in French. I know what I am doing; I believe in my expertise and my analysis. I want my ideas to be taken seriously, but that is hard when I have not mastered the language, as I should. Presenting my ideas to a client can be a nightmare, since I am much less subtle or articulate in French. I usually rely on my humor and social skills to connect with people that I do not know well to facilitate presenting difficult ideas. Luckily I have an assistant who is currently helping me with anything that I need to write in French.

It takes a great deal of self-confidence to overcome the fear of rejection despite an inability to articulate a point of view or comfortably produce a spontaneous written note. Developing fully in a new context can be one of the most rewarding aspects of living internationally, but it takes intense patience and effort. And often by the time Global Cosmopolitans are satisfied with the result, circumstances demand that they move again.

Global Cosmopolitans routinely face two classic relational challenges. The first is finding a way to be competent with other people despite obvious gaps in cultural or linguistic knowledge. To connect with their new culture, Global Cosmopolitans often have to change roles from the one who knows to the one who needs advice.

The second classic aspect is lack of language, an obvious challenge to building authentic relationships. An adult hidden from view by a child's command of language can feel limited and infantile. A narrow range of expression and lack of subtlety can greatly affect communication. But even Global Cosmopolitans who speak a language well can experience invisible challenges. "I learned Spanish at age five. I left Spain at age eight," Sara writes. "I hardly remember my experience there, but my playground Spanish is fabulous. My accent is perfect, but I have a child's voice and vocabulary."

Global Cosmopolitans also face the complex puzzle of defining which parts of themselves to bring into a relationship without losing a sense of who they are as a whole. For example, Miki, who has struggled as a Japanese outsider, decided that she could be a "Global Cosmopolitan Japanese" by becoming active in the international community in Japan and by creating a website to share her knowledge about living there. Global Cosmopolitans also find that talents, personality traits and languages can remain hidden. Instead of feeling like they are fully in a relationship, they can feel like nobody really knows who they are. They must defy the popular expression that a leopard can't change its spots, taking on the appropriate coloration to blend in with their surrounding context while still remaining a leopard. Robert described the challenge this way:

People generally see me as very upper-class British, an image I developed in boarding school and at university there. My parents are of Hungarian and Russian origin, although they raised me in New York and Hong Kong. I worked so hard to be accepted with my peers in boarding school that it is hard for me to let go of that mask. Hidden away is that ability to see beyond borders and the certain sensitivity that my parents have given me.

103

The habits I developed back then both serve me well and, at the same time, they get in my way.

Global Cosmopolitans face the challenge of being an active member of a team, particularly when a new language and culture are added to the typical jitters of arriving at a new job. "I make new friends at work and I love to feel like I am part of a team. I know that I am shy, but as soon as a door is opened, I can be quite socially skillful." But in her new context, this woman has lost the social ease that she contributed to making her teams work. She is seen as competent, but she is "really an outsider." Global Cosmopolitans can also find that adaptation patterns that have worked in the past, such as observing, can seem strange in team relationships. "I realized that trust would quickly become an issue. I needed to find a way to add my ideas to the team right away, yet I was busy struggling with my need to learn about how things worked and how to articulate my point of view."

Career decision-making can be particularly complicated for a Global Cosmopolitan, whose career choices can often be anywhere in the world. As they start to get to know themselves, they know what the tradeoffs can be.

I was just offered the perfect post-MBA career opportunity, a job in China at a top-tier consulting company. But the choice was not a simple one. I do the analytic work easily, but how do you figure out if you really want to be a consultant when you feel so inadequate speaking the language and knowing the subtle aspects of cultural communication. I look Chinese, but I have a limited ability to speak since I was raised in Canada. I know that people will expect me to understand, when I do not have clue. I am ambivalent. I know that I am highly motivated by adventure and having opportunities to learn at every turn. I also know that I want to know something about my family origins. If I can find a way to feel relaxed with my team there, I know that I will be able to handle the stress and the crazy working schedule. I also know that this is the time for me to live in China. I am not married and my parents are still young and do not really need me. In a few years, everything could change.

Challenge Three: Understanding Different Ways of Relating

I come from a small village in China, where my parents were sent after the Cultural Revolution. My grandfather stayed in Shanghai. My parents had me live with him so that I could go to better schools. He taught me everything and, yes, I was an excellent student and went to an excellent university. I had one way of relating to my parents and the people in my village and another way to relate to my grandfather and even another way to relate to my friends at university. Working with Chinese from different backgrounds was easy, but taking the giant step of doing an MBA and working in Europe still has its challenges.

Global Cosmopolitans can feel confident and competent in how they relate to people, only to take a leap into a different culture and discover a gap they never knew really existed. Having changed from village to city, city to university and university to work, the Global Cosmopolitan quoted above knew the skills he needed to figure out how people around him related differently to each other. But this time he faced the added complexity of different cultures and languages. Until he felt more comfortable, he hesitated to speak and take risks.

Relating to people with different value structures and different ways to demonstrate values is one of the most difficult challenges, especially for people new to international living. Reconciling different cultural notions about right and wrong, good and bad, direct and indirect, can be particularly challenging for people who have to be true to their own values to be true to themselves. Even veteran Global Cosmopolitans who understand the notion of subcultures and check their own stereotypes can be surprised by clashes in values. "I do not lie," an American manager new to working in France recounted. "That is what I naively believed about myself." He needed to ask permission for his child to miss a day of school before a vacation. An assistant urged him to say that the family had to fly out early because the mother was extremely sick. "She explained that the school administrator could not accept my straightforward note without an admissible excuse. She would know that it was a lie, but that was okay."

Global Cosmopolitans sometimes dramatically confront differences in religious backgrounds that leave them feeling powerfully alienated. The example here is Zeynep:

Zeynep's parents met in Boston when they both were students. Born in the United States, Zeynep then moved to London with her family, but Zeynep mainly grew up in Turkey, where she was surrounded by family and people who knew her well.

She moved to the United States to study finance and then to Saudi Arabia to work in finance.

With each move, the ways people related to each other changed. Dating, dressing, relations between male and female friends and other issues posed a continuing set of challenges.

She adjusted to being completely covered when she worked in a bank in Saudi Arabia. The rules about female behavior did not stop her from getting the experience she wanted, although she knew advancement options were limited.

An MBA in Singapore seemed like the next right step. She felt comfortable dressing like the other students, wearing shorts and T-shirts.

She looked like her classmates and made friends with them.

And then she took a class trip with them to the Abu Dhabi. All the adjustments she'd made in her life didn't prepare her for what happened next.

"My friends from school made fun of the women that were completely covered in the airport," she writes. "I ran into the bathroom crying. It was so upsetting. I was dressed like my friends, but I felt like they were making fun of me."

While she adapted so well to looking and sounding like everyone in each new context, bringing her worlds together gave her a painful shock. She had found a way to live with the different behaviors depending on the external norms, but she was not ready to be a sophisticated interpreter for her friends. She needed to look at how she put the pieces together to create a sense of who she was. She also knew that she needed to think about what her role would be in helping others understand the choices she was making.

Challenge Four: Relationships between Couples, Families and Friends

Weighing who they are in relation to others is particularly challenging when Global Cosmopolitans need to make career decisions. These relational issues often surface during times of multiple transitions in a Global Cosmopolitan's personal and work life.

I see myself as a loving and giving person who is very much in love with my husband. We both are French and share many values about life and raising children. I love the adventure of moving around, but now that we are living in Japan with three small children, I am at my wits' end. Work has always been an important part of my life and my sense of self. I am not working, and I do not see possibilities for this to happen soon if we stay here. He has a great job, the children are happy and I am miserable. I have lost the person that I am, and I am afraid that the only way to find her is to move back home to France now!

Many of the relationship issues that Global Cosmopolitans face in their personal lives are universal. The woman whose comments appear above can find plenty of company among other women staring at the career track with small children circling their feet. But the universal issues of couples, families and friends have a distinctive Global Cosmopolitan style. In this instance, for example, professional mothers in their home cultures wrestle with finding acceptable child care and flexible schedules to accommodate their new responsibilities. But the French woman above is in Japan, cut off from family support and professional connections, her job options limited not just by language and culture but also by regulation of foreign workers. The only possibility she sees for herself is to return to France and be like the other professional mothers she knows. But to return, she must tear apart the happiness of the rest of her family. Not surprisingly, one of the most common reasons foreign assignments fail is spousal unhappiness.

Aware of the impact on family of multiple moves, many couples pay close attention to the importance of decision making. They try to find ways to provide realistic options for themselves as well as exploring the potential effect on their children. Knowing that moves can involve surprises, losses, gains and many reactions that are impossible to anticipate, they understand the importance of making decisions together.

Different Notions of What a Relationship Is

Family and cultural styles can also complicate managing differences and conflict. Cultural differences can often be used to open dialogue early in relationships, but fear of conflict can also lead couples to avoid potential problems. Some couples can't figure out how to begin to address them.

Long-distance relationships demand a very particular creative touch. The upside of the strain Global Cosmopolitans feel on their personal relationships is that they gain experience trying to find working solutions. Yet many couples face deep challenges when they are faced with long-distance relationships. Finding good professional opportunities in the same country is not always easy. Many students working on their MBAs do so without their life partners. Technological advances in communication have helped ease the burden somewhat, but sporadic visits and long calls are often an inadequate substitute.

My husband could not come with me this year. He had just started a new job and had to fulfill the requirements of his visa. I moved here, knowing that I would miss him, but I did not understand how much it would hurt until I got here. I missed the physical proximity and I missed sharing our lives. I knew that he had some challenges at work and I had many questions about what I wanted to do next. We had to learn how to time our phone calls. Bad timing could be a disaster, leading to misunderstanding and conflict. We were in very different time zones, which meant I had to wake him up if I just wanted to say goodnight.

How could you marry someone who speaks a different language and will never fit in here? That's a classic question Global Cosmopolitans face from family and friends. It illustrates how once they are in couples, Global Cosmopolitans face uniquely complex relationship challenges. They must maintain their relationships through repeated transitions, involving not just geographical moves but also changes in their personal lives and development. A Romanian consultant who traveled to London and Australia after finishing his studies at Harvard explained that his relationship issues at work were simple compared with those at home. On one hand, the woman he loved fit his new life as an international consultant. But she shared no language or cultural connection to his family in a small town in Romania.

Global Cosmopolitans have a lot of work to do to insure the vitality of their life as a couple and family. Couples over time can struggle to manage their individual differences against the backdrop of work, family, friends and children. But Global Cosmopolitans, especially couples from different cultures, face the added challenges of their complex life paths, cultural mandates about how things should be done and the connections and disconnections inherent in global mobility. Even normal decisions that couples make can be more challenging in an international context, such as spending time with old friends who speak a language that the other member of the couple does not understand.

Moving and having children can change the family chemistry even more. "How much do I want to move?" or "How much do I need a home?" can become nightly discussions. The same is true with discussions about raising children. One parent might consider the importance of extended family nonnegotiable. The other might feel like extended family will smother their attitudes and values. One woman might feel like neither a good enough mother nor a good enough daughter living so far from her parents. Another woman might feel like her mother could never understand the person and parent she has become. And ideas about raising children that once seemed so fixed and true can change according to life experience and the continuing challenges of adult development.

Many Global Cosmopolitan couples follow the course of choosing a country different from either of their own. But then they face the issue that their children will identify with a culture that neither parent fully understands. "The hardest job I have is parenting my three children," a consultant in Paris writes. "Neither of us is French, and we have different yet equally strong values that our parents gave us. We want to teach (our children) what we believe in, and at the same time we know that they will have to integrate into the French community." They also face tough choices about moving on once the children are established. "Moving to France as a third country option has worked in many ways," one student writes. Now the question arises "Is this it? Is this home for them now?"

Family of Origin

Whether they are in couples or not, Global Cosmopolitans face relationship challenges from their parents, siblings and childhood friends. One of the first questions Global Cosmopolitans typically hear from them is "Why don't you come home?" Rashid from Uzbekistan is a classic illustration. He has been highly successful, thanks to the support of his parents. He has learned how to compete in the most challenging work environments from Moscow to New York and to London. But now his parents want him to bring his new skills and status home and marry locally. Rashid knows he does not belong to their world anymore. On the other hand, he has trouble thinking about marrying a woman who could never blend with the world where he grew up. His girlfriends, all from the United States or Europe, share who he has become, not where he is from. Of all the Global Cosmopolitan challenges he has faced, Rashid feels that this one is the hardest.

After the first polite question or two from family or friends, Global Cosmopolitans sense no genuine curiosity about their experiences. They listen to constant stories from others, but are seen as boring or bragging when they offer their own. Interest, when it does come, sometimes happens because family and friends want inside information to arrange vacations. Global Cosmopolitans often cannot attend special birthdays, weddings, anniversaries, graduations, funerals and other ceremonies that bind people together. When other people are helping drive cancer patients to chemotherapy or cheering children at a big sports event, Global Cosmopolitans can offer only long-distance support. They might see themselves as loving and caring, but family and friends can find their absence inexcusable and write them off as distant, cold and self-centered.

Many Global Cosmopolitans have become adults in a world both literally and figuratively different from that of their parents. While successful in their academic and professional careers and personal development, they feel judged in their personal lives. They feel pulled by the messages of the cultures they grew up in:

A good son would marry and settle down near home.

It is your responsibility to take care of us in our old age.

Your country needs you. It is time to come back and take care of social injustice at home.

A woman your age should be married and starting a family.

Challenge Five: Managing Multiple Relational Networks

Developing the know-how to manage multiple networks is a key skill for Global Cosmopolitans. On a personal level, friends and family can be the sources of resilience that Global Cosmopolitans need in order to learn, grow and maximize the value of their experiences. Given that they are often the ones on the move, it is up to them to develop and maintain the relational connections. They have to do this task with sensitivity to all sorts of cultural differences. In cultures where traditionally an absent person is forgotten, Global Cosmopolitans might need to be physically present. Friends from other cultures might just need to be nudged from time to time on the internet.

One of the great values that longtime Global Cosmopolitans bring to the workplace is their extensive list of contacts worldwide. These contacts allow them to create business opportunities. But not all of their networks are for business. Liv is able to create strong relational ties wherever she goes. "I can understand a lot of different people," she says. "I make friends quickly and with people from different parts of my life. It leaves me feeling very lucky." She rewarded herself for this talent by celebrating her birthday in Borobudur, in Central Java, surrounded by family and good friends from around the world. The challenge of finding ways to bring this diverse group together was an exciting opportunity for her.

Rapidly changing technology has given Global Cosmopolitans an ability to keep in touch that is amazing compared with even a decade ago. But it also requires a commitment of time and energy. Social networking sites as well as investment in travel can become a necessary means to combat the isolation of being far away and on the road for work. That was true for Nicole, who over the past two years moved from Germany to Singapore to France to England and back to Germany. Now looking for work in France, she has benefited from the time she put into her networking. "I am one click away from knowing where my friends are," she writes. "When I go to Paris or London, that is what I do."

THE GLOBAL COSMOPOLITAN RELATIONAL TOOLBOX

My name, Lian, means "to connect" in Mandarin. I was twenty-one when I made this discovery. I thought that my name and personality could not have been better aligned. I had just begun to understand how much I enjoyed making connections between worlds. I loved learning languages to connect with other cultures. I relished linking friends with mutual interests. I was beginning to explore and appreciate my connection to history, including my family's background and the many lives surrounding me. I was also starting to connect with deeper parts of myself, uncovering my life passions, my different selves and life potential. These were all forms of connections I savored then; today, these types of connections continue to delight me. I am truly a connector in name and spirit.

Given their extensive experience with connection and disconnection, Global Cosmopolitans develop an ability to grow from relationships that they develop wherever they travel. Many build on skills that they started to develop because of challenges in their early years, benefiting from childhood roles such as negotiator, diplomat, translator, bridge builder, even entertainer. Equally powerfully, Global Cosmopolitans find themselves in situations where their old identity is stripped completely and they must find a way to reinvent themselves. Taken together, the roles and competences that Global Cosmopolitans develop in the face of connection and disconnection become a handy relational toolbox. Over time, these tools give Global Cosmopolitans the extraordinary confidence and flexibility they show in their interactions with others.

I have the best consulting job that you could imagine coming out of my MBA program. I am on an amazing learning curve. My colleagues are smart, very smart. They have been encouraging right from the beginning, which I know contributes to the development of my confidence and ability. I know that in order to make some major career decisions, I have to look at this business idea that I have. I do not want to quit, but I do need to find a way to have some time off to put this business proposal together. If it does not work, then at least I will know that. If it does work, then I'll have some different decisions to make. Here is where my ability to use my self-knowledge and my ability to get people to support me will be the keys to getting positive working arrangements. I know that it sounds arrogant and that I want it all, but I do believe that if I manage the discussions well, we can find a solution.

By now the message should be abundantly clear that Global Cosmopolitans do not develop their strengths through lives that read like a succession of travel brochures. Confidence like that expressed above comes wrapped in any number of personal and professional challenges. Each challenge can give them an opportunity to learn about themselves; each lesson can reinforce their ability to handle change and complexity. A CV or résumé describes the outward journey, but the challenges in these chapters describe the silent, inner journey that is the root of strength and resilience. Experience is an exceptional teacher. Understanding the lessons and skills learned can give Global Cosmopolitans both confidence and ability for future relational challenges and opportunities.

At the same time, Global Cosmopolitans face changing circumstances while they move forward. They need to make sure they are not trapped by the past. Sometimes the old lessons they learn simply don't apply anymore. They need to find ways to look objectively at themselves and identify old patterns that might be holding them back. Surprisingly, many discover those obstacles in the personal strengths they cherish most. The next section of this book looks at why challenges don't always lead to strengths and why strengths can sometimes become challenges.

PART III

THE INVISIBLE JOURNEY: NEW PATHWAYS TO GROWTH

"I need to accept my inner complexity and personal inconsistencies. I cannot do that by rejecting my past but by interrogating it with curiosity and sympathy."

7

PARADOXICAL NEEDS: FINDING THE ROOTS OF CHALLENGES

I live between two seemingly contradictory fears: the fear of being excluded and the fear of being just like everyone else. If I feel excluded, I become very unhappy and squarely place blame for my misery on the surrounding environment. If I am included in a categorical grouping, I become indignant. It rarely occurs to me to question my own actions or behavior for creating the feeling of exclusion or stereotyping. It could be perceived as self-confidence or arrogance, but I am simply repeating what I felt as a child.

I have suffered from being an only child. I was brought up as a moderately spoiled youngster, but had you asked me then, or even now, I would have traded all those rewards for a brother or sister. Hence I grew up with the strong desire to integrate with as many persons as I could. Furthermore, the prevailing circumstances at the time of my upbringing (exile to France during the war) pressed me to blend into groups of children who were from a totally different culture than mine. Consequently, I have developed Global Cosmopolitan qualities such as the fine ability to interrelate and build connections with outsiders. My energy and liveliness swell significantly with the feeling of belonging to a community. I would be one of the group members who always put in his time and effort to come up with the best plans and activities. At work, I would consistently be the team's dynamo.

This chameleon attitude has brought with it some benefits such as a very wide and extended network of acquaintances as well as a minute cluster of foes. But by pleasing others, I have lost a significant chunk of my true self. I observe that what I stand for is very flaky, of secondary significance, definitely less important than what others stand for. I look for contentment in the eyes of a third party much more than self-satisfaction. Hence I have become a social prostitute, giving people what they want, in return for their approval and support of my person.

Funnily enough, my "whatever you want me to say" behavior, which was supposed to rally as many people as possible around me, has backfired. For example, some individuals who have known me for quite some time started doubting the authenticity of my opinions. I know a few colleagues who have stopped asking for my take on matters, since I would tell them what is music to their ears and not what I deeply believed in.

Furthermore, I have always adopted a "yes sir" mentality at work, at the expense of my physical and moral well-being. I remember working with a workaholic manager who would always ask for massive tasks to be accomplished in a very short time period. At first, I performed those assignments with a smile on my face since I wanted to prove my worth and capabilities to the manager: a badly calculated move; there was no way back from the reference point I had just set. I had just shot myself in the foot. From that point on, high-intensity requests were thrown my way. My manager would say, "Walid is my man. I can rely on him in any circumstances." When I left that job, I was morally and physically a wreck, just because I couldn't say no in the first place.

With each transition to a new culture, Global Cosmopolitans must find ways to reestablish themselves, consciously or not, to meet their basic psychological needs. Sometimes those needs feel like they pull in opposite directions, stirring a feeling of helplessness or loss. This tension can lead to issues such as ambivalence, emotional paralysis, a wish to hide one's true self or an inability to trust. But this tension can also be seen as an opportunity to change behavior and make different choices. This whole forceful struggle can take place beyond the awareness of the person experiencing it. "I am simply repeating what I felt as a child," Walid writes. He does not question his own actions or feelings. He simply repeats. And the result for him is a life guided by paradox, neither side of which provides a satisfying resolution.

The focus of this chapter is on paradoxical needs and how they are experienced by Global Cosmopolitans. Although many needs have a universal quality, such as a need to belong and a need to differentiate oneself, others have been applied more directly to the lifestyle of Global Cosmopolitans, such as a need to move on and a need to stay. The next chapter looks at how Global Cosmopolitans adapt to basic needs such as these. It also describes a different paradox: how adaptation patterns that contribute to multiple strengths can sometimes create new challenges.

Developing awareness of paradoxical needs helps Global Cosmopolitans explain their underlying issues and emotions. People change, experiment with new behavior and mature with a greater understanding of their dilemmas, attitudes and actions. This awareness is important because internal conflicts such as those described in this chapter set up many of the challenges, the learning opportunities, through which Global Cosmopolitans develop the abilities that they bring to the business world. Over time, as they find their own place and learn how to live with the contradictory forces within themselves, Global Cosmopolitans increase their capacity to deal with constant change and uncertainty.

For Global Cosmopolitans, confronting contradictions is a normal part of living across cultures. As a result, they have a head start on confronting the contradictions they find within themselves. As they focus on the management of paradoxical needs, they can intensify and clarify how they have created the story of who they are and learn how to communicate their needs to others in a constructive manner.

BELONGING AND FEELING DIFFERENT

Walid's words at the beginning of the chapter illustrate the paradoxical need of "belonging and feeling different." Global Cosmopolitans like Walid need to belong in their current context while at the same time knowing that they belong to different worlds. They can look, sound or feel different. Sometimes their difference is invisible outside but difficult to live with inside. Walid has been pulled in two directions by his need to blend into groups and his need to be himself.

Walid knows that finding the balance he wants will not be easy. But his comments below show how his new insights about paradoxical needs provide him a key to Global Cosmopolitan professional success. These insights help Global Cosmopolitans fulfill the potential that their international mobility has given them. Walid is determined to manage his need to belong and feel different, he says, "to live a life of my own making." He writes:

I need to have a clear sense of where my identity lies and stick by it. No need for proving myself to anyone who's not in my closest circle of intimacy. No need to be either loved or cherished by everyone; this would dilute any distinctiveness, traits and individuality I am trying to cultivate. In addition, I should get used to being more direct, straight, authentic and saying what's in my mind, even if this will place some of my interlocutors out of their comfort zone. The words coming out of my mouth should be mine and not what someone else wants to hear. I should also acknowledge the fact that I am a mere number within the corporate world, that managers won't stop in their exaggerated pursuit for requests unless I say, "Stop, that's enough." I believe this will be one of the most daunting tasks at hand, but this is where it all starts.

Some Global Cosmopolitans resolve the tension of being different by trying something different that moves their identity in a new direction.

Joana went to Germany from Romania to complete her university degree. She had always been surrounded by love, positive attention and approval, so her first big move was a major shock for her. She felt like a complete outsider. She felt like she made many mistakes in trying to establish a social life. Since she had no experience trying to integrate into a totally new situation, she concentrated on trying to belong. Although she loved to take care of others, she could only enjoy this activity to a point. To be happy, she knew that she had to assert herself and her interests in her own way. She was miserable. And then she started to dance. She decided to assert her difference and tell her story through performance.

CONTINUITY AND CHANGE

Other paradoxical needs emerge because of the nature of a global lifestyle. The case of Markus, for example, illustrates the paradoxical need for "continuity and change." Global Cosmopolitans need to change without losing their personal stability. On one hand, they grow and develop from their international mobility; on the other, they need the time for personal integration to feel that they have a sense of their core identity that allows them to manage the different selves which they accumulate in their moves. The amount of stability and security they feel by knowing who they are affects the risks they feel they can take. Markus reflects this paradox:

Both of Markus's parents are German, but he has never lived in Germany.

Although he visited Germany frequently as a child, he never lived in Europe until he went to a boarding school and then Cambridge University in England.

He grew up in Africa, in three countries that have all changed names in his lifetime. He remembers having local playmates but went to German and international schools.

Markus started working as a consultant in London; then he moved with the same group to Brazil before going to France for his MBA.

Still in the early stages of his business career, Markus has already had seven countries and three continents woven into the fabric of his life.

Through all these moves, Markus developed a mode of survival that served him well in business. His logic and agility in complex situations reflect the tools for understanding and meaning he found in childhood.

But at the same time, all this mobility has made him highly aware of the importance of people and place.

Markus was concerned about how constant adaptation has affected him over time. After he finished his MBA in France, he carefully chose Australia to work as a consultant and develop a home base.

He was looking for a different balance in Australia. He wanted his new home to provide the continuity he needed so that he could develop the relationships he felt were missing from his life.

For Global Cosmopolitans, life is a balancing act between the growth and development they experience from change and the time they need to bring the threads of their lives together. They need to feel and show their own personal coherence and to manage different aspects of who they are. Global Cosmopolitans wrestle with how to feel whole and yet remain flexible enough to use their different selves when the situation requires it. They question how much stability they need before they can take on more risks.

The paradox of integration of continuity and change is immensely complex for Global Cosmopolitans. The way they view themselves and their future possibilities is greatly affected by culture and language. Languages that are either lost completely or else limited in their ability to fully express thoughts and feelings can cloud the active memory that they need to feel connected and whole. Sometimes adapting to new cultural circumstances requires them to change dramatically. They can lose track of the core from which these changes took place.

Some Global Cosmopolitans become virtually addicted to change as the only path to find opportunity, adventure and learning. Sometimes they see change as the universal solution to boredom. These narrow viewpoints can limit personal and professional choices. By paying attention to their own rhythm of change and integration, Global Cosmopolitans can see their lives in a new way. They become aware of how they have limited their options and can identify new ways to grow and move forward. This broader range of life choices helps resolve the tension between the need for continuity and the need for change.

Having grown up in a small Italian town, Luigi has always been hungry for ways to change himself or his situation. After university he had his first taste of living abroad, and he loved it. From then on, change became part of his life: moving countries, learning languages, changing industries, even trying his hand at an entrepreneurial adventure. His MBA experience finally gave him a chance to step back and consider how much he actually needed, or even wanted, to constantly move and change. His parents were getting older, and he missed them. He thought about how his many moves had affected his relationships. He started to consider whether he could find a way to live closer to home and yet not be bored. To find the answers, Luigi looked closely at his concerns about re-entry and discovered unresolved issues within himself.

He knew that he had avoided certain problems by moving. He had a short attention span, which explained why he was easily bored. But hopping around to avoid boredom left him feeling unconnected. The path forward required him to develop parts of himself that he had been able to ignore by constantly changing his lifestyle and surroundings. He had to concentrate his attention on finding work and relationships that engaged him more. He also knew that he missed his parents but had never established his own space when he was around them. He started exploring professional opportunities in Milan and hoped that his years of freedom would help him be near his parents without feeling invaded by them.

MOVING ON AND STAYING

For many MBAs with global lives, deciding what to do next revolves around the dilemma of "moving on and staying." The paradox behind this dilemma again concerns the need for change that allows growth and development and a need for personal integration.

International moves both enrich and complicate their lives. Some Global Cosmopolitans become so identified with constant change that they fear staying even though they think it would be a wise choice. "When I change countries I develop, but when I stay in one country, I fear stagnation" is a common theme. Goncalo, whose comments appear below, performs exceptionally well at work and enjoys his international mobility. But like many Global Cosmopolitans, he has other needs and considerations that he doesn't share in the office. His paradoxical need to move on and to stay shapes the way he thinks about his future. Goncalo writes:

I like to lead a busy, internationally mobile life but need to have a link to Portugal. In all the years I have been abroad I knew I could at any time go back for a weekend and organize a big reunion with my old friends from German school. They always make an effort to see me when I am there, as my visits home are often an excuse for the old group to meet again. During a big part of the years I spent abroad I never used to note any major changes in the lives of the friends living there. They went to the same bars and discos and restaurants and beaches. The same couples were together. Life was the same. Over the past couple of years, however, I have noted some major changes in most of these. As people started working and moved out of their parents' place, couples started breaking up, new friends were made and the routines changed. Friends started getting married to people I met at the wedding only. I started to go back and feel that distance was being built between Portugal and me. When this started happening, I began to seriously question if I should continue to stay abroad or if it was time to move back. I think that this capacity to adapt and learn from diverse environments could be a point of difference from other managers which has helped me to succeed and feel accomplished in my professional life. I therefore fear that by moving back to Portugal I will not be able to leverage one of my main assets and will feel frustrated and bored by being stuck in a monocultural environment where this diversity is neither needed nor appreciated.

The fear of losing his link to his closest friends is only part of the tension that Goncalo is experiencing. At home there is pressure of another kind. Goncalo feels the need to be home to help out with his family, but he also feels that being away from his parents makes his life easier.

As my parents get older, I feel this emotional pressure-cooker heating up and becoming unsustainable. On the other hand, being away makes it personally easier to deal with my mother's possessive nature. I can see them whenever I like and I do so quite often but do not need to worry about or manage the complicated weekly family dinners and lunches. I try to help them as much as I can from a distance and sometimes even feel I am more useful where I am; I tend to quickly lose my patience when talking to them very intensively over a period of several days.

So does he move on? Or does he stay in Portugal? And if he stays, how will he keep himself from becoming bored without the stimulation of international moves? Global Cosmopolitans might have a great deal of experience moving on, but to resolve the tensions of this paradoxical need they must also learn how to stay put and develop themselves in one context.

INDEPENDENCE AND DEPENDENCE

Goncalo also knows that he is ready to find a meaningful relationship. As he puts it, "Freedom is useless unless it is shared with someone."

Over the past three years I have, for most of it, lived my dream life: cool job, plenty of free time, nice single apartment in the center of Paris and all the freedom to do whatever I liked in my thirty-five days of vacation (thank you French labor laws!). I traveled for two months before joining INSEAD. I had enough money and no girlfriend, no pet, no debt. I used this freedom to do lots of things I always wanted to do: climb mountains, run marathons, travel around almost every weekend, flirt with a few girls. I now have the feeling that it is pointless to do more of the same. It will not be as fun, and you quickly take things for granted and do not even appreciate all the good things life throws at you. Life quickly becomes a collection of boxes ticked and challenges conquered. These last three years were a great way to end a chapter in my life; now I would like to find someone to share the achievements and pain. It is the first time in my life that I feel genuinely ready to jump into a relationship and make the necessary compromises to make it work. I guess it's the first time in my life where I would welcome some loss of freedom. In some respects it's like money and inflation: if you have too much money running around it loses value and you need to reduce the money in circulation to re-appreciate the currency.

The need to be and work alone and the need to live and work with others are common feelings faced by everyone. I call this paradoxical need "independence and dependence." But for Global Cosmopolitans, the puzzle becomes more complex with each change of culture. Their need to be self-reliant even at a young age, in some cases reversing roles with their parents, has been described in this book. Global Cosmopolitans are often rewarded for their independence in their jobs but suffer when career advancement requires them to depend on others. "Dependence" might seem like a negative word, but teamwork, mentoring and networking can be essential to corporate success. Global Cosmopolitans might know their work or personal lives are out of balance, but as Miki's experience illustrates below, they feel torn between the independence they are proud of and the dependence they know they need.

I needed to have the independence in my life, especially when it required changing locations and managing the transitions. If I hadn't had such a sense of independence, I would not have enjoyed and learned from all the transitions I experienced. However, as time went on, I started to wonder if my sense of independence might also be my weakness. I had a lot of tasks all the time, as I was the first member of the office. Consequently, I tend to carry all the tasks and not be able to delegate. Was it because I was the most experienced in the office, or was I missing some skill? The answer was the latter. I repeated burning myself out at work, and I didn't know how to get out of it. Being able to do things by myself and being able to let someone else do it usually does not come hand in hand to me. I need to learn how to do it and to assess what I should do by myself and what I should let other people do.

Global Cosmopolitans need to find ways to be themselves and be in relationships with people from highly different backgrounds. Along with personality differences, they can have language gaps and different cultural ways of resolving differences. Different cultural norms and styles of dealing with emotion are not always appropriate in the country where Global Cosmopolitans work. Without appropriate emotions, Global Cosmopolitans have difficulties motivating people or even gaining attention at meetings. Discussing difficult issues is limited at best by a lack of awareness about emotional cues or the potential for conflicts. Global Cosmopolitans must find ways to balance what is both culturally and personally appropriate. They can be quite creative when the tension touches the need to be independent while knowing the importance of their dependency on others. This multilevel puzzle illustrates the type of learning opportunities open to Global Cosmopolitans; resolution of complexities such as these provides the skills that they can take into the workplace.

IN CONTROL AND OUT OF CONTROL

For many Global Cosmopolitans the need to be independent and dependent shows up as the need to be "in control and out of control." Rima had a happy and protected childhood in the UAE until turmoil forced her family to live in a variety of European countries at a moment's notice. Looking back, she sees the pressure she felt to always be in control and follow new rules. As a manager, she has been rewarded for her sense that she can control any situation, but in her personal life she feels constrained.

Rima acknowledged that she felt scared when she was not in absolute control. But to balance her life, she resigned herself to finding a wider range of possibilities. Here she explains the dilemma caused by her struggle:

Control is very important to me. I like to be in control in three ways: being organized, efficient and never wasting time; knowing that I make my own decisions and do not defer to others; and being in control of my sense of self through development, change and achievement. It makes me feel good to think that I am in control. Conversely, when I lose control, I hate that situation, yet I find it unthinkable to ask for outside help since I am so used to doing everything myself.

CONNECTION AND DISCONNECTION

Staying connected to the past in a meaningful way is a challenge for Global Cosmopolitans, particularly when languages can be lost and found and when pieces of family history can fade without linguistic, contextual or relational reference. Tensions arise between wanting to stay connected to one's roots and living in the present. Global Cosmopolitans also struggle to stay involved and caring in the present while knowing that another transition might be imminent. The need to maintain important connections with people over time, space and language becomes a challenge because of frequent moves. Global Cosmopolitans must find a balance between maintaining an ability to develop relationships and supportive networks and yet being able to let go.

Marta was born and raised in Mexico, dreaming of a future as far as possible from her negative view of traditional Mexican womanhood.

And she made it.

Instead of building a life around men and children, Marta became an investment banker in New York City.

She wanted success. She wanted respect. And she wanted to have relationships with men without falling into a traditional role.

She found the success and respect. She loved her identity as smart, tough and atypical.

But her dream-come-true fell short of the reality she'd imagined.

She hated New York City. She hated the lifestyle of an investment banker, and she was not motivated by her work.

She had begun to crave a connection to her past. She wanted to make a difference in the lives of other people, particularly in Mexico.

Central to her core was a new sense of mission. The time had come to switch careers.

As Marta weighed the change, the tension in her life began to build. She struggled with how she could connect with her past without losing what she had built in the present.

She liked the benefits of being an investment banker. She was afraid to let go of the tough, smart, atypical identity her job gave her.

Most of all, she grew up in a highly traditional household and was afraid that other people would see her, and she would see herself, as the model of Mexican womanhood she had once dreamed of escaping.

Marta's story illustrates a specific kind of connection and disconnection, a tension between tradition and breaking out, which is frequently described by Global Cosmopolitans. By becoming an investment banker, Marta succeeded in creating the tough, smart, nontraditional story she had imagined, only to discover that a piece of her identity was missing. While some Global Cosmopolitans have grown up in homes where their parents provide models of maintaining relationships across oceans, cultures and languages, Marta has no such example to follow. She feels lost in the city, lost in her job, disconnected from a sense of purpose and from important people in her life. To reinvent herself, Marta knows she needs to confront the other side of the paradox. Her challenge is to find the balance between connection and disconnection.

"Connection and disconnection" is a classic illustration of how paradoxical needs underlie the challenges from which Global Cosmopolitans develop their strengths. The previous chapter addressed the challenge of connection and disconnection, a fact of life that Global Cosmopolitans face: as they move to and away from different worlds, they need to develop an ability to make and maintain relationships and support networks. But Marta's story shows that behind the challenge is a deeper need, an internal conflict between the connection and disconnection of her own identity.

For Miki, whose challenge as a Japanese outsider has been described earlier, the internal struggle between connection and disconnection looks like this:

It is indeed true that I constantly carry a strong sense of responsibility for my family. However, it is also true that I take actions about whatever I feel strongly about. For instance, in retrospect, I remember one of the key motivations I had for going on a year-abroad exchange program during university time was to go away from my family. Was I feeling responsible for my family then? I'm sure I was. So was I selfish to leave the family? Or was my urge to take what I thought was my path at the time stronger than the sense of

125

responsibilities I had for my family? I think all these reasons are true to a certain extent. I'm selfish and have a strong sense of independence. However, I do feel propelled to return home after a few years because of the family responsibility I carry. My sense of family responsibility is very strong and burdensome in my life at times, because it has recurrently prevented me from pursuing my own personal or professional plans. As bizarre as it sounds, having a certain level of selfishness does help me move forward in my life.

KNOWING AND NOT KNOWING

Global Cosmopolitans constantly face the reality of not knowing what is readily apparent to the people from the culture where they live. They can also lack the linguistic, contextual or relational aspects of previous pieces of their lives. They need to feel comfortable with this reality and compensate by developing detective skills that allow them to understand complex situations when puzzle pieces appear to be missing. As they move away from family roots, they also can lose their ties to their own family history.

One illustration is Stephan, who discovered an ability to understand complex problems without a lot of information after he dug into secrets about his family's past.

Born in South Africa, Stephan attended university in France, returned to South Africa to work and then returned to France for his MBA. Feeling that his reaction to violence and oppression was inappropriately powerful and confusing, he dug up the nature of his European roots and the experience of his parents and grandparents and started to weave together the missing pieces of his personal puzzle. His parents immigrated to South Africa from Europe but refused to talk about their past. They were depressed, they were fearful and they always argued about justice. He needed to know their truth, and finally he heard the brutal reality of their survival during World War II.

Knowing and understanding the impact of the past on his present has helped him with the importance he places on the need to know, to understand certain problems in depth and his ability to act responsibly in potentially controversial arenas. He thought about becoming an investigative journalist, but he saw a different application for his need to understand and to know. His unusual ability to find the truth and to understand the source of complex problems without much background information has served him well as a consultant. It has also allowed him to understand his parents and get closer to them, their stories and the meaning of his own past.

There is a saying that the only way to learn to walk is by losing your balance. "Knowing and not knowing" describes the tension that results when Global Cosmopolitans must take their first step in unfamiliar surroundings. Knowing and not knowing is one of Global Cosmopolitans' most peculiar and commonly shared reactions in the face of change. When a mountain climber prepares to climb a new peak, everyone can see the mountain. But Global Cosmopolitans constantly find themselves in the exact opposite position. When they arrive in a new culture, all the things they don't know are readily apparent to all the people surrounding them. They are sent with the expectation that they will perform as well as they did in their old, familiar circumstances. There is only one person in this whole equation who is standing at the base of the mountain looking up.

The concept of knowing and not knowing is so integral to the Global Cosmopolitan experience that it has already been presented both as a challenge and as a strength. But what psychological need lies behind this challenge? What does it feel like to let go of the familiar and know that even things you think you already know might not be true in your current context? Nigel describes the paradox of knowing and not knowing this way:

I love learning about new situations, new environments and, in general, being the naïve new boy, allowed to be ignorant because of my unfamiliarity with my circumstances and hence having an excuse for not competing. Although I love experiencing new situations, I usually need some pushing or prompting; my desire to be in control means that I prefer to do things within my normal sphere of knowledge. And, of course, because I prefer to be in control, when I am being pushed, I am usually resistant to this pressure. And when experiencing the new situation, I am often not happy either: witness my initial feelings on traveling to New Zealand or starting to work in London.

When people love to do something, they are eager for it to happen. Typically they seek it out as often as they can and enjoy it thoroughly when they do. But as Nigel's comments above illustrate, love does not necessarily mean happiness. Because of the hidden pressures he feels beneath the surface, Nigel loves change but is reluctant to experience it; his love of the new is laced with tension about moving into the unknown. His words illustrate why Global Cosmopolitans are experts at change and complexity but typically feel ambivalence just like everyone else.

Knowing and not knowing can trigger fear, pain and insecurity. Not only are Global Cosmopolitans moving into a new culture, with different linguistic, contextual and relational aspects but they are also moving away from their community ties and family history. Inarticulate in their new surroundings, Global Cosmopolitans can forget that they were once knowledgeable, fully competent persons. Before Gilles, a French engineer, could build a bridge in Vietnam, he had to build a bridge both to the team he was leading and to the locals who could give him the inside knowledge he needed. Yet, he arrived speaking no Vietnamese and had no direct knowledge about the culture. Not surprisingly, Global Cosmopolitans in situations like this one need to compensate for the discomfort of not knowing by developing detective skills that allow them to fill in the missing puzzle pieces in complex situations.

This chapter has presented some of the paradoxes that explain why Global Cosmopolitans face personally constructed hurdles when they are confronted with change. Recognizing these hurdles and remembering why they exist can be difficult for Global Cosmopolitans because of the uncommon complexity of their internationally mobile lives. The use of paradoxes can help Global Cosmopolitans look back at their experiences in a new way to gain fresh insights. Because of the common nature of their experiences, Global Cosmopolitans frequently mention a cluster of paradoxical needs that create internal tension in the presence of change.

The next chapter looks at the issue of paradoxes from a different point of view. Global Cosmopolitans can gain new insights by analyzing the potential downsides of strengths, a paradox that this book refers to as "two-edged swords of mobility." Awareness of the limitations of strengths can open up possibilities for a broader range of responses to the challenges that Global Cosmopolitans face.

8

TWO-EDGED SWORDS OF MOBILITY: WHEN STRENGTHS CREATE NEW CHALLENGES

Joseph has a special gift for negotiation. He has a way of finding clarity and consensus even with the most difficult clients. He is solution oriented, helping people feel comfortable with outcomes. He is recognized for his talent and ability to negotiate in extremely difficult situations.

He didn't learn this art at Oxford University.

He didn't learn it studying for his MBA at INSEAD.

He didn't even learn it as an adult.

He learned it growing up in a home where he wanted to protect his family from suffering in exile and where conflict was a perpetual guest. The more the conflict grew, the more skillful he became at negotiating around it.

Joseph's parents had been exhausted by the struggle to build a new life after they decided to flee the political turmoil in Lebanon. They tried living in France but eventually decided to settle in the United Kingdom.

Joseph was just an eight-year-old boy when they moved, leaving behind all their family, friends and resources. While his father traveled back and forth to Lebanon to maintain a family business, Joseph quickly took on the adult responsibility of negotiating to provide for his family's needs. With his winning ways, he helped his mother take care of financial problems. He also managed to get scholarships for himself and his siblings to excellent schools.

Bright, skillful, adaptable and charming, Joseph excelled at school and then at work. Everyone at the office knew him as the expert negotiator, the one who could bring calm to any situation and find win-win solutions for even the most trivial of problems. He was always there to deal with conflict in very tough negotiations.

With his clients, he could rise above conflicting positions. But what nobody at work knew was that Joseph had lost his magic touch at home. He was so concerned about calming conflict with his parents that he was ruining one of the most important decisions of his life.

While working in China, Joseph had fallen in love with a Chinese woman and wanted to marry her. But his parents insisted that he marry someone from a more similar family background.

He was close to his parents. He wanted to please them. But this decision was nonnegotiable.

Joseph simply avoided conflict by avoiding his parents.

He ended up causing everyone—the woman he loved, his parents and himself—a great deal of pain.

"I am a great negotiator," Joseph writes, "but I cannot deal with conflict in my own family."

This dilemma is what I call Joseph's two-edged sword.

The concept of two-edged swords, for issues with both positive and negative aspects, is present in languages throughout the world. The irony is how often we fail to recognize two-edged swords of adaptation within ourselves. In general, one edge represents a strength which is well developed and used in a positive and constructive way. The other edge represents the potential downside of that same strength. Understanding the paradoxical nature of strengths provides opportunities to comprehend and to see ways to develop both sides of the sword. While the source of the strength or the reasons for its development can be complex, recognition of two-edged swords of adaptation can open doors to personal understanding and possibilities of developing other sources of competence.

Anyone, whether or not she or he has changed countries, might develop a two-edged sword like this: "I am a perfectionist at work and when I am helping others, but I have not perfected how to take time for myself." But Global Cosmopolitans also develop what I call "Two-Edged Swords of Mobility" as a result of the shared complexity of their experiences. One side is a valuable adaptation to the challenges of change and complexity in their lives; the other can be underused, underdeveloped or, as in Joseph's case above, unhelpful. To reach their full potential, Global Cosmopolitans need to understand both sides of the blade.

HOW CAN A STRENGTH LEAD TO A NEW CHALLENGE?

A positive adaptation to changing cultures such as "I am good at eliciting opinions" might have worked at one stage in life. But this strength becomes problematic if the flip side is "I am not so good at expressing them." The downside might become apparent because of growing awareness of the need to be more expressive in a relationship or because of feedback at work. In either case, recognizing the problem provides an opportunity to work on it.

Joseph's paradox is just one example of when a Global Cosmopolitan strength becomes a limitation. Since a two-edged sword cuts both ways, favorable consequences on one side can lead to unfavorable consequences on the other. Global Cosmopolitans have described their swords from multiple perspectives:

I am an excellent observer, but I need to engage in life.

I am such an expert at dealing with loss that I worry that I do not let myself experience it enough. It makes me wonder how much I care or even understand why others have trouble just moving forward.

My story is one of a transforming person. I can go anywhere. I can do what people need me to do. I need to feel less changeable.

I can move anywhere, anytime, but I cannot stay in one place for too long. Can I stay in one place for a while without getting bored or feeling boring?

I know how to find my way through the transitional journey between one place and the next. I can be seen as cold, since I try so hard to move forward that I sometimes forget to let myself experience the loss. While I know that those feelings do not threaten me as much anymore, I need to work on being more expressive. I also need to work on my networks. I am not cold and uncaring, and in spite of multiple moves, I want to keep the connections to the different people in my life.

I am flexible and willing to adapt, but this affects my ability to get what I want or to clearly state what I'm interested in doing.

I am a superb analyst, but I feel cut off from the emotional world of others.

I know how to adapt to situations and people, but I lose my point of view and myself.

Two-edged swords are related to but significantly different from the paradoxical needs elaborated in the previous chapter. They are related because paradoxical needs often underlie the strengths from which two-edged swords arise. That's why they often use similar language such as adaptability, independence or moving and staying. But the two paradoxes are fundamentally different in how they are experienced and what they mean for personal development. Paradoxical needs are a tension between two seemingly contradictory forces. The invisible pull creates a challenge that Global

Cosmopolitans must resolve. Two-edged swords, on the other hand, develop as an adaptation to a challenge. The strength can be highly visible, like a friend and protector, but it can overshadow the need to develop the other side.

My identity as a Global Cosmopolitan has most certainly been a double-edged sword. On one hand, I gained an early appreciation for different cultures and an avid passion for travel. From growing up in Zambia when the country was in the throes of economic depression to backpacking through the mountain kingdom of Bhutan, my experiences have given me a unique global perspective and the ability to relate well to people of different cultures and backgrounds.

I consider this a significant strength, particularly relevant in a world that continues to shrink economically and culturally. I also count my ability to learn quickly and succeed in vastly different settings as key strengths. I doubt that either of the above would have been possible without the experience of having lived in several continents.

On the other hand, the constant moving has meant that my religious, cultural and national identities have been in a process of ceaseless evolution. I have now called fourteen cities in five continents home. My religious views, fundamental to my family, changed early on, partially due to my time in Africa and being in touch with other cultures. Moreover, I do not identify with being Indian anymore, and I don't believe I have the sense of belonging anywhere in particular.

Finally, the fact that my ideals have evolved so much over the years through different experiences, I believe, is a big contributing factor in me not knowing what exactly it is I want out of life. This of course happens to be the most worrying development of them all.

In the case of Global Cosmopolitans, change can feel normal. But change is also a trigger. It sets off earlier patterns of adaptation. People often reach backward to move forward, relying on what is easy, what works, what gives them both confidence and the knowledge that they can deal with the change. The more the adaptation works, the stronger and more confident they feel. They can feel so confident, in fact, that the strength becomes central to their identity.

Lessons learned at one stage in life can interfere with change and development at a later stage. Left unquestioned over time, the strengths that emerge from those lessons can create new challenges of their own. For example, a toddler's brute grab for a desired object might work with playmates but find little success in school and even less in adulthood. When grabbing fails, it creates a challenge that provides a new lesson for the next stage in life. The result is a new strength to move forward, at least until that lesson fails and the cycle begins again. This adjustment process is the cycle by which a person's ability to manage complexity matures over time.

The old expression "There's no arguing with success" explains why the paradoxical nature of strengths often remains hidden. The emotional intensity caused by the separation and loss associated with international mobility can reinforce certain adaptations that are characteristic of Global Cosmopolitans. Each success reinforces the strength and reduces incentives to look for downsides or the likelihood that there might be better adaptations.

When Global Cosmopolitans reach backward to move forward, they find an accumulation of experiences and emotions without a fixed language or cultural cues. They can become lost in remembering why they respond the way they do. Each successive change can move those reasons deeper into the dark as the turning point that sparked the adaptation becomes completely obscured. Some adaptive strategies, regardless of how well they actually work, take on a mythical aura of inevitability, as if they were like height or eye color. Even if Global Cosmopolitans are aware of their limitations, they typically don't link them with their strengths.

At work, the very strengths that make Global Cosmopolitans experts at constant change can potentially create hurdles for them to move ahead professionally. A frequently cited two-edged sword describes autonomy: "My strength and my weakness is my autonomy in new situations. I can usually handle new situations very well, but I do not know when and how to get help." However, moving up the career ladder can call for mentoring, teamwork and other capacities that sometimes conflict with cherished adaptive strategies such as autonomy.

To broaden their capacities and their power base at work, Global Cosmopolitans benefit from understanding how to shift from a focus on well-developed strengths to a place where they feel less secure. "Success has helped me look at my dark areas; it has given me the courage to explore and develop other strengths, just as getting passed over for promotion can be used as an opportunity to learn."

To develop an awareness of the two-sided nature of their strengths, Global Cosmopolitans can benefit from recognizing where they were in the developmental process when the lesson took place. By moving forward from that turning point, they can see how well that adaptation has worked for later challenges.

This adjustment process must be done with care. Strengths, like Joseph's ability to negotiate discussed at the beginning of this chapter, are key building blocks in the structure of a person's identity in life. There is a delicate balance in developing awareness of two-edged swords without allowing this awareness to immobilize the strength.

Ameya, who enjoys challenges, found it rewarding to challenge the most vital pieces of his identity.

Ameya is used to winning.

He left India to train as a champion tennis player in Florida while he pursued his studies. Now he is a successful Marketing Development Manager for an international company in Switzerland.

He has been enthusiastic about pursuing an international career but eventually plans to return to India to take over his family's business.

Part of what makes him a winner is his adventurous spirit and the boldness it gives him. So how can such a vibrant part of his identity become a limitation?

Here, in Ameya's words, is the two-edged sword of his adventurousness:

Whether I'm landing a plane at one of Florida's international airports or mountaineering in the Garhwal Himalayas, or executing a market entry strategy, my courageous spirit constantly helps me to move forward and grow. This adventurous yet pragmatic attitude gives me the strength to take important personal as well as professional decisions, but it also leads me to do too many different things at the same time; this often results in a feeling of confusion and helplessness. For example, while I was pursuing my tennis ambitions, it was easy to stay focused, but when I started working in the unstructured environment of the family business, without realizing my limitations as a new entrant, the lack of concrete goals led me to take on too many challenges and get frustrated.

Many Global Cosmopolitans would name adventurousness as one of their key personality traits. And many of the people who hire them are looking for exactly that kind of a person. After all, being adventurous is an adaptation ideally suited to the border-jumping jobs that Global Cosmopolitans do. But Ameya illustrates that the form this strength takes can greatly affect a person's job performance and satisfaction. On one edge of the sword, Ameya can be a champion. On the other, he can be confused and helpless. His strength becomes a challenge when he lacks concrete goals.

The twist, though, is that Ameya also has a two-edged sword that concerns setting concrete goals. When he was a tennis champion, he learned the lesson that goals helped him maintain his focus. Because of his need for high achievement, he has applied that same lesson repeatedly with great success. High achievement is often used by Global Cosmopolitans to gain recognition and approval in a new culture. It can be praised and rewarded. But it can also be a trap. Looking back, Ameya sees that the lesson he learned as a tennis-playing teenager has limited him as an adult professional. It is only now that he realizes how his relentless focus on goals has always cut him off from other people. He writes:

Whether I was playing tennis, studying or involved in business development projects, I worked relentlessly to fulfill goals within pre-set timeframes by motivating people and optimizing the processes that were critical to success. While this single-mindedness works as my strength, it can also affect my ability to relate to people. For instance, I often find it hard to take time off to build on relationships because of my over-involvement in my work. As I have a high need for achievement, I tend to adopt an extremist attitude to ensure that I excel in whatever I do. As a teenager, for example, I always reminded myself that spending time with friends was a waste as it did not help me to improve my tennis game. I also accepted the myth that if I excel in tennis, everything else will follow, including the most desirable girls. This tendency to shut out things that seem irrelevant so that I can completely focus on a few goals has been an enduring theme in my life and also functions as a two-edged sword.

From the fresh perspective of two-edged swords, Global Cosmopolitans identify paradoxes in some of their most treasured abilities. Even their talent for speaking many languages can become a two-edged sword. The strength is obvious for anyone who needs to work and live in another culture. But Global Cosmopolitans also discuss feeling lonely or misunderstood, sensitive to language gaps and frustrated when the subtlety they need is not accessible to them: "I learn new languages and new cultural ways of behaving quite easily. There are times, however, when I feel lost or lonely in translation."

Single-minded motivation can bring outstanding results, but its two-edged sword brings out a less-favorable side in Global Cosmopolitans. Consider the common Global Cosmopolitan motivation of pushing personal limits and seeing new possibilities. The excitement of seeing and experiencing new possibilities is a strength when life is relatively simple, but increasing responsibilities later in life can create the need to manage the resulting complexity. For instance, many Global Cosmopolitans feel less desire to experience the new as they feel an increasing need to develop important relationships. They begin to experience growing concerns about a personal lack of focus, depth and ability to make decisions. "I am always seeing new possibilities," said Roberto from Brazil, "but people often have to tell me to stop looking at alternatives and just do it." Global Cosmopolitans like these need to learn how to make a decision and live with it. Over time, they start to learn how to gain more depth from an experience and how to make decisions without always pursuing new possibilities.

Risk taking is another motivating force for Global Cosmopolitans that has not only obvious advantages for international mobility but also limitations:

I think that I have become addicted to risk taking. Setting up a factory in a new country or living in a totally different culture were the risks that I started loving and needing more of. It gives a certain excitement to my life. Now I want to channel that need to take risks in another way. How will I find the buzz if there seems to be less drama to the risk or at least less mobility?

Achievements are often a way that Global Cosmopolitans learn how to manage transitions in childhood. But achievement orientation has a downside, too.

Whenever I moved as a child, I kept finding ways to achieve. That made everyone happy, including me. I will always be achievement oriented, but there is more room in my life to find other roots to happiness as well.

I know how to bring my strengths to a new situation. I make my mark in a new country by making sure that I have visible achievements. Now, I need to realize that I can let up and learn other ways to be noticed besides needing everything to be so outstanding.

Another pattern seen in childhood adaptation is learning how to wield power. "I know how to be noticed in a new country," Thierry noted.

From a very young age, I learned how to take powerful positions so that I could get recognized. I seek recognition with the same skills that got me into elected responsibilities in the various schools I attended. I have had plenty of practice with every move. What has changed is my self-confidence that I do not have to work so hard to be seen and recognizing that I need to develop relationships that are closer to me.

One of the reasons Global Cosmopolitans enjoy international mobility is that their jobs often come with high levels of responsibility. They are rewarded for their ability to work autonomously, to be decisive and to remain in control in unfamiliar surroundings. But these strengths can cut people off and limit their perspective. The example here is Daniel:

Providing a clear vision, energy and taking fast decisions that I took responsibility for were some of the qualities that led to progression and promotion at work. The resilience to maintain views and challenge the status quo I believe is also a strength. The flip side has been the difficulty in involving and adopting others' ideas to bring them with me. Moving too quickly to black and white can miss options or incur mistakes in diagnosis, although, when situations change or additional information comes to light, I do adapt quickly and am not fixed in my views.

ADJUSTING STRENGTHS AND THEIR LIMITATIONS

Ever since I can remember, I have been someone who gets bored easily. Sometimes it is because my mind works so quickly and sometimes it is because I just do not care. Whenever something feels repetitive, I want to change. After finishing high school in Germany, I decided to go to the United States for a year to study. The change brought about so much stimulation that I was never bored. That experience marked me. I am less bored and I can now admit that, thanks to that and subsequent moves around the world, I cannot imagine another way of life. I am organizing my professional life so that I know the door is always open to international moves. I can move anywhere, anytime, but I cannot stay in one place for too long. I need to work on developing my confidence that I can stay in one place for a while without getting bored or feeling boring.

Boris, who moves constantly, keeps changing the people in his life, so he has no outside perspective that can help him hear these words. Instead he keeps repeating his childhood ideas about defeating boredom. Thinking about two-edged swords helped Boris articulate that his ability to move constantly has a downside. But that awareness is only the beginning. The real question is what to do next. Boris takes his insight a step further; his real issue is building confidence in himself so that his enjoyment and satisfaction do not depend on perpetual motion.

Through this process of self-understanding and sharing two-edged swords of mobility, Global Cosmopolitans confront the phrases they have been reluctant to hear. These issues have often made them feel stuck or act inappropriately for the situation. Sometimes these dark shadows can threaten someone's entire sense of identity.

Looking at the origin of these issues, often by understanding key turning points, can help Global Cosmopolitans reinterpret their life stories. They can identify patterns of adaptation to constant change, look at them from a new perspective and see new roads open in their future. Juan, for example, knew that he had superior skills of observation. By acting on the insights he developed through looking at two-edged swords, he learned how to become both an insider and an outsider and felt better about his work and personal life. He writes:

I left a privileged family situation in Cuba to move to the United States when I was very young. The move was traumatic. I lost all sense of understanding, since I did not know a word of English. I just watched. I have become an excellent observer. I see every detail, and, just as I did as a child, I then try to see them from a different perspective. Although my observational capacity has served me well in life, since I could be counted on to notice everything, I suffered the consequences of always being an outsider, an observer. I suffered from lack of involvement. Getting involved in teamwork has helped me see the skill that I have that I can bring to projects with others. I am able to understand a problem from many different angles. I have realized that others do not observe with the same intensity, so they miss aspects of a problem that I can bring to the discussion. Now that I have found ways to use this skill in my professional life, I find myself more engaged in what I do.

Global Cosmopolitans whose strengths are focus and achievement orientation have learned to pay attention to their emotions and to remain safe with the feelings that result. Others who have shown remarkable resilience in the face of family turmoil and tragedy have discovered that they can learn how to relax and enjoy the moment they have earned through their powers of resilience. Some Global Cosmopolitans are virtually addicted to taking on impossible tasks and making them possible; they learn to enjoy the possibility by identifying a broader range of ways to motivate themselves. People who have had to take control to rescue themselves or their families from difficult situations can learn to give up control and believe that others will help. "The good news is that with each attempt at trust, my world keeps opening up to the possibilities that working together creates," says Amir from Israel. "The anger is disappearing and I no longer feel so alone."

"I know how to focus on achievement, but I have to be reminded about the feelings of the people around me." The illustration here is Philip, who grew up in four African countries before going to a French boarding school for high school. He considered himself French, yet he was terribly rejected by his peers at school. He shut his emotions down and focused on achievement. The result was a great deal of responsibility at work. But he has reached a stage in his career where drive is not enough. He cannot do everything on his own. He needs to learn the skill of learning from other people. He needs to learn to work with others since the nature of his projects is much more complex.

I returned from growing up in various countries in Africa to go to boarding school in France. I had always been very self-assured and happy. I was French, or at least I thought so, until I went to a boarding school. I did everything wrong socially, and was terribly rejected by my peers. I felt alone and miserable. I shut my emotions down, and became very focused, achievement oriented and in a hurry to get on with my life. Now, over twelve years later, I am happily married and have just had my first child. My focus on getting ahead has allowed me to have incredible responsibility at work. I have a fabulous CV. Now I need to trust my feelings and pay attention to the feelings of others. Too much of my time goes into this drive and achievement orientation, even at work. In order to get ahead at this crucial turning point in my professional life, I have to pay attention to my emotional intelligence.

"I know how to adapt, but I do not know how to bring my different and unique voice to my work and my life." The illustration for this two-edged sword is Judith, who moved every few years as a child and felt a strong need to be accepted. She became so adaptable that people would mistake her for a local soon after she moved to a new country. This skill comes so naturally to her that she hardly notices she has it. She thinks of this adaptability as her greatest strength, but sometimes she adapts too much and doesn't bring her own perspectives to a situation. Now that she has more professional experience, she feels the need for change.

We moved every few years when I was a child. It was painful to leave my friends and situations where I knew how to do well. I think that it was my need to be accepted that contributed to my adaptability. At age three, when I moved to Spain, in a matter of weeks I was mistaken for a local. I even changed my name so that I would fit in. At age five, the same thing happened when my family moved to Italy. This pattern of adaptation continued throughout my childhood. My parents could rely on me to be the perfect daughter. My ability to adapt to new situations is definitely my strength. It is so incredibly natural for me that I hardly notice it. However, sometimes I adapt too much to what I perceive is what others need and do not bring my different perspectives to a situation. With each new professional move, I can adapt to the needs of the people I work for. Now, with sufficient professional experience, I want to be able to share my own ideas faster and take the risk of not adapting to the ideas of others.

As we moved around, I also learned how to be very independent. I could not count on my family to help with the process of adapting. I learned the new rules much faster than they did and they did not have the same needs to be accepted as I did in the new cultural environments that we lived in. Again, at work, my ability to start a new project in a new country is so easy for me. I can do it myself, and I do not need to rely on others. However, now, my work demands are more demanding and I need to learn how to allow others to take certain responsibilities.

My relational skills are outstanding, thanks to my adaptability to new situations. I have learned how to understand how people function in very different cultural contexts. My ability to understand others and work with others is excellent. Sometimes, I see the changes in their behaviors before they see it.

Developing an awareness of two-edged swords can be painful, but Global Cosmopolitans like Miki feel rewarded for their efforts. Looking at her extraordinary strength of adaptability raised some questions for Miki when she focused on its two-edged nature:

Is this a gift? I doubt it. To me, adapting to one culture/environment comes so naturally, without any thinking process. If I was more down to earth and had a strong self-identity, I could probably assess more clearly whether a new place is really comfortable or if I'm pretending to feel comfortable in it.

Miki took this awareness a step further, discovering how both sides of her sword could help her gain a better understanding of herself:

Such insecurity of not having an identity is not a pleasant side to discover, but I'm glad by going through the self-assessing process, I've discovered this insecurity that I have and that it could be one of the core anxieties that lies below many of my other issues. In spite of everything, I do recognize that my adaptability skill is a strength. It is very helpful, especially in a world that has become as global and cross-cultural as it is. However, adaptation comes too naturally for me that at a certain point, I feel that I don't have a solid identity that refers to one country or culture. That, I feel, is a weakness.

MYTHS AND PERSONAL GROWTH

Sometimes what people think of as the essence of their identity is more perception than reality. Examining the developing awareness of what I call "personal myths" can shed light on this process.

I am irresponsible and not committed. This has been my storyline. Now that I am thirty-five and have lived in five countries over the past seven years, the secret is that I want to change. I am lonely, and I know that I am not as irresponsible and not committed as I have been telling myself and others.

Just as our strengths are not as strong as we might believe they are, many stories that become part of our identities are not necessarily as real as we might like to think. They are based on perceptions and memory, built with personally selected details. Someone else might describe the same events entirely differently. Yet these stories can become the core of one's identity, or at least central to it. These are not lies; they're myths. The manager quoted above, for example, has been living with the myth that a life unencumbered by people or place has made him free.

Myths can develop when people draw the wrong lessons from life experiences or they keep using lessons after they have served their purpose. These powerful stories evolve slowly, unconsciously, compressing the intricacies of real individuals into simplified molds of the people we'd either like to be or fear we might become. These internal characters personify self-concepts such as being adaptable, perfect, high achieving, interesting or, in the case introduced above, irresponsible and not committed. Strengths can become central to a Global Cosmopolitan's identity, the mythical proportions externally reinforced by outsiders who benefit from the strengths and are unable to see the other side of the two-edged sword.

Global Cosmopolitans seek coherence in their life stories like everyone else, but they must find unity and purpose amid complex change. What worked in one context at one stage in personal development no longer works, yet they might keep telling themselves and others the same story. Myths can easily form that block possibilities for future growth, their grip on identity so powerful that they can persist even in the face of illness and death.

Since myths can have a profound effect on whether Global Cosmopolitans reach their potential at work and home, learning to counteract myths can be essential for future development. Giving voice to his secret desire to be responsible and committed changed the life of the manager above so much that he has shared his story frequently with others. Instead of being free, he honestly felt lonely and less irresponsible than he had pretended to be. Opportunities changed for him, and his move has been reinforced by the different kinds of freedom he had experienced. He has developed a love relationship and has been given considerable responsibility at work. He could be both free and committed, which is something he could not envision before that.

Many two-edged swords contribute to myths that can feel central to one's identity story. Being able to look at both sides can be easier if Global Cosmopolitans can see that the questioning does not mean losing important pieces of one's sense of self. The following quotes illustrate how other Global Cosmopolitans have broken through myths and begun to identify new avenues to growth:

On being interesting: *For years I believed that the only way for me to be an interesting person is to keep moving and having an exotic lifestyle. I need to explore other ways to see myself as interesting. Is it possible to work on my self-image?*

On being adaptable: *My story is one of a transforming person. I can go everywhere. I can do what people need me to do. I need to feel less changeable.*

On being a high achiever: *Whenever I moved as a child, I just kept finding ways to achieve. That made everyone happy, including me. Now I want to look for other ways to define achievement.*

Transforming myths into momentum to move in new directions is challenging, particularly when the myths have been highly successful and personally defining. But the central stories that Global Cosmopolitans have been telling themselves and others can become burdensome. Stories of living in five countries in seven years can convey an image of being highly cosmopolitan; the freedom can be so exhilarating that a Global Cosmopolitan starts to feel defined by the lifestyle. But at some point, the frequent moves and transitions, the constant disconnection and noninvolvement, transform the freedom into a limitation. Seeing this change provides an opportunity for a new kind of freedom, one that detaches identity from lifestyle and allows it to be linked in a deeper, more meaningful way.

Global Cosmopolitans often do not realize that they are carrying burdensome myths. "I received feedback doubting my capability of handling and/or managing conflicts," Sara recounted. She'd always prided herself on how she handled family disputes and considered conflict management one of her strengths. She continues: "After I received the feedback which was opposite from what I thought of myself, I started to doubt if I really have such a skill."

Counteracting myths requires a fresh look at reality. Most Global Cosmopolitans who move constantly have no effective way to check the stories they tell about themselves. Their relationships change with each new context. As a result, childhood theories and adolescent myths risk becoming entrenched. After receiving feedback about conflict management, Sara looked with a fresh perspective at conflicts from her past and discovered a pattern she hadn't noticed:

I seem to draw a clear line between "problems" and "conflicts." Problems are issues that seek solutions, whereas conflicts are collisions or nonconformities of something that are deeply rooted, such as cultures, values and identities. Many times such conflicts do not have any solutions. Even if there is one, it takes a long time and substantial effort on both sides to reach it. After categorizing the issues into two, I tend to immediately embark on trying to solve problems, but I do tend to avoid conflicts. I certainly consider this side of me a weakness.

Understanding the effects of paradoxical needs, two-edged swords and myths takes Global Cosmopolitans deep into the roots of their identity. They begin to see the sources not just of their strengths but of their limitations, too. From these insights, they can shift their silent, internal journey onto new, more productive paths. They can rid themselves of emotional burdens that have weighed them down. This adjustment process, once learned, can be used throughout life when different stages call for new approaches and solutions. The final part of this book explores these stages and provides specific ways for Global Cosmopolitans to move forward.

PART IV

MOVING FORWARD: BRINGING THE INVISIBLE JOURNEY OUT OF THE DARK

"My past is not a linear groove into which I slotted myself, or was slotted years ago, and which will spin me like a rifle bullet to some terminal destination. Rather, it is an old shed full of junk and hidden surprises, which I revisit to look for the tools I need day by day. Some of them inflict wounds on me and are to be avoided, others are broken beyond repair, some are damaged but reparable, and then there are others, half hidden and dimly perceived, which are barely touched or brand new, waiting to be tested and put to good use."

9

MOVING FORWARD: A PORTRAIT OF TWO CRUCIAL DECADES

Just when Josh thinks he has an idea of who he is and what he wants, everything starts to change at once.

The son of an American mother and a Swiss father, Josh grew up in San Francisco but had close ties to Europe. He visited relatives in England. His family spent a sabbatical year in Germany when he was eight and another in France when he was a teenager.

Life had looked straightforward when he met Carrie in his second year at Stanford University. They finished their studies, got married and found great jobs in New York City. But Josh wanted more. He combined his dreams of returning to Europe and becoming an international business consultant by getting his MBA in London.

But now that Josh is thirty, he's learning how little family sabbaticals and family visits to Germany have prepared him for the complex realities of being an adult Global Cosmopolitan.

Complications started right away. Carrie kept her job with a hedge fund but ended up spending long periods away from home. This was not how they wanted to begin their married life. Then, without warning, Josh's mother died. His mother had been a source of strength. His loss and the break-up of the family estate left Josh feeling heartbroken and rootless.

When Josh finished his MBA, he didn't feel ready to start his own business. So he landed what he considered the perfect post-MBA job, a position in London with a prestigious consulting firm. Now, two years later, he feels like he has no control over how he uses his long hours at work. He is prepared and restless to move forward with his entrepreneurial dream. But Carrie wants to start an MBA. She is concerned about losing the security of Josh's paycheck.

They also have talked about starting a family, but graduate school will probably delay that decision. When they do have children, they feel like they'll need a home base. Right now, they love living in London. Yet it does not feel like a place for them to settle down.

Josh likes living in Europe. But especially now that his mother is gone, he needs to feel anchored by his friends and family. His friends from childhood have gone in different directions and can't really understand his life, but he needs to be part of theirs. Carrie doesn't understand Josh's need to spend their precious vacation time with his friends. She feels their different work schedules barely give them enough time to see each other.

In fact, Josh and Carrie disagree about too many things these days. They still feel love, friendship and goodwill for each other. But they can see how their differences affect their ability to make important decisions together.

Josh is at the dawn of the two crucial decades in which people typically establish a place in the world. Like other ambitious people his age, he has big dreams. But his anticipation about the future is wrapped in uneasiness. He is starting to have difficulty savoring the present because he is usually caught up in thinking about what's coming next.

He wonders how he is going to have time to do everything and still have time for the family and friends that are so essential to his existence. Right now, Josh wants to make some space for himself in his marriage. That way he can figure out how he and Carrie can work through their differences, and he can move forward with his professional dreams.

Everyone goes through periods like Josh's where suddenly, sometimes inexplicably, the world shifts. Like many other young professionals, Josh thought everything was resolved, and yet nothing feels resolved. He is struggling with issues about place, attachment and identity. According to psychologist Roger Gould in his book *Transformations*, people reach their thirties and crash headlong into a childhood myth: life is simple and controllable. In fact, life at this age is anything but simple, but the loss of that key assumption can be overwhelming. Josh feels the intensity of the challenges and opportunities in his life. He also feels the weight of deciding and taking responsibility for his decisions. He is both excited and afraid. For the first time in his life, he is beginning to see how hard it is to have it all.

Many young professionals share these issues, but Global Cosmopolitans like Josh must factor in both concerns and possibilities created by distance, by being different and by their multiple cultural experiences. This chapter provides snapshots of Global Cosmopolitans as they transition into their thirties and forties, dealing with the competing pressures and needs of their lives. They are living out the consequences of past decisions while they continue to make choices that have tremendous impact on the patterns of their lives.

An anecdote from another context suggests a path that can help Global Cosmopolitans to move forward. When Michelangelo unveiled the first half of the Sistine Chapel ceiling, his frescoes stunned the assembled crowd and became the talk of Rome. But one onlooker was less than satisfied. It was Michelangelo himself. Without the heavy scaffolding to block his view, he saw his work for the first time as other people would see it. He realized how small and cluttered his figures and scenes appeared from the floor. Today's visitors to the Sistine Chapel see the result of Michelangelo's reflection and re-evaluation. The figures on the second half of the ceiling stand an average of 4 feet (1.2 meters) taller. There are fewer people in the bordering parts of the ceiling, and their size has expanded accordingly. The first fresco Michelangelo painted with his new approach became the most famous part of the ceiling: the Creation, with its iconic touch between God and Adam. It was only by stepping back that Michelangelo finally saw what he wanted.

By taking the time to step back, Global Cosmopolitans can look at the personal portraits they are creating. This reflection and re-evaluation is particularly important when major life changes and choices are concerned. Dreams can provide a certain structure for the choices. But each life phase creates possibilities that challenge and extend the foundations on which identities are built. Transitional moments provide the ideal time for reflection to take place.

Transitions can become an even more delicate balancing act for couples. The tension that Josh and his wife experienced while working through their differences is a common theme for Global Cosmopolitans. Couples can react to changes or potential changes differently, which can heighten the need for relational skills and mutual understanding. But these periods provide couples advantages as well as challenges. The tension can lead to constructive discussions about what the problem is and what the choices are. Working together to find something that both people can commit to becomes a process that can be applied and reapplied to major changes at later stages in life.

According to life stage theory, Josh and Carrie are actively going through their thirties crisis. They had been feeling like such a team. What scared them more than anything was to see how certain differences could affect their relationship. Everything that they thought they knew about commitment, responsibility and, in particular, responsibility in relationships is being reexamined. At the same time, both of them are feeling more dependent on each other and building a solid relationship together.

Josh was ready to quit his job to create a new venture. He was not concerned about financial security. They had money in the bank. He figured something interesting would happen and they would be fine. He grew nervous when Carrie started to feel scared, and he thought that his relationship was threatened. And Carrie did feel scared. She needed to have money in the bank to feel secure, and they would be spending their savings.

Josh had enjoyed years of being in the limelight, feeling supported by loving relationships. While he could see that some of the differences in their personalities helped them find an important balance in their relationship, he was at a loss to understand a fundamental question: how can I be myself, take care of myself and build a loving supporting relationship with Carrie?

Learning how to deal with conflicting needs became Josh and Carrie's first priority. They want to find a path together. They know that their relationship is painful right now, yet they have decided to look at their own needs and decide how to build a relationship with the space to work together on moving forward. The questions about personal identity, attachments and relationships, professional and personal development, and lifestyle will continue reappearing in their lives. They need to learn how to step back together and look at the questions that arise. As Global Cosmopolitans, they will need to factor in the daunting issue of place in light of the context that they are living in as well as where they have been and where they think they might be next.

While everyone can see the potential for challenge in periods of change, the greater complexity of global living requires even more sophisticated soul searching, decision making and creative solutions. Cultures provide life scripts for how most adults are expected to assume their commitments and responsibilities. But Global Cosmopolitans have no single cultural script to follow. Their languages of interpreting their lives are uniquely constructed for their own use only. This means that making sense of what takes place has mental images blurred by different cultural frameworks that are now part of their makeup.

Klara's motivation to think about her identity story came from settling into marriage and knowing that she was about to have a baby. Writing her life story underlined the importance of knowing who she was and how culture mattered to her. She knew that her quest for pulling together her identity story was complicated by her lack of national identity. She had just turned thirty, and every aspect of her life was about to change. With all of the transitions she felt that she was going through during her INSEAD year, Klara tried to imagine what she would say to her unborn baby about who she was.

Most of us identify with our nationalities, or our professions, but few are able to really define and know the "I" that they are referring to. In my case, growing up without a national identity has undoubtedly contributed to my unease about who I am. I cannot say that I am a Belgian or an American, even though that is written in my passports. Neither can I claim to be a German or a Hungarian, despite those countries being the roots of my origins.

My lack of national identity (and now of profession too!) has left me with precious few external factors on which to base my identity. However, the world is an ever-changing place: external factors such as professions, friends, and countries are in a constant state of change. I believe that if I continue to search outside of myself, my reference point will always be changing. My search has finally led me to the conclusion that the only viable, long-term anchor of my identity must be somewhere in myself, inside of me.

This chapter looks at Global Cosmopolitans as they deal with the competing pressures and needs of their complex lives. It begins with an exploration of how life cycles affect adult human development. It looks at how Global Cosmopolitans confront these universal stages with personal questions that stem from the pressures of an international lifestyle. Although every life stage is marked by a transitional phase, this chapter focuses on the two crucial decades when most people determine their place in the world. It looks at the thirties and then the forties, describing how they are distinct but complementary.

LIFE STAGES: ASKING NEW QUESTIONS, FINDING NEW ANSWERS

Global Cosmopolitans have different reasons to consider or reconsider the path of their international journey and what it means for their future. Those just starting out are determining what their future might look like. Those still on the move might want to understand the implications of a new professional opportunity or the personal consequences of following a life partner. Those who are questioning their choice to live globally might feel a need to have a home base for their children or to be close to aging parents. How free people feel to choose their path also depends on economic and political realities. Some companies make it harder to go home. Some countries do, too. No two stories are alike except that they often share a common theme of conflicting needs.

Global Cosmopolitans typically see their world as a lifelong process of personal development. Although they consider geographical change as central to their growth, they are also affected by the different life stages that are common to all adults.

The life stage perspective on adult development is quite useful for understanding the experience of Global Cosmopolitans. While the uniqueness of the Global Cosmopolitan journey is not treated in the literature on adult development, Global Cosmopolitans tend to relate to the descriptions of adult development presented by Daniel Levinson's notion of Seasons[1] or Gail Sheehy's concept of Passages.[2] Both describe a predictable and invariable succession of life stages posing predictable issues and challenges. Each stage ushers in a process of realignments as individuals continue the adventure of their lives.

Each new life stage changes the nature of the internal dialogue about "who I am now" and "what is important to me."

Of the many questions that arise at each life stage, some need to be considered immediately while others are placed on a back burner, often to be revisited later in the life cycle. The questions do not remain static but evolve as individuals mature and change their life focus over time. This framework raises particular questions or suggests additional dimensions for Global Cosmopolitans in addition to those that they share with a broader population.

Everyone finds these transformations challenging, but the greater complexity of global living requires even more sophisticated decision making and creative solutions. For Global Cosmopolitans, the task of writing the script they will follow is particularly pressing as they enter their thirties and forties. During these crucial decades, Global Cosmopolitans are hoping to live out many of their personal and professional dreams. The complexity of international mobility pushes their need to know who they are and what advantages they have in building their life journey. The more opportunities they have to prove themselves and gain confidence at work, the more likely they are to find creative outlets for their unique approach to life. As they gain more life experience, they become more conscious of the trade-offs and benefits of their lifestyle. They often are more aware of their invisible as well as visible strengths. Along with this awareness comes greater acceptance and maturity.

In a sense, moving forward internally parallels moving geographically. Their new life stage redraws the context of their world; their mental map no longer describes the terrain. Because Global Cosmopolitans experience different cultures, they understand how profoundly context affects development. With different ways of knowing and seeing the world, they understand that what they know about themselves is not static. Their life experiences have taught them that perspectives change, sometimes radically.

The following sections will look at Global Cosmopolitans as they move forward in their thirties and forties. Along with describing some of the complexity of those decades, the sections will give a sense of the creative possibilities that Global Cosmopolitans have found. These crucial decades are a time to reflect, learn and communicate. Through self-awareness, self-acceptance and a healthy need for reinvention, Global Cosmopolitans can use their adaptive capacity to advance their careers and transform their lives.

GLOBAL COSMOPOLITANS: MOVING FORWARD AROUND AGE THIRTY

Putting other people first is central to Ricardo's identity. Working for the benefit of society and consideration of others are key family values rooted in his parents' and grandparents' societal position in Colombia.

Now he is working for a global company in France. The rules of relating are different there. He needs to be careful, and he is having trouble living up to his ideals. Normally spontaneous, he is challenged when he has to think carefully about what he wants to say. If he waits too long then the passion that he uses effectively gets lost.

A competitive man with challenging work, Ricardo would love to put the people at the office first.

A caring husband, he would love to put his wife first.

A proud father of a newborn baby, he would love to put his son first.

As much as his instincts tell him to make everyone his top priority, he is starting to see that he simply no longer has time to do everything. He feels conflicting needs in every part of his life. While he knows that he must keep the generosity of spirit that is central to his identity, he has started to see that he needs to learn to be attentive to his own needs.

Ricardo has discovered that if he is to help other people as much as he can, he must start by putting himself first. Time management is crucial. He has resolved to set limits on people's demands and to stop constantly putting other people's ideas and needs before his own.

By refining what it means to help, Ricardo has found his way forward.

After making their way in the adult world for a decade, Global Cosmopolitans like Ricardo are starting to see the consequences of their earlier decisions. They can still see their dreams off in the future, but more than ever they wonder how, if ever, they will get there. Their commitments have loaded them with more day-to-day responsibilities. The patterns of relating to people that they learned in childhood have been tested by the complexity of geography and culture. While they might have a greater sense of confidence and personal consolidation based on their experience so far, the questions and decisions that await them are often more complex than anything they have faced.

As the complexities mount, a gnawing feeling can settle in that the assembled pieces of life just don't fit together. People at this age are discovering that there isn't time for everything. They want to live their dreams for work and personal life, and they need to figure out how to best accomplish what they have set out to do. Some Global Cosmopolitans are weighing their future in the context of committed relationships. Others are wondering when and whether they can share their journey with someone else. The crucial question in the early thirties revolves around the statement "I need to know who I am."

This life stage has serious implications for work. Global Cosmopolitans around thirty are considering and experimenting with career definition and reinvention. They are weighing career opportunities that can vastly alter the direction of their lives. They have a clearer sense of the political realities at the office. "I have gone to the best schools in India and in France," writes an MBA student from India. "I have an excellent track record in France. Yet can I ever get the responsibility that I want in France? I will always be the other." He plans to return to India in a few years. Meanwhile, he has stopped worrying about long-term implications of job decisions and started searching for challenge and opportunity. He has exchanged his government and aerospace experience for an internship in the fashion industry. While initially not interested in fashion, he realized that it would allow him to build bridges between different worlds. He knew he had found the right place.

For the Global Cosmopolitans that I work with, this period can be the first time they start to identify invisible strengths and build on them personally and professionally. Living without a single national identity, they begin to recognize the limits of external reference points and are motivated to look inside themselves to find the source of their stability. They begin using their creative edge of difference to bring excitement and motivation to their global journey. Even if they do not plan to make major changes in their lives, their greater self-awareness helps them see fundamental paradoxes like personal myths and two-edged swords. Aware of the compromises, they start to take responsibility for the choices that shape their global journey.

ENTREPRENEURSHIP: SEEING THE OPPORTUNITIES BETWEEN THE LINES

If Global Cosmopolitans have ideas that are different from the mainstream, they know that eventually they will have to find ways to convince people at work. They have enough professional experience to feel a growing sense of confidence, but they see how quickly the cycles of motivation and boredom can move. A central issue becomes finding work that they feel will motivate them over time, even if that means starting a company of their own. The entrepreneurial option also attracts Global Cosmopolitans who find that what might traditionally lead to success does not make them happy. By knowing what they have learned so far and benefiting from those lessons, Global Cosmopolitans can look between the story lines of their lives and see new opportunities for themselves.

To get a sense of this important decade and its creative possibilities, consider the case of David:

David convinced all the right people that he was the perfect man to be transferred from Paris to Chile. The day he got his dream assignment, he and his wife uncorked Champagne and celebrated with their toddler son and newborn daughter. But the next morning, he discovered he'd been too convincing.

The Director for Europe, a man David didn't even know, decided that he was the perfect man to help with a massive, high-profile merger in the transportation industry in Europe. There was no choice. David soon faced a tumultuous arrival in Amsterdam with dozens of work groups and no time to think. It was a time of terrible tension, lost sleep, canceled vacations, exhausting negotiations and endless meetings. But it was also a time when the many lessons of David's life came together in a remarkable way.

From his first job in Frankfurt, David brought to Amsterdam the language skills that he needed to learn Dutch. From his second job in Singapore, David learned sales from a boss who was an expert, and he made career decisions that made his family top priority. He also learned the power of emotional attachments with friends. His close circle explored mountains, beaches and discothèques. David suffered when he drove to the airport to move to Japan. "I don't cry often," he writes, "but that evening I cried the whole way."

From his third job in Tokyo, he learned he had the political instincts to overcome resistance, winning the respect and support of managers more than twice his age. He also learned the power of harmony, calm and focus. "In Japan, I learned to take my time, be patient and share with people before I jumped in."

All these lessons came together in Amsterdam: salesmanship, political instinct, harmony, focus, patience, motivation, confidence. At each step of the way, David learned to face the tough decisions he needed to make, to take responsibility for them and to accept the risks involved.

David, now thirty-four, did not return to his transportation company when his sabbatical to study for his MBA ended. Instead he convinced all the right people that he was the perfect man to start his own company.

He understood the lessons he brought with him. He had the stability he needed with family and friends. This time, when he uncorked the Champagne, he knew no boss could change his plans.

This time, the boss was David.

MOVING FORWARD: VOICES FROM THE FORTIES TRANSITION

No matter what the choices have been to this point, they seem to come up again around forty.

If the early thirties is a time for re-evaluation, the beginning of the forties is a time for realignment. Global Cosmopolitans worked in their thirties to define themselves; a decade later, their identity becomes even clearer. They can see their chosen path from the perspective of time; they have built up an accumulation of experiences, relationships and skills. They have a closer alignment with what they want and what they don't want. They know that they have handled challenges in the past. They have had practice resolving conflict with others and within themselves. They are often known in their profession and have contacts around the world. They exude a certain confidence. They are ready to take responsibility for their actions and make the most of their lives. With a better idea of how the pieces of their lives fit together, Global Cosmopolitans in their forties typically focus on the pieces that are missing.

By now the stakes are even higher, especially with respect to global mobility. As time becomes more pressing and options narrow, people at this age are clearly making choices with consequence. Some issues that they haven't dealt with unexpectedly reappear. They get tired, for example, of old destructive patterns and decide to do something about them. This decade often involves juggling different lives besides just their own. Dramatic events can change their thinking about relationships, family of origin, impact of professional life or their ability to keep relationships healthy. The complexity can be overwhelming. For couples, alignment at this age is particularly delicate. Couples often struggle to find the strength they need for the increased complexity of these later years.

While the complexities of the thirties push the need for Global Cosmopolitans to know who they are and what they can gain from their differences, the complexities of the forties push the need to go beyond what they already know and find personal fulfillment. The crucial questions at this stage involve satisfaction and meaning. Global Cosmopolitans by age forty have a lot invested in the past and a different view for the future than they had a decade ago. For this life stage, growing into oneself can be the biggest challenge of all. By this I mean that people approaching their forties want to feel like they are consistent, that the choices they make will match their identity story no matter what or where they are. Because there is no certain, secure world around them, Global Cosmopolitans need to know the sources of their personal resilience. They typically are moving forward on multiple dimensions, such as better time management, a stronger relational fabric, living attuned to their values, community involvement and social responsibility, even health issues.

If an outside event, a move or an unexpected challenge has not raised any questions, turning forty can sometimes be a nonevent. Moving forward at forty can mean just continuing with their personal portrait and clarifying details while leaving the core intact. But for other people, this age can provide a reason to take stock. For many people, the magic number 40 can open up to certain issues that might have been put on hold.

After making their way in the adult world through their thirties, Global Cosmopolitans are starting to see the consequences of their earlier decisions. While they can still dream about future possibilities, their commitments might have loaded them with more day-to-day responsibility. The patterns of relating to people that they learned in childhood have been tested by the complexity of geography and culture. While they might have a greater sense of confidence and personal consolidation based on their experience so far, the questions and decisions that await them are often more complex than anything they have faced.

Feeling the need to realign their current situation and reconsider the path of their global journey, Global Cosmopolitans in their forties can feel overwhelmed and lonely. Given the complexity of their stories so far, they know that there are no formulas. Not only do they have their own issues to address, but they often need to address the needs of the important people in their lives, including spouses and children, as well as people in their family of origin and friends. This can be a time to look for new solutions and a time for tapping the creative edge of difference that has developed as a result of their lifestyles.

MOVING FORWARD AT FORTY: USING GLOBAL COSMOPOLITAN STRENGTHS

From a life-stage perspective, men and women in their forties are in parallel stages of development. But Global Cosmopolitan women make particularly fascinating case studies, because their international lives are often shaped in conjunction with the needs of families. The pressures they feel to live up to societal expectations, the need to shift roles and professional status as they cope with the arrival of children, and the desire to integrate their professional and personal fulfillment create powerful transitions that can provide equally powerful transformations. As they find both good questions and good solutions, they also develop a context of mutuality and support for experimenting with new ways to move forward. Both men and women at this life stage have to seek out people who understand quickly what their challenges are all about.

The cases presented here involve women who have studied and worked in at least three cultures and languages. While their personalities and cultural backgrounds vary, they are all Global Cosmopolitans attempting to pull together the pictures of their lives. Their different voices articulate different pieces of the forties puzzle. Location plays a fundamental role in their transition, since they are all moving or planning to move. But location is only the tipping point. They are working on what changes they want or need to make for the next decade.

The case of Ana illustrates how the tough, but frequent, transition at this life stage is not the exotic but the familiar. Global Cosmopolitans who have spent years away from their "home" do not anticipate the realignment that moving back entails. Reentry in the thirties can be challenging because Global Cosmopolitans often feel lost and misunderstood. One of their central skills, their cultural capability, is not necessarily valued. They must compete against their peers who never left and wonder how they could catch up. Although they have often held positions of responsibility in another country, they feel the need to prove themselves again. They wonder whether they will still be able to live out their dreams. When Global Cosmopolitans return in their forties, they confront the reality that they can't step back seamlessly into their old surroundings and move forward from there. Life is not the same as when they left. Reentry for people in their forties has a feeling of finality, like they have made their last move and they are under pressure to make the most of it.

Ana is the family entrepreneur.

She had a thriving design business in Hong Kong and Indonesia combining ideas from the different countries that she had lived in, which spanned three continents. Whether her clients were Asian, European or American, she used her experience base to build on their sensitivities.

She is smart, ambitious and hard-working. But when a great opportunity came for her American-born husband to transfer to Spain, her native country, she couldn't wait to pack her bags and take their children home. Even if they stayed for five years, this would be her opportunity to create a home they could always have.

Except that Spain wasn't home, at least not the home she remembered.

Ana had been gone for twenty years. As much as she knew about the rest of the world, she discovered she had much to learn about Spain.

Suddenly the expectations of appropriate behavior confronted and confounded her. Simple interactions, such as exchanges with the concierge in her apartment building, became confusing. The concierge expected someone Spanish to know all about the rules of behavior, but Ana had learned other rules given her global experience.

The way she saw it, she simply was not acting Spanish enough.

The same disconnection surfaced at her children's school. Ana felt she was an excellent parent, but she had to relearn the expectations of the Spanish school system. While the children considered themselves Spanish, they had lived in Asia and spoke English better than Spanish. They relied on their mother for the unwritten rules of behavior, and she did not know if she could deliver.

Her husband was having fun living and working in Spain. He had a responsible and high-profile job for the same company where he had worked in Asia. His new life called for him to use his global skills.

And Ana's new life? It called for her to work at being Spanish again.

She is using this opportunity to look at how she has developed across her different experiences. At the same time, she wants to find an outlet for her passion for interior design.

Her first two projects are personal, creating homes for her family in the village where she was born and in Madrid. They have kept her involved, but she is on the lookout for another way to put her skills together in Madrid.

One of the changes that she had anticipated was the need to restart her professional life again. She knew from experience that it would be challenging. But that same experience of reinventing herself many times before had taught her that she could do it again.

Her background as a Global Cosmopolitan had given her strengths that would serve her well in this transition. She could see the world as both an insider and an outsider, understanding that the cultural gaps she was experiencing were not wrong but different. Most important, she knew how to be comfortable knowing that she did not know. With time, as she had experienced many times before, Ana knew she and her family would find the security, familiarity and direction they needed to move forward.

Sasha had developed a self-awareness that allowed her to take a pragmatic approach when a major transition moved in the opposite direction to the future she had imagined for herself. This adaptive ability is essential in Global Cosmopolitans, whose lives are buffeted across borders. In Sasha's case, as with many Global Cosmopolitans, a network of global contacts means that many places in the world will have familiar faces. But for someone like Sasha, it takes extraordinary adaptive capacity and creativity to turn the merely familiar into a real home.

The notion of the perfect place to live often shifts over time. By the time they have reached their forties, many Global Cosmopolitans have experienced the different charms and disadvantages of different cities and countries. Some continue to look for the perfect context, but many take a pragmatic approach to their location. They enjoy what they have now and see any future moves as another chance to gain a new perspective on the world. Sasha illustrates this pragmatic approach. She was tired of moving around the world and wanted to create meaningful relationships and a sense of home. She missed home, but she did not miss her traditional upbringing. She knew that she could no longer fit in. She found the perfect job in a biotech firm in Sweden, where she hoped to create the feeling of being at home.

From one day to the next, Sasha's boss decided to move the entire business to Hong Kong. She had to accept that without her job, her emotional investment in Sweden might not pay off. Hong Kong was not her first choice as a home, but she went anyway. She knew she could rely on her network of friends there to help her settle in.

Sabine was able to move forward because she possesses the Global Cosmopolitan strength to find solutions by putting the pieces of her life together in a novel way. Her ability to look at her adopted culture as both an insider and an outsider has allowed her to identify a successful business opportunity. Despite the complexities of a radical change in location and life roles, she was able to move forward by identifying the places in between, both personally and professionally.

Growing into one's self can be the biggest challenge of all. Taking the time to question and look at the pieces that might not have fit the thirties identity story can sometimes bring out the best and most creative responses to using that piece of the story. Even in the most secure of situations, experimenting with a different lifestyle or accepting that personal needs require life changes can be quite difficult. For Global Cosmopolitans, making changes in the absence of certainties and a secure world requires a belief and knowledge of sources of personal resilience.

Sabine has been able to show extraordinary resilience in her forties transformation. She is starting to experience the light of her new pathway. She has had her up-and-down moments over the past couple of years in transitioning from a corporate high flyer to a focus on her roles of wife, mother and student, but now she has her new business up and running, she is thrilled.

Sabine likes to see the opportunities between the lines. She loves the adventure of creating her life.

Going back to Argentina isn't an option right now. Her entire family lives in Germany. And since she has never lived there, she knows that Germany will never be home. But Sabine has a history of combining the adventure of a new environment with possibilities for personal growth.

When she had an opportunity to move with her company from Argentina to a management position in Spain, she jumped at the chance for a new adventure. Later Sabine left a senior management position in France to take advantage of a move to join her husband in Singapore. This transition gave her the time to think about what she wanted to do next.

Although she already had her MBA, she decided to get another masters, in art management, when she first moved to Singapore. She finished her studies right after the birth of her son. She created her own business at the same time. Working with a local Singaporean of Indian origin and an English artist, she has put together a team of people with different skills to start an advisory company. Sabine loves people who are different, and her company reflects this. The Singaporean government, seeing the value of this proposal, has supported her start-up, when funds become available, hoping to develop creative efforts in Singapore.

Emily's case shows how Global Cosmopolitans can move forward in tremendously creative ways when they are aware of their personal needs. As different as the Global Cosmopolitan identity stories are at this age, so are the solutions. Global Cosmopolitans move beyond the day to day and look at their lives in new and bigger ways. They rotate different aspects of their lives to rearrange their roles and relationships. Because they need to belong and yet remain true to their sense of self, people in this decade can learn to move between their different roles, adjusting to their circumstances. Consolidation in the forties means finding creative answers to complex questions.

Emily found a way to use her need to be independent to create the perfect job:

It wasn't like Emily to be restless and bored. And yet that's how she felt in the years that she and her husband worked in Switzerland.

Born in Hong Kong, Emily's first international adventure on her own was as an undergraduate student at Princeton College. She followed that experience with an MBA in France and ended up working in private banking in London.

When Emily married, she kept her high degree of independence. Initially, she and her husband enjoyed their work in London. But when they both got jobs in Switzerland, the enjoyment was distinctly one-sided.

Emily searched for different possibilities and ended up working in Paris and commuting to see her husband on the weekend. From that beginning, she has since created what feels like the perfect job, given the complexity of her situation. She splits her time between Geneva and New York, working in private banking again.

She has the independence she needs. She also can spend more time in New York, where she has found a close circle of Global Cosmopolitan friends her age.

The dream job that Cristina created for herself happened because the Global Cosmopolitan lifestyle she'd had since childhood had given her a creative edge of difference. Cristina works hard, and she loves what she does. A theme throughout her life about being different is now serving her well. She has friends from around the world and she creates events and situations where she comfortably brings them together. But it is the identity piece that is so exciting for her. She has found a way to be different, enjoy it and actually have it be her core asset at work.

I have learned what my unique advantage is. Initially, I had to learn how to work in an English consulting environment. To some degree, it seemed to me it meant focusing on the rational, leaving the emotional aspects of business at home. Being a Latin American female engineer, both dimensions were an integral part of me: the rational and emotional. However, I started finding different ways of bringing the two to work, and it seemed to work. I developed deep relationships with key clients, perhaps because they saw there was something different in my style. There was more trust. We talked more openly about important, even if sometimes difficult, things. In Colombia I grew up acquainted with diverse people, some of them powerful and influential. Hierarchy never seemed to be a boundary or a barrier for me; I felt comfortable with people at any level early on. So I seem to find easy access to people, develop rapport and relate to clients' behavior.

I have a reputation for being a bit unconventional, having an unusual angle or perspective and doing things in atypical ways. But I think part of my job, precisely, is to enable my clients to think differently, perhaps even feel differently, and on that basis come up with new solutions and approaches. Now I have my own business where I combine strategy and leadership consulting as well as coaching, while also working in the academic world. It is great; I get to do what I love and what I can do well. It is the perfect combination for me. Each person is so different; I love creating a mental map of what makes him or her up and how they work. It allows me to use my curiosity in a constructive way, while helping them think strategically about their business.

I think I am incredibly lucky. I get paid for teaching others some of the skills I picked up through life. I get paid for being me!

Liv and Claudia want to take charge of the forties transition, reconsidering the complications and realities of their lives. The skills they bring to work of planning, organizing and making things happen they bring to their personal lives. They talk about the importance of learning from their experience, using the confidence and competence gained to help them move forward creatively. With all of the challenges that they have experienced, they see that they have developed and learned skills that will help them with their current dilemmas so they can continue to realize their dreams.

Claudia has high expectations. She is as tough on herself as she is on others at work when she wants a change to take place. Now that her children are getting older, she is reconsidering many aspects of her life, from what the values are that she wants to give to her children, given the different cultural messages that they are growing up with, to how she and her husband see their lives now. She wants to find good solutions that meet their different needs and an outlet for her professional ability and needs. He is successful and happy continuing his professional life in France. She is concerned about whether this is the right place for her.

Claudia and her husband have been married for ten years. While they might have been clear about their choices ten years ago, now, with a certain awareness of what it means to sink roots in another culture, to raise three children in another culture and to get perspective on their professional development, they are ready to step back, evaluate and discuss how their individual perspectives and experiences have had an impact on how they see their lives and their choices.

Although she was born in the United States, she has always felt very Italian, since she has parents that are Italian and she spent most of her youth there. She returned to the United States to go to Princeton. She decided to work in the United States for a while and took a job with the World Bank. There she met her Peruvian husband.

They decided that they needed to be on neutral territory to build their own family. Claudia wanted to get her MBA and eventually be closer to Italy and her family. Claudia's husband was able to get an interesting situation as a lawyer in London, while Claudia was able to get her MBA.

They decided to build their relationship and family in a third culture, England, where they would be raising their three daughters. Some of the biggest challenges to their successful integration into life in England have come from their different cultural mandates and experiences. While she has put together a professional life in London, she is getting ready for a professional move. She knows how to make things happen and needs a bigger scale to do that. While Claudia has taken on the role of managing the various complexities of the relational fabric of their family life, she is ready for a change that might shift the balance that they have created.

Liv is planning the next steps in her professional life by using her Global Cosmopolitan strength for kaleidoscopic creativity. She knows that every environment has different merits, and as her life develops, she will see the pieces differently. She looks back at her life that way, as a kaleidoscope with different patterns and adventures.

A single mom, Liv has had to realign priorities daily. There is her children's education and her professional opportunities to consider, along with her personal life. Liv knows that she will soon have to reinvent herself again. Leaving won't be easy, but she is confident that she can build another home that will be better for everyone.

Liv describes how ideal her current situation is:

Everything is aligned here. That is important to me. Where else in the world can I find nature like this, along with the spiritual side and the human side.

It captures so much. I am not afraid to lose it. When you have lived in many places you are always thinking about moving. But I will have a big shock when I leave.

When the children do reach an age when they need a stable educational environment, she says that the most likely move will be to Geneva; it isn't home, but it is where she had a fabulous schooling environment when she was a child. She considers it an easy city to live in, with a highly international environment and a beautiful natural setting. An important factor, of course, is that her mother still lives there.

All these changes have raised big questions about the next chapter of her life. Where is home? What does home mean? What parts of her identity are most important to her now that she is raising her children? She knows that she has to adapt and plans to use the skills she has developed over a lifetime to do that. She is conscious that being a good mother is her most important role right now. Her important lesson from growing up is the need to give her children a value base.

In the hotel business, one has to focus on what the next move will be. The challenge now is that remote adventures are not plausible. I love opportunities to create, but I need to keep a perspective on what locations are plausible, particularly when I consider the future education of my children.

Of course, many men experience powerful transformation at this stage in their lives, too. Andreas did not want this transition to slip by. He saw it as the moment to take charge of his life. He knew what lifestyle he wanted, and he knew that he wanted more than the professional success that was coming so easily his way. Global Cosmopolitans like Andreas can realign their priorities in their forties to create a life that reflects who they truly are.

In Austria, where he grew up, Andreas dreamed of two things. He wanted a high-flying career. And he wanted to live in California. When he was earning his MBA in France, he decided his ideal life would be a great high-tech job in Silicon Valley. He expected both money and fame.

Andreas found responsible and enjoyable jobs in the high-tech industry. His work took him to Europe and the United States. But he found contentment when he took the time to develop other sides of himself.

He took up yoga and decided to help people with leadership and life training. Just as he had dreamed when he was growing up, he bought a house in Southern California. He made friends in record time, inviting forty people to celebrate his fortieth birthday in his new home.

He might not have earned the fame and money that he expected a decade before. But he is pleased with his choices. Andreas wants his next position in the high-tech industry to be near his new home. It took him longer than he expected to arrive where he is now; he wants to stick around and enjoy it.

Ten years ago, Andreas was thinking about the future. Now he is living in the present and content with his life.

The next chapter introduces concrete ways in which readers of this book can make the lessons of mobility more visible. Like Michelangelo looking at his ceiling, Global Cosmopolitans need to find ways to step back to move forward. Their interior journey requires different planning from moving forward on a traditional journey.

10

GLOBAL COSMOPOLITANS: UNLOCKING THE POWER OF STORIES

IMAGINING THE JOURNEY

Imagine a woman who has just returned from cycling around the world, look-ing much the same as when she left, yet something about her has changed.

To propel herself through different countries, cultures and experiences, she needed to know when to change gears, use more effort or conserve energy, and maintain and repair her equipment. She needed to find food, clean cloth-ing, shelter and medical care.

She needed more than just a bicycle. She also had to rely on different aspects of who she is as a person. The journey certainly would not have been easy. But she would have learned a great deal about what it takes to make an amazing voyage.

She might not be aware of everything she has learned right away: life on the road may have become so normal that she hadn't noticed all the effort she put in. Along the way, she just adapted to having an interesting and effective ride.

But she is highly aware that she was thriving during the experience. She has come back with a sense that life is an opportunity to learn, that every day can be a new adventure. She has a sense of accomplishment, maybe even a feeling of being energized. She will probably talk about what she has seen and the highlights of the experience. Or show you pictures of far-flung places and newfound friends. If you are interested in food, she will tell what she discovered about the many different kinds of rice she ate and the many different styles of cooking. She'll tell you a few stories about mishaps in dif-ferent countries. She'll probably share how her perspective has shifted after seeing the world's challenges, like poverty and global warming, from so many different angles.

She learned about being alone and what it was like trying to make new friends with people who were different and who spoke different languages.

167

She has funny or scary stories about how she ran into trouble by not understanding the rules, or how she managed to win the trust of someone very different from herself. If she has some good stories and knows how to tell them well, she might keep you captivated, especially if you are interested.

But there are also things she won't talk about.

She might feel a newfound sense of competence that is hard for her to describe, particularly if she feels it might threaten or alienate people. She might have big ideas, like ways to save the world's resources, but she doesn't want to give other people the idea that she has moved into a world where they do not belong.

She might feel alone, like a stranger in surroundings that should feel familiar. She might see how people have moved on with their projects and their lives in ways that no longer interest her. Maybe the loss she feels is all too painful and she doesn't want to talk about it right now. Maybe she feels like she can't possibly make other people understand. And perhaps she's right.

She might be eager to think about how her journey has changed her, the new ways it has prepared her for life. Maybe she doesn't want to forget how she dealt with the difficulties and challenges she faced, because that knowledge makes her feel unique and more confident and creative than when she left.

But perhaps she is afraid that she has changed too much and doesn't want to talk about it. She might be concerned that if she is fundamentally different, she will change the key relationships she currently needs to flourish. She might be concerned that the people she left behind can't play the same role in her life now that she has returned.

Is she really different after this voyage? What key elements have stayed the same?

Is she ready to take time out for the personal exploration she needs to answer those questions? Will she be able to remember and articulate experiences that cross so many cultures?

And are people at work and at home ready to open a dialogue to find out who she has become and what she can contribute? Are they willing to take the time to decode a complex global identity that transcends standard cultural expectations?

The cyclist is a useful image to describe Global Cosmopolitans who have been on a unique voyage and are preparing for inner journeys of personal exploration. The image represents the potential of the learning environment in which Global Cosmopolitans live.

The nature of a bicycle journey is different from a plane or car journey. It requires effort, a will to push the pedals and propel oneself forward. It also requires balance; a cyclist who has lost her equilibrium needs to take the time to reestablish it or she will not get far for her struggles. Her journey is not about speeding through to a destination. It is about the journey itself, about being in contact with the people and surroundings. It is about being curious and aware of that which is unique and that which is universal. A cyclist can reach places that a plane and car cannot. Often the best learning experiences happen off the beaten path.

In return for her distinct efforts, the cyclist reaps distinct rewards. At times, she is sweaty and uncomfortable and wishes she'd never done it, but at other times the journey is the greatest joy imaginable. Such a journey requires cleverness, creativity and flexibility to handle the constant adaptation and learning at every stop. It requires an ability to forge relationships that count. The cyclist's unique opportunity to take a closer look at each new place is what ultimately yields a broader outlook, a global perspective.

Finally, the cyclist's journey can teach a unique set of life lessons. One important example among many is how much security a person is going to need, or not need. Sometimes after a journey of constant change, the cyclist discovers that she needs some stability and knowledge that her life will not always be changing.

Each Global Cosmopolitan is the cyclist, with his or her distinctive journey marked with anxious moments and joys. If they want people at work or in their personal lives to value their experiences, Global Cosmopolitans have to define that value and figure out how to communicate it effectively. This need is particularly strong when Global Cosmopolitans have settled into a single country and are working in jobs without a direct international connection. Valuable skills and insights can easily disappear. The result is a feeling of unused capacity and job frustration.

It is not enough for Global Cosmopolitans to have a shapeless feeling of confidence and accomplishment or a collection of exotic snapshots and travel snippets. Other people will never understand what Global Cosmopolitans themselves cannot express; Global Cosmopolitans need to know why they feel the way they do. Along with all the other skills that they have learned from living globally, they need to develop their own personal power of knowing: knowing their own story, knowing the story that others tell about them and knowing how to communicate their story appropriately.

Global Cosmopolitans cannot always be relied upon to articulate their uniqueness on their own. They may be unaware of much of the intellectual and emotional work they have done. They consider it day-to-day living. Their belief in their ability to handle any situation can inhibit their ability to articulate why they feel the way they do about themselves. Capacities can remain buried or lost because Global Cosmopolitans don't realize they have these abilities or can use them. The goal of effective dialogue in the workplace is to make sure that the company, colleagues and the individuals themselves understand these valuable differences and unique abilities.

Family and friends, too, can provide Global Cosmopolitans with the support and stability they need after a life of constant change and complexity. That connection works best when Global Cosmopolitans feel they are understood and accepted for the individuals they have become.

GLOBAL COSMOPOLITANS: KNOW YOURSELF; KNOW YOUR STORY

"Know yourself; know your story." This phrase is the essence of how Global Cosmopolitans can tap the creativity, benefits and sources of resilience that they have accumulated on their international journey.

By knowing their stories, their strengths can become more visible. By knowing how to *tell* their stories to other people, they can build stronger relationships inside and outside of work and forge professional opportunities to use their distinctive abilities in new and more meaningful ways. Through their stories, Global Cosmopolitans can ultimately understand how they learn and how change affects them. Understanding their past can help them build their future.

But developing the power of knowing is not an easy process. Global Cosmopolitans who want to experience this power must begin with a decision to devote the time to know themselves. Global Cosmopolitans have to pay attention to their identity stories and adjust them over time. The more they know, the smoother the journey can be. It is their responsibility to learn what they need to know; nobody can do it for them.

Global Cosmopolitans weave their identity stories or narratives from a collection of threads that represent their life experiences. Their stories emerge from the way they weave those threads together in a particular role at a given time and place. They can feel alone in reconstructing memories because the details blur amid the shifting languages, people and places in their lives. International mobility makes

170

the patterns of identity particularly intricate and hard to find since no one culture or language can clarify them.

The workbook at the end of this book addresses the distinct challenges Global Cosmopolitans face when putting together their identity stories. The exercises are designed to provide targeted ways to explore elements that shape an individual's identity. When a Global Cosmopolitan's identity story is complete at one point in time, it describes in specific detail the work that he or she has done to see opportunity in difficult times, to take risks, to construct a life in the face of uncommon complexity and change. These details reveal the answers to broader identity questions:

Who am I after all these experiences?
What are stable sides of my personality and what is still evolving?
What pieces of my identity travel with me everywhere?
Which pieces appear depending on where I am and who I am with?

This self-awareness process is a powerful tool that Global Cosmopolitans can revisit over time to redefine their understanding of themselves. Maintaining this personal power can provide them with continuing motivation to develop as they move through the different stages of life.

KNOW THE STORIES THAT OTHERS TELL ABOUT YOU

But the story Global Cosmopolitans construct from their own memories is not enough to experience the full power of knowing, because it represents only one side, which, while unique, may contain significant distortions. They also need to know the stories that other people tell about them. Other people's perceptions can have more influence on a person's possibilities for development in relationships and at work than whatever reality Global Cosmopolitans might hold about themselves. Others will make certain assumptions about who Global Cosmopolitans are and what their possibilities might be. The power of knowing how others perceive them can provide Global Cosmopolitans an opportunity to understand the reactions of others and, at times, to shift these perceptions.

Professional environments often provide formal and informal performance reviews and other forms of feedback. Good systems can be useful, but given the complexity of Global Cosmopolitan profiles, formal systems can be misleading. For obvious reasons, companies try to keep their formal employee review process objective and universally applicable. Global Cosmopolitans need essentially the opposite. They need to be aware of the subjective rationale behind people's perceptions of them. And they need feedback that recognizes the uniqueness of their identity. People differ in their ability to get appropriate feedback at work. But if organizations cannot provide this kind of feedback, Global Cosmopolitans benefit by knowing how to ask for it. This is even more difficult outside the work environment, where no formal processes are even suggested to generate such feedback from family and friends.

A key component of constructive feedback, again, is the use of stories. Global Cosmopolitans might tell their story one way, but the people who know them might have a very different story to tell. It can be a powerful learning opportunity for Global Cosmopolitans to find out what stories have been created about them by people who know them in different ways. Global Cosmopolitans can compare their own versions of events with what they hear from other people. Sometimes Global Cosmopolitans believe they know how people will describe them, but often these assumptions are at slight variance or even diametrically opposed.

Hearing the stories that other people tell gives Global Cosmopolitans the possibility to have an impact on the way their story is framed and understood. With this knowledge, they have an opportunity to correct any misconceptions held not just by others but by themselves. Lily, for example, is Chinese. When she arrived to live in the United States, she believed that she talked loudly, spoke too quickly and was difficult to understand. Years later and with an improved fluency in English, she held onto that image and adjusted her behavior without checking its impact. She hesitated to speak until she got the key feedback that she was actually too soft spoken, very easy to understand and extremely interesting. Rather than back away from team meetings and risky ventures, Lily was ready to participate to the fullest.

Global Cosmopolitans do not necessarily have to adapt to their new awareness of how others see them. But even when they choose not to change, they learn a powerful lesson about how to understand the reactions of others. More distinct outlines of their identities emerge as Global Cosmopolitans begin to understand what they can approach with a flexible attitude and what they cannot or do not want to change. If this process is managed well in a work environment, it can help Global Cosmopolitans decide whether they should continue on their current path or stop and think about doing something different.

Listening to feedback can be difficult for Global Cosmopolitans. Perfectionists can be highly self-critical and assume that the feedback process will confirm their worst fears rather than be positive or give a very different but constructive view on behavior. Culture can play a role, since there are many different cultural stances on appropriate ways to give feedback. Given the mixture of cultures that Global Cosmopolitans engage, sensitivity to the different cultures at play can be crucial. Yet sharing feedback can also be a way of creating a more honest relationship with another person

KNOW HOW TO TELL YOUR STORY

One step remains if Global Cosmopolitans want to bring their different ideas and perspectives into their professional and personal lives. It is crucial for them to be able to tell their identity stories in an authentic, appropriate and effective manner. Global Cosmopolitans can experience the full power of knowing only when they can make other people understand what they have learned about themselves. This means taking responsibility to move beyond a simple sense of who they are and actually being able to convey their authentic selves.

The fine art of communicating is empowering at two levels. In a professional context, Global Cosmopolitans can convey their work-related interests and capabilities. But in a broader context, effective communication builds relationships. Although physical distance and cultural difference are central to their experience, many Global Cosmopolitans suggest that their resilience is linked to the important people in their lives. Yet finding relationships where they feel understood can be challenging. Global Cosmopolitans who know how to express who they really are can help people understand them and find mutual benefit. Understanding and mutuality are essential to helping people feel connected and involved.

Some of these important people will not change their perceptions, but Global Cosmopolitans can still look for creative ways to work on these key relationships. They can use their communication skills to create bonds that grow over time. They may be so skilled at helping people find common interests that they take this ability for granted. But they need to use this same bridge-building capacity for themselves. By taking the time to articulate their identity stories, Global Cosmopolitans can communicate across differences to find common ground with the significant people in their professional and personal lives.

Global Cosmopolitans who have completed this self-awareness process can use their knowledge to create more meaningful possibilities for themselves. As they look at their own stories and listen to feedback from others, they can begin to ask serious questions about how they learn and change over time.

OPENING THE DIALOGUE

It is evident why Global Cosmopolitans might want to understand more about themselves, but why should other people set time aside to know them better? There is an investment of time, but it can be the fastest way to capture the Global Cosmopolitans' potential contribution and create possibilities for richer relationships.

What is the mutual benefit in the workplace? Consider Daniel, brilliant and ambitious. When focused, he can climb mountains and not just in the metaphorical sense. He has organized climbing expeditions all over the world; the higher the mountain the better. At work, he is a highly competent analyst. But his passion and ability to take on complex projects is not reflected in the work he has been asked to do so far. He is getting restless and thinking about leaving, maybe even starting a mountain-climbing business. He knows his current company has the kind of projects that could motivate him. What he needs is the opening to talk about what he knows and loves in order to map out a path to the next level.

Not every Global Cosmopolitan will be ready to explore their identities at work for various and legitimate reasons, ranging from different notions of what is appropriate at work to differing abilities and desire for personal disclosure. They might not see how it will help or how to do it in a safe and effective way. But many ambitious and talented people are eager to be asked to show their expertise and will seize the opportunity for effective mutual dialogue. These individuals need the chance to realign their lives and chart a better course. For example, William has had a fast-track career that has led to many worldwide responsibilities. A little coaching helped him recognize the change that was taking place.

I sold myself to my company as a man who could move anywhere, anytime, and I believed it. I have been doing that for over ten years. Now I realize that

174

I have already lost too many people in my life, and I have to admit to myself and to my company that I would like to stay in one place for a while. I never thought that I would say that, but now that I am thirty-five, I really have to redefine who I am and what I have to offer. Our recent discussions have helped me realize that there are many different avenues for using my expertise.

What is the mutual benefit for friends and family? Consider a case like Alexi, whose family relations have reached a painful stalemate. Having left Romania for a better life, he studied in the United States and worked first in Singapore and then Australia. He wanted to move to Europe to be closer to family, so he left a satisfying career in Australia and moved to England. Alexi was devastated to find his family seemingly uninterested in the sacrifices he had made to live closer to them. They did not want to meet the woman he loved and kept talking about a woman from home that they said would make a perfect wife. Alexi wanted the love and approval of family, but he knew he could no longer go home to live. He started calling less and less, feeling unappreciated. He understood that his parents and friends were worried that he had changed, that his new life in a different language and culture had pulled him away from them. He knew that he had to make the first step to create a dialogue, since he wanted an opportunity to create a connection to the people he still loved and the place he still called home.

BUILDING MEANINGFUL AND EFFECTIVE DIALOGUE WITH GLOBAL COSMOPOLITANS AT WORK

Global Cosmopolitans want the opportunity to use their capabilities and knowledge to create meaningful careers while contributing to global organizations. Many competent Global Cosmopolitans end up leaving to look elsewhere for work or become entrepreneurs because their corporate jobs have left them feeling cut off from their deeper dreams and talents. Meaningful and effective dialogue is crucial to understand what motivates Global Cosmopolitans and what hidden or unused skills they can contribute to an organization.

For this professional alchemy to happen, a trust that the personal exploration process will be mutually beneficial is essential. After all, a common two-edged sword is the ability Global Cosmopolitans can have to "read" other people and tell them what they want to hear. Global Cosmopolitans need to believe that their openness and candor will benefit them in the long run. The framework, stories and exercises in this book will help them clarify their thinking, but the cyclist mentioned earlier has many ways to describe her story. Only you can determine what you want to know from a business perspective. How can you help them appropriately share their stories?

The goal of effective dialogue in the workplace is to make sure people understand where the individual Global Cosmopolitan's difference and unique ability lies. The way that Global Cosmopolitans can best contribute to their professional environments is not found in their passports but in their stories. Their stories can articulate who they are, what they know, how they learn and what they think they can add.

Interviewing is often seen as inefficient compared with using the services of an assessment center. The use of questionnaires and personality tests can provide interesting discussions for personal development, but these tools do not tell the whole story. What makes Global Cosmopolitans unique in the workplace is precisely how different they are from the mass of people those tools were designed for. The real differences and advantages they offer, including expertise with complexity and rapid change, often become lost in the conversation.

While much has been made of cultural sensitivity and diversity in the workplace, certain assumptions and culture consciousness can actually be counterproductive for Global Cosmopolitans and border on stereotyping. What you see might not communicate the complex cultural picture of a Global Cosmopolitan. This is particularly true if they still need to develop the language and style that allows them to assert a greater picture of themselves. For example, Chen, a Chinese woman working in London, developed a reputation as a standout financial analyst. She was ready to leave her investment bank because she had difficulty getting Europeans to accept how intuitive and creative she could be.

The more companies understand the creative edge of difference in their Global Cosmopolitan workforce, the better they can leverage it. This knowledge can be of value throughout the organization, from managers to human resources professionals to team members, even to potential backers. It can help managers get a better grasp of the capacities of the people they are hiring and, in tough economic times, of whom they are deciding to let go.

This book is not a global management book. It suggests a platform on which to develop a global professional. The analysis of the Global Cosmopolitan phenomenon shows how much companies can exploit the differences that Global Cosmopolitans provide. While it is ultimately the responsibility of Global Cosmopolitans to communicate their interests and abilities, it is in the interest of business to understand the resources at their fingertips. Is this person a good fit for our global team? Does this person have the know-how and skills to build bridges between cultures? Does this person have the ability to manage complexity? What is his added value to our team? Will this be the right time to send this person to a new culture? These are just some of the questions that global organizations should consider every day.

CREATING THE RIGHT ATMOSPHERE TO GET TO KNOW THEIR STORY: SOME POINTERS

Talking about your life, telling your story, works best when it is mutually beneficial. Global Cosmopolitans are not likely to open up and take chances to talk about themselves unless they know there is genuine interest, sufficient trust and respect on the part of their employer. Global Cosmopolitans who are skilled at reading other people often resort to telling them what they want to hear. They need to believe that their openness and candor will benefit them in the long run. Companies can signal their sincere interest by committing to bring Global Cosmopolitan expertise to light and pledging to find ways within the organization to use it.

Start the conversation with what is appropriate to talk about. The process of examining identity and even investigating possibilities is sufficiently sensitive that it is important to avoid pushing Global Cosmopolitans into a territory where they are not ready to go. A discussion about how to proceed can be useful.

Take a few minutes in the beginning to let them pull together the outline of their story. It is an opportunity to see how they pull the story together and possibly check an assumption or two that you might have. This sends an important message that you are ready to listen and learn and understand.

Effective dialogue requires checking assumptions, but that can be tricky because making assumptions about people is a normal part of trying to establish a conversation. For example, while it can be reassuring to know certain things about a person because of the nationality that normally defines them, it is far more productive to create a space where they can talk about self-definition in their own terms, rather than depend on a cultural perspective that limits the discussion or, even worse, sounds like you have just emerged from a refresher course on cultural diversity. Asking questions about personal assumptions, as well as listening to their stories, can kick-start an interesting discussion.

Give them opportunities to demonstrate their power to look for "the space in between." This is the creative space between one culture and another, one perspective and another. Given their experience of difference and their experience of not knowing what everyone else knows in a new cultural setting, Global Cosmopolitans become experts at bringing together the best of two different cultures to solve a problem. Presenting a problem that requires this kind of thinking can give companies a new idea of what Global Cosmopolitans are capable of accomplishing at work.

Global Cosmopolitans do not readily communicate the breadth of their possibilities. Their capacity to adapt to change and complexity comes so naturally that they fail to recognize it as a unique skill; their general sense of self-efficacy, which means a firm belief that they can handle any situation, might inhibit them from being able to articulate the foundation on which this belief is built.

Listening to that story with an open mind is challenging; the temptation always exists to jump in and make a point. But the way to gain the greatest benefit is to get to know the individual and to help them articulate what about their inner journey is relevant. This book's lists of strengths, skills, abilities and types of knowledge that result from the Global Cosmopolitan's internal journey are designed to help align their possible talents with current and future professional possibilities.

Storytelling is also a means to see culture relevance. It is a quick way to understand the different cultural paths people have taken. Storytelling is also a means to understand when culture is not the relevant factor. An American born in Vietnam felt like the economic deprivation his family went through when they arrived in the United States was the defining feature of his background. Although he was clearly bicultural, the dominant issue for him at this stage in his life was the split between how his family suffered without resources and how he was living now, with an abundance of resources. He had managed that split as a scholarship student and felt that was where he learned about dealing with difference.

EXTERNAL RESOURCES

There are also external resources that companies can use to assist Global Cosmopolitans in their process of self-awareness and communication. Coaches are often used to assist people with challenges at work or with plans for major transitions. This assistance can be combined with a

360-degree feedback to help people get a better perspective of how they are perceived. Coaches can help Global Cosmopolitans integrate that feedback and frame the changes they plan to make.

In-house training or off-site courses are often provided by major multi-nationals to enrich employees' understanding, skills and perspectives. Unfortunately programs geared to Global Cosmopolitans are yet to be well established, but the potential exists for a rich learning experience.

Employee assistance programs are often made available to both employees and their families for relocation assistance or in antici-pation of a major transition, although they are geared not to Global Cosmopolitans but to people that are starting out or looking for an expatriate experience. By considering the insights about the Global Cosmopolitan phenomenon, these programs can help people discover their sources of personal resilience and give them a positive framework within which to view their upcoming change.

FAMILY AND FRIENDS: GETTING TO KNOW THE STRANGER YOU KNOW SO WELL

The building blocks for Global Cosmopolitans, their resilience and adaptive capacity, are often related to the quality of the relation-ships in their lives. While some people experience initial freedom and excitement in their early years of traveling, many ultimately see the need to feel rooted in loving relationships that provide a missing backdrop of stability. Some Global Cosmopolitans have loving rela-tionships that are part of their global journey. Some are on the road alone, their family and friends not taking the trip with them. Most Global Cosmopolitans describe the importance of both worlds, work-ing hard to maintain relationships with the people who have made a difference for them over their lifetime as well as the new family and friends that they have created as adults. Since human connection can be seen as the center of psychological growth, family and friends can be the keys to a successful Global Cosmopolitan life. They *are* home for many Global Cosmopolitans, even if they do not say it. But that does not mean Global Cosmopolitans will return to what family and friends consider home.

As Global Cosmopolitans move around the world, there are family and friends who do not take the voyage with them. While they might have encouraged their life adventures, they still might be waiting for the Global Cosmopolitans to return.

Whether a person was born a Global Cosmopolitan or chose to become one can affect family attitudes about international mobility. Global Cosmopolitans are often trailblazers breaking with centuries of family tradition. But they can also be choosing not to pass a family's globetrotting tradition to their own children, opting instead for the stability and continuity they never had.

Friends might be recent or from long ago. They might have never moved, or they might be Global Cosmopolitans themselves. Friends might speak a language that a spouse doesn't speak or one that the Global Cosmopolitan is regretfully forgetting. All these people will see a Global Cosmopolitan who looks the same on the outside. But each one will get to know different facets of the Global Cosmopolitan's complex inner identity.

"When are you coming home?" Five words, so innocent on the surface, can be loaded with hidden meaning when spoken by family or friends. The question might be interpreted as a subtle way of saying that the time for fun is over and it's time to grow up and settle down. It might be jealous or critical, worried or angry. It might just mean "I miss you." That five simple words could cause so much confusion shows the extent to which Global Cosmopolitan relationships can benefit from an effective mutual dialogue.

The goal for family and friends should be to communicate at a deeper level with the Global Cosmopolitans in their lives. Family and friends can benefit from understanding the pressures and complexities inherent in the relationships of Global Cosmopolitans across time, distance and language. Standard relationship bonds—keeping in touch, celebrating rites of passage and being supportive when friends and family are in need—all become more difficult with international mobility. Even seemingly simple decisions, like where to spend vacations, are more complex. The people described in these pages show that Global Cosmopolitans are both normal and different at the same time and that many other people choose to live the way they do. Their curiosity to see the world from new perspectives can override the desire for security and belonging to one place.

Family and friends can be an important source of feedback for people whose context is constantly changing. Through values, family heroes and traditions families can provide continuity from past generations to future possibilities. Difference doesn't have to draw relationships apart. Believing that there is sincere and genuine curiosity can help bridge the loss of physical proximity. Effective dialogue with family and friends has the potential to manage the complexities of global relationships. It might mean a loss to everyone, a change from the way things used to be, but that change can create space for new solutions to grow.

UNLEASHING THE POWER OF KNOWING

The Global Cosmopolitan Workbook is designed to lay the groundwork for effective dialogue and personal growth. These exercises can apply to anyone, and I would encourage readers of this book who would like to develop a greater self-awareness and self-acceptance to try them. But the workbook is particularly relevant to Global Cosmopolitans, because it includes opportunities to articulate the complex challenges that have shaped them. In the workbook, Global Cosmopolitans can discover how to turn their expertise for change and complexity inward to find the power of knowing themselves.

The life of a Global Cosmopolitan is a journey across cultures, borders and boundaries. The purpose of this book has been to show that their journey is internal as well as external and that lessons learned in either journey can make its counterpart richer and more meaningful. It is a journey full of adventure and surprises. It is a journey full of challenges, uncertainties and loss.

But most of all, it is a journey full of beginnings, where every destination is a new point of departure.

THE SEVEN C's OF CHANGE AND DEVELOPMENT

While Global Cosmopolitans have traveled the Seven Seas, they often lack a comprehensive framework for the personal and emotional journey that accompanies their global experience. This book has examined many of the elements of that parallel journey. One way of pulling together these pieces into a coherent whole is through what I call the Seven C's of Change and Development. This is a recurring process, which cycles through *Complexity, Clarity, Confidence, Creativity, Commitment, Consolidation* and *Change*.

The Seven C's of Change and Development is useful both as a descriptive and as a diagnostic tool. The more an individual has a framework for telling a story—in this case a change story— the greater their ability to articulate it clearly. This also increases the likelihood of being understood by another and creating a

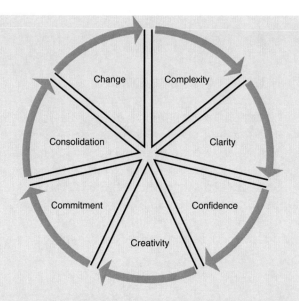

genuine dialogue. The Seven C's framework also affords insight into difficulties encountered in the change cycle, those moments when individuals get stuck and need support or assistance.

STAGES OF A CHANGE AND DEVELOPMENT CYCLE

Each of the Seven C's describes a stage of the change cycle. At each stage there are elements that must be resolved to allow the process to continue. For each stage, it is important to understand the task, what facilitates accomplishment of the task and what might derail or slow down the change effort.

The cycle is set in motion by a trigger event, which may be internally or externally initiated. Some external stimuli are quite positive, like the unsolicited offer of a dream job or an encounter with someone special. Less positive stimuli might include the death of a friend or family member, an illness or an unexpected job loss. Equally, internal events can also set the cycle in motion. An insight about your home or work situation arising from reflection or unexpected feelings of restlessness can be as much a trigger as any external event. The unforeseen consequences of earlier decisions or internal feelings that have been building over time can also become the event that launches a change cycle.

The trigger for change is not always obvious and immediately perceived. The signals that point to a need for change may be missed or misinterpreted. The fear of loss or the uncertainty of new situations may lead to denial or an inability to confront the requirement for change. Often what appears, as a surprise, is simply the sudden recognition of a pattern of signals that have long been present.

However, once the need for potential change is perceived, the change cycle begins. The cycle is complete only when a new direction is established and one is living a change.

COMPLEXITY: IDENTIFYING AND UNDERSTANDING THE VARIETY OF IMPLICATIONS CREATED BY A CHANGE

The task of this stage revolves around the struggle to become aware of and understand the complexity surrounding an anticipated change. The prospect of change moves one from the relative stability and known dimensions of the current state to the consideration of numerous variables and the uncertainties of an unknown future. These new elements expand the complexity beyond the individual to considerations of the impact on significant others affected by the change.

It is essential to find ways to understand and accept this new complexity. Failing to do so leaves individuals overwhelmed and seeking the relative simplicity and certainty of the status quo. Other unsuccessful coping methods push prematurely toward simplifications that lose or suppress important aspects of the prospective change. Positive resolution of the task at this stage is often facilitated by techniques such as preparing lists and considering systematically elements of the change process. The challenge at this point is to avoid panic and manage anxiety in the face of many new and unknown factors. Resolution begins in the following stage.

CLARITY: BRINGING COHERENT UNDERSTANDING TO THE COMPLEX ISSUES RAISED BY CHANGE

Now it becomes important to find frameworks to organize and prioritize the numerous issues created by a prospective change. It is not possible to maintain the large number of competing issues in mind at once. The establishment of priorities is the first step toward bringing clarity to the confusion generated at the initial consideration of a change. With increasing clarity, a positive circle of anxiety reduction follows. The more that clarity emerges, the less anxious one feels. The less anxious one is feeling, the easier it is to find greater clarity. To the contrary, unmanaged anxiety is a significant cause of derailment at this stage, leading an individual to abandon the change effort because of an incapacity to cope with a large array of issues and impacts.

Equally important at this stage is recognizing useful resources that can help bring clarity. While many friends and colleagues may wish to help, their ability to listen may be hampered by their own feelings about the prospective change and its impact on them. They may be tempted to advise on the basis of their own needs or their own desires to pursue similar changes.

A previously developed and strong support network is an important resource to manage this process. Relationships with individuals who can listen without judgment are difficult to develop in the midst of change. The development of such relationships would require significant investment at an earlier time but promise a big payoff at this stage.

CONFIDENCE: DEVELOPING THE BELIEF THAT ONE CAN BE SUCCESSFUL IN THE CHANGED SITUATION

The ability to confront the problems and risks that have become apparent requires a high degree of self-confidence. While many aspects of the change may be out of one's control, it is important to feel sufficiently capable of managing the process in order to proceed. On one hand, overconfidence yields a risk of plowing ahead with insufficient sensitivity to important or newly emerging information. Too much self-doubt yields a helplessness in the face of difficulties that allows the change to be subverted. Failure to assume a sense of control can imply that the individual is a passive recipient of the change and has little or no ownership. Without sufficient confidence, constant rethinking or other forms of paralysis result.

While a significant part of confidence is conditioned by life history prior to the change in question, self-confidence can be facilitated by small actions at this point. Alliances that provide personal and emotional support are significant. Concrete resolution of some small problems associated with the change can build a sense of successfully confronting issues. The ability to focus on a successful outcome of the change rather than spending extensive time concentrating on the possible pitfalls is often a major help in moving ahead. Self-confidence is critical to building and maintaining the necessary energy to proceed through the next stages of the cycle.

CREATIVITY: FINDING NEW OPTIONS OR SOLUTIONS

At this point the process requires the generation of appropriate options to achieve the desired change and overcome those obstacles that threaten to undermine it. These options may be creative new approaches or the adaptation of past successful strategies. This stage requires an openness to new ideas and the willingness to seek innovative solutions to the problems at hand. The magnitude of the change may seem overwhelming and suppress any energy to seek new approaches. As a result, one may retreat to previously successful strategies that are not suited to the current context. At the other extreme, innovative but unrealistic solutions may be designed in an effort to solve all possible aspects of the change. It is essential to find an appropriate balance between creativity and realism in generating options.

At this stage, once again, personal relationships can be a significant resource in designing realistic and innovative options. Other individuals who have faced similar obstacles can provide information as well as the benefit of their own experience. Others who are willing to brainstorm with you can facilitate your own thinking into innovative approaches. Finally, trusted others can provide important reality testing of ideas that you have developed.

COMMITMENT: TAKING THE FIRST STEPS TO IMPLEMENT THE CHANGE

Having taken the time to generate options, this is the time to choose and act. Forward movement at this point is necessarily based on the realization that there is no one right or perfect answer. Rather, successful change is based on commitment to a good, realistic solution that is skillfully implemented. Then, choices are translated into commitment by taking first steps. These first steps often close options or preclude a return to a previous situation and, as a result, confirm the commitment to the change process.

This realization can lead individuals to get stuck in self-doubt and backsliding, but the closing of escape options may generate so much anxiety that paralysis results. This is often evidenced in second-guessing and an inability to act. This is a particularly difficult step in the change cycle. It is the feeling of stepping into the dark of an uncertain future and naturally breeds anxiety. For some, the recognition that this step is neither right nor wrong but simply the choice of a different path is soothing. For others a push to take the first step allows the individual to get moving and access internal energy to keep going. The first step is often the hardest; however, there is no change without one.

CONSOLIDATION: ADOPTING THE NEW IDENTITY AND EX-IDENTITY THAT THIS CHANGE REPRESENTS

As William Bridges points out, all changes feature an ending and a new beginning. While some aspects of identity must be set aside or abandoned, the understanding and acceptance of this loss contributes significantly to moving forward. Similarly, one must begin to adopt important characteristics of the new role into one's own identity. Individuals in a new company who say "we" in referring to a previous organization have not yet made this change. Divorced individuals referring to themselves as "we" are still clinging to their identity in a couple. While such transition does not take place quickly, it is facilitated when one begins to adopt the new identity and communicate it to others. Derailment occurs when one has difficulty letting go of an old role. Others often recognize this before it becomes obvious to the individual in the process of change. Trusted friends and colleagues can help build awareness of these residual aspects that are difficult to shed and that block the change process. However, these same people may be the sources of resistance to change if they cling to the past basis of their interaction for fear of losing the relationship. Further resistance may come from friends and colleagues who recognize that they must change in order to maintain valued relationships with a person in a change process.

While it may seem contradictory, change requires individuals to ensure that certain parts of their identity and life space will remain the same. Recognizing factors that preserve a feeling of being anchored provides the stable basis for safe experimentation with other aspects of the new identity. This stability can be linked to items as small as familiar foods. More significantly, the linkage to people, places or a sense of core values can provide a safe platform to permit change in other aspects of identity.

Some individuals move more easily through this passage to a new identity by focusing less on loss of self. Rather they feel that the change is developmental and brings them closer to a true self or to possibilities that they might now achieve. While accepting that change implies loss, this framing of change as forward movement yields significant benefit in this consolidation stage.

CHANGE: LIVING THE CHANGE

As the consolidation proceeds and one is living the new identity, it is necessary to face any unintended consequences of the change or new challenges as they arise. While there are still elements of a transition taking place, the change needs to feel like, and be seen as, a new beginning. This is not a static state. Rather every new beginning plants the seeds of subsequent changes.

Therefore, successful change should be an energizing experience that furthers the motivation for subsequent changes. For Global Cosmopolitans and an increasing number of others, change is the steady state. Discomforts and mistakes along the way should be framed as learning opportunities. If they become feelings of regret, loss and an aversion to future movement, the change cycle becomes increasingly threatening.

It is equally important to help others accept the change. When a young woman makes a significant departure from her current situation, friends and family only knew her in a previous context. They knew how to work with her, get her attention and influence her. Her change requires adaptation and new behavior on their part in recognition of new elements in her identity. The change may alter her availability to them or present new and unfamiliar behaviors. Helping significant others manage the loss of the person they knew and the acceptance of a new person is an important task. If it is not accomplished, these key relationships may become a drag on development and eventually disappear.

TAKING THE STORY OF CHANGE FORWARD

The Seven C's of Change and Development is a framework for structuring a story, a story about change. It allows a deep reflection on the change process and the challenges along the way. It can be used as a map for understanding as well as a basis for communicating the change story to others and bringing them along.

Knowing how to tell the story of the change can make it easier to engage others appropriately in the process, particularly when looking for understanding or assistance. Ultimately, this may form the ability to teach others about a new identity and the change process in general.

Given individual differences and the variety of change situations, there is great variance in the amount of time necessary for a cycle of change. There is no single answer on how long that should take. Some people linger in one stage unable to resolve the fundamental tasks at that point. Others speed too quickly through a stage and must return to confront the unresolved issues. Still others remain at a stage to absorb the learning necessary to proceed successfully through the subsequent stages. Finally, some choose to slow their progress to allow time for significant others to accompany them. For those seeking a clearer prescription, the unsatisfying answer is "As fast as you can; as long as you must!"

One additional utility of the Seven C's framework is to facilitate learning about the change process. Learning from past change can contribute to greater facility and skillfulness in managing future change. For Global Cosmopolitans, change is often a fundamental theme in their lives. Change is normal and is often triggered quickly and unexpectedly. The acquired skill in navigating the Seven C's of change is a cornerstone of their resilience and success. Their ability to learn from experience facilitates the continuous cycle of change in their lives as well as the growth and development of the unique competencies that characterize this group.

THE GLOBAL COSMOPOLITAN WORKBOOK

INTRODUCTION

- *Start by Creating an Insight Book*

- *The Art of Storytelling*

SECTION I   SELF-ASSESSMENT EXERCISES

- *The Past as Prologue: Turning Points and the Road to Identity*
  - *Step One: Lifelines*
  - *Step Two: Analyzing the Lifeline*
  - *Step Three: Looking for Patterns*

- *Exploring Identity: What's in a Name?*
  - *Step One: Identity Group Labels*
  - *Step Two: Different Groups, Different People*
  - *Step Three: Labeling Your Global Identity*
  - *Step Four: Naming*

- *Invisible Rules, Silent Voices*
  - *Step One: Drawing a Genogram*
  - *Step Two: Collecting Data to Fill in the Blanks*
  - *Step Three: Working the Genogram*
  - *Step Four: Messages from Parents and Cultural Contexts*

INTRODUCTION

This workbook provides basic techniques for a guided exploration of the concepts elaborated in this book. These insights can be useful to Global Cosmopolitans, their employers and colleagues, and their family and friends. Professionals such as therapists and coaches may also find useful techniques for working with Global Cosmopolitans. While particular exercises are geared to the experience of Global Cosmopolitans, they have been designed to be of use to a much larger audience. Any individual desiring to explore his or her strengths, identity and the paradoxes faced in composing a life can usefully pursue the exercises described in this workbook.

Sharing this exploration process with others, particularly those accompanying you on your life journey, can provide additional perspective and insight. Therefore, these exercises are well suited for discussion in pairs or groups and can be adapted to a class or workshop setting. If yours is a solitary voyage through this workbook, I would encourage you to share at least the personal issues and insights raised in the exercises.

START BY CREATING AN INSIGHT BOOK

The stimulation of everyday life prompts a wealth of reflections and associations that are quickly lost to the recesses of your mind. As a first step, create a notebook that you can carry with you to note insights. At the end of each day, take time to look over what you have written and add reflections on your day. Your insight book is also a good place to log the feelings generated in the course of daily work and social interaction. While a notebook is highly recommended, some people prefer a BlackBerry, an iPhone or a PDA. It is important to have a single place at hand to note down ideas, associations or stories that spring to mind during your day.

THE ART OF STORYTELLING*

Increasingly, people are rediscovering the power of storytelling. Once, stories were the manner of conveying culture, history and personal identity. The advent of PowerPoint, Twitter and other technologies has limited the use of stories as well as the attendant skills of shaping and communicating them. Yet the speed of reading lists, bullet points and summary statements is matched by an equally quick loss of recall. Stories well crafted and told become aids to memory and endure significantly longer.

Storytelling is an art that can be developed. The following exercises provide practice in crafting your personal story while allowing you to uncover pieces of your life and their impact. This skill will be valuable to you because storytelling is also a bridge. Your stories connect you to your own past, present and future. They also connect you to people who have no other way to understand how your personal journey has shaped you.

Developing stories about who you are and your life experience is a part of each exercise. An exercise at the end of this workbook is writing a personal narrative. This is an opportunity to take some time for yourself to elaborate your story and to refine your identity story.

You can gain insight into your Global Cosmopolitan identity by taking time to focus on the following exercises on different aspects of your personal journey. The exercises are drawn from the materials I use in my classroom and clinic to help Global Cosmopolitans understand their complex lives. They contribute to your exploration of self-awareness, understanding of others and ability to communicate effectively your own identity.

---

*Do not feel constrained by the spaces allotted here for your responses. Use additional sheets of paper, a notebook, or an electronic file to elaborate your responses or to capture important details you don't have room for in the book itself.

I   SELF-ASSESSMENT EXERCISES

THE PAST AS PROLOGUE: TURNING POINTS AND THE ROAD TO IDENTITY

Step One: Lifelines

One way to gain perspective on your development and your identity is to look at the significant turning points in your life. A turning point could be defined as an episode, experience or meaningful moment when you underwent a significant change in your understanding of yourself.

Definitions of turning points are highly personal. Examples of significant events are a geographical move, a family or relational crisis, a significant success or failure, an illness or a political or economic crisis. A significant event could be an intense emotional event such as the loss of a significant person or a divorce. Taking developmental steps in life such as changing school, work or profession can also serve as a turning point.

Lifelines

What are the key events in your life? What are the meanings and lessons associated with them? Look at the lifeline below.

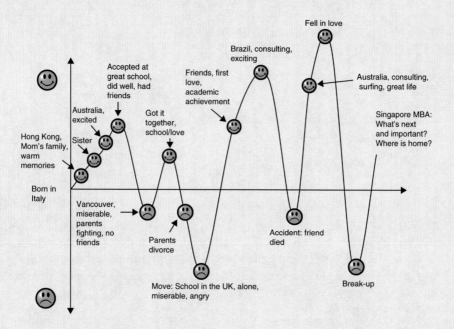

Draw your own lifeline capturing the major events and turning points from your birth to the present, as you define them, as well as your emotional engagement in the drama of your life.

Start with your birth and extend a horizontal line across the page, ending with your present situation. This line represents the passage of time. The vertical axis represents the general positive or negative feeling component, the emotional highs or lows connected with the event. Use a word or phrase to note the events and the high and low points, as illustrated above.

Step Two: Analyzing the Lifeline

Look at your lifeline and highlight your turning points. This gives you an opportunity to picture the emotional high and low points over time and to consider what have been the significant or meaningful moments in your life, when you believe that you have changed or developed in a significant way.

While all turning points are significant, for the purposes of this exercise, list the three which were the most momentous.

1. _____

2. _____

3. _____

For each turning point, imagine that you are preparing a presentation of five minutes or less to help other people know you better by describing your turning points.

- Describe the turning point and its impact on you
- Describe the lessons you learned from the experience

Story 1:

_____

_____

_____

_____

_____

_____

_____

_____

Story 2:

_____

_____

_____

_____

_____

_____

_____

_____

Story 3:

_____

_____

_____

_____

_____

_____

_____

_____

If you have the time and inclination, share your lifeline and the stories of your turning points with another person. If you are hesitant to discuss the whole picture or to discuss certain stories, do you understand why?

Step Three: Looking for Patterns

This is an opportunity to stop and observe patterns that have emerged from working on this exercise. Consider the following questions:

1. As you look over your lifeline, do you see any pattern to what triggers a turning point?

_____

_____

_____

_____

_____

2. A lifeline can help you see a pattern to your emotional high and low points.

   - Can you see a pattern to your emotional high and low points?
   - Do you see any personal strengths that helped you recover from the low points?

_____

_____

_____

_____

_____

3. What contributes to your ability to learn from life experience?

_____

_____

_____

_____

_____

EXPLORING IDENTITY: WHAT'S IN A NAME?

Step One: Identity Group Labels

A significant aspect of identity arises from the groups to which one belongs. Given their international mobility, Global Cosmopolitans often have to create an identity from a broader array of groups that represent parts of their past and present. These exercises will help you think about the different groups that make up your world.

Look at the list below. Fill in the blank on the right to note the label or labels that feel appropriate for you.

Nationality (e.g. Venezuelan) _____

Home town (e.g. Paris) _____

Geographic designation (e.g. African) _____

Family status (e.g. married) _____

Sports interest (e.g. squash player) _____

Profession (e.g. management consultant) _____

Work context (e.g. Google) _____

Religion (e.g. Buddhist) _____

Political affiliation or attitude (e.g. liberal) _____

Leisure activity (e.g. theatre) _____

Physical attribute (e.g. left-handed) _____

Others _____

_____

Review the list above. Select the five labels that feel most salient to your identity today.

1. _____

2. _____

3. _____

4. _____

5. _____

Step Two: Different Groups, Different People

Aspects of identity are shared in different ways, with different people and in different situations. Each new context and relationship is an opportunity to highlight different sides of who you are. Moving to a new cultural context can challenge your ability to share certain features and perhaps suppress others.

Think of two new group situations that you participated in recently. What features of your identity did you attempt to highlight? What features did you attempt to suppress? Can you explain why? Now briefly write down the stories.

Story 1:

_____

_____

_____

_____

_____

_____

_____

_____

Story 2:

_____

_____

_____

_____

_____

_____

_____

Step Three: Labeling Your Global Identity

Globally mobile people often seek new ways to address issues of similarity to and difference from those around them. Here are some labels that people have suggested.

- Nationality (e.g. Italian, Italian/American, Brazilian)
- Geography (e.g. South American)
- A displaced national (e.g. an American in Paris)
- An expatriate
- An exile
- Global Cosmopolitan

Feel free to create your own: _____

Pick two labels that feel comfortable to you. Explain why they are descriptive of you?

1. _____

_____

_____

_____

_____

_____

2. _____

_____

_____

_____

_____

_____

_____

Step Four: Naming

Families, countries and cultures have different naming rules and traditions. Do you understand the significance of your name to your family or to you? What stories do you know about the choice or significance of your name?

One naming story:

_____

_____

_____

_____

_____

_____

_____

_____

_____

Some individuals are quick to rename people if their name sounds "foreign" or is hard for other people to pronounce. Some simply like to give nicknames.

1. What do people call you? What are your nicknames?

_____

_____

_____

_____

_____

_____

2. What is the significance, if any, of these names? Do they link you to a place or to certain relationships? Do they offend you?

_____

_____

_____

_____

_____

_____

3. If someone knew the cultural context or meaning of your name, how would they know you better?

_____

_____

_____

_____

_____

_____

INVISIBLE RULES, SILENT VOICES

Step One: Drawing a Genogram

A genogram can be used as a visual representation of a family's history. This type of visual mapping of significant people, events, relationships and patterns can provide a wealth of information about the people and the stories that have had an impact on your life and your visions of the future.[1] Through genograms, you can develop greater awareness of how your decisions are influenced by family history, tradition and values.

On the next page is an example. Some of the conventional symbols used are explained in the key.

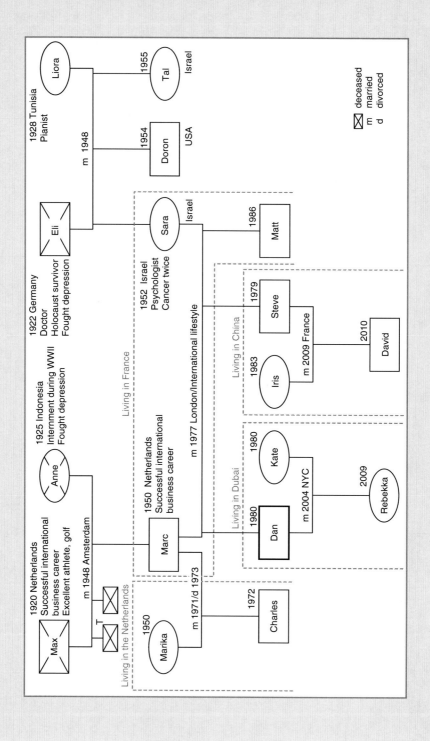

Your Genogram

Start drawing your genogram with the data that you have at hand. You might want to draw the genogram on a separate sheet of paper so that you have room to add relevant information. Begin by drawing your current family situation and going backward in time to your grandparents' generation; previous generations can be included if you have some of that information. Include other significant people, even if they are not immediate family, such as significant family friends or other important relationships. Label the dates of birth and death, as illustrated in the example with the information that you know.

Once you have placed the significant people, you can start to detail some of the connections and significant events as illustrated in the example. Use the standard symbols to illustrate certain events and relationships.

Note important relational events such as marriage, separation, divorce or adoption. You can trace important family patterns such as level of education and profession. You can also try to identify patterns of interest to you, such as health-related issues or substance abuse. All of these factors affect the family system and are part of a family's history.

Step Two: Collecting Data to Fill in the Blanks

People differ in their knowledge of family details. This can be an excellent opportunity to learn more about your family. Think about the questions that you have. Some of the questions might be untangling confusion or perceptions formed many years ago. Others might be linked to your current concerns. You will almost certainly have to talk to family members and other people from your past to get all the information you need.

This detective work should be led by your own concerns. During the data collection process, the following questions might help clarify some important aspects of your personal history:

Significant Background Information

- What was the ethnic/religious background of family members?
- What languages were spoken?
- What is the pattern of socio-economic status of your family?
- Has war or political upheaval had a significant impact on your family story?

Health and Well-Being

- Are there significant physical or emotional health patterns in the family?

Geographic Stability and Mobility

- Where do your family members currently live?
- Is there a history of significant geographic moves in your family?

Patterns of Professional and Personal Success

- Are there certain professions that seem dominant in your family history?
- Do you see patterns of perceived professional success or failure?

Family Relationships

- How would you characterize family relationships? Were they close? Distant? Cut off? Highly dependent?
- How did/do people communicate with each other?
- How stable were their relationships at home and at work?
- Did secrets have an important function in your family?

Preparation for Information-Seeking Interviews

1. As you look at the picture of your family, what is the missing data?

_____

_____

_____

_____

_____

_____

2. While you might have many questions about your family history, what are the three key questions that you would like to investigate further?

1. _____

_____

2. _____

_____

3. _____

_____

3. Whom can you ask?

_____

_____

_____

_____

_____

_____

Step Three: Working the Genogram

After completing the genogram, what have you learned from the people, their stories and the context of their lives? For example:

1. Who are the people who have had the most impact on your sense of identity? How do you think they have influenced your career or personal life?

   _____

   _____

   _____

   _____

   _____

   _____

2. What stories about individuals in your family have had a significant impact?

   _____

   _____

   _____

   _____

   _____

   _____

3. What do you know about the context of previous generations (family situation, politics, history, economic conditions, spiritual beliefs, etc.)? How do you think their context affected them?

   _____

   _____

   _____

   _____

   _____

   _____

Step Four: Messages from Parents and Cultural Contexts

This exercise looks at what your parents said or did, and how that has affected how you behave or judge the behavior of other people. It also focuses on where those messages come from.

Think about the messages that you received from your parents about appropriate behavior. Write down a message that you received for the following categories:

1. Table manners _____

2. Gift giving _____

3. Being a good friend _____

4. Giving or receiving help _____

5. Managing conflict _____

Imagine you are having a discussion with your parents. What do you assume that their messages are?

1. What would make them the happiest?

_____

_____

_____

_____

_____

2. What would disappoint them?

_____

_____

_____

_____

_____

3. What advice would you like from them about your next professional steps?

_____

_____

_____

_____

_____

Global Cosmopolitans describe having multiple cultural scripts about appropriate behavior. Learning new rules and adapting your own behavior can be difficult, particularly if the rules are attached to strong messages about right and wrong.

The voices of appropriate behavior are there: "Be nice to people and they will be nice to you, wait for your turn, do not brag, share your food, respect privacy and do not ask questions too directly."

Describe a situation when you had to navigate conflicts between your parents' rules and the rules of a new culture or larger social context.

_____

_____

_____

_____

_____

_____

Describe one situation at work that requires finding a way to adjust to the new rules.

_____

_____

_____

_____

_____

DEVELOPING COMPETENCE

Step One: Potential Roles for Managing Change

Old Roles on a New Stage

While change always requires the acquisition of new roles, global mobility requires many more roles to be mastered. You might have learned the script for a new role as a child when you had to find a way to adapt to a new situation. For example, some individuals identify with the role of being an adventurer when change is involved. Some adults who have developed this role as a child may see its immediate relevance to a new setting. Others may need prodding to figure out how to make this appropriate as an adult.

Here are some other roles that Global Cosmopolitans assume which can be applied to some extent to any change process:

- *Negotiator*: Asking for and negotiating to get what they need
- *Translator*: Identifying differences and restating them in ways that are clearer or understandable to others.
- *Humorist*: Using humor to reduce tension and bring people together
- *Diplomat*: Conducting business smoothly across contexts
- *Bridge Builder*: Closing gaps between people or groups
- *High Jumper*: Taking on and succeeding at increasingly difficult assignments
- *Professor*: Teaching about new ideas or different perspectives
- *Orchestra Leader*: Keeping many facets of their lives or the context in harmony
- *Detective*: Collecting clues to find out or clarify what is unknown
- *Entertainer*: Taking center stage to provide leadership or structure to a situation

What is a role that you take in new situations? What successes have you had in the past with this role?

_____

_____

_____

Being an Ex

Part of the change process can involve giving up a role or leaving behind an aspect of one's identity. Leaving behind what is known, even if the change is perceived as positive, can be difficult. However, recognizing the loss of a clearly defined role in one situation and successfully adopting a new, appropriate role in a new situation can build self-confidence to repeat this process. I call this Being an Ex.[2]

Leaving school means that one is no longer identified as a student, becoming an ex-student. Getting married means that one is an ex-single, with whatever that entails for identity. Leaving consulting, one is no longer a consultant, or is described as an ex-consultant. Changing jobs from IBM to Sony, one becomes an ex-IBMer. Sometimes confusion arises when the individual says, "We always did it this way," as he or she has not accepted this ex-identity.

List three ways in which you would describe yourself as an Ex:

1. _____

2. _____

3. _____

Based on your own experience, what advice could you give someone to help them let go during a change?

_____

_____

_____

_____

_____

_____

Step Two: Learning from Experience

While all individuals have life experience by simply existing from day to day, the ability to grow and learn from that experience is not universal. Global Cosmopolitans describe the variety of knowledge, attitudes and skills developed from their experiences of moving among and living in different cultures.

Change and mobility can contribute significantly to the development of perceptual skills and a more global mindset. These abilities are built upon the recognition that individual cultures have patterns of thinking and behaving that are different from, rather than better or worse than, another or my own culture. Further skills develop from the experience of reacting to change itself. Although reading and classroom education can sensitize individuals to the following abilities, Global Cosmopolitans report that their development comes largely from active reflection on their personal experience.

Assess yourself on the following abilities, which are largely learned from experience. Score your skill level from 1 (poor) to 5 (excellent). In each case, take a moment to explain what specific elements led you to choose that rating. Finally, if you wanted to improve that rating, what might you do?

1. **Peripheral Vision**: the ability to view people and issues from a broader perspective (a wider field of vision) to incorporate the context into your understanding.

   a. Rate Yourself: 1   2   3   4   5

   b. Explanation: _____

   c. Improvement: _____

2. **Kaleidoscopic Vision**: the ability to see things from different perspectives. This is fundamental to understanding interaction with groups who do not share similar backgrounds, culture or other elements of diversity.

   a. Rate Yourself: 1   2   3   4   5

   b. Explanation: _____

   c. Improvement: _____

3. **An Insider/Outsider Perspective**: the ability to fully engage in a context while retaining the capacity to step back and observe the situation in a dispassionate manner. This affords a self-check on one's involvement but also risks providing a place to hide from engagement.

   a. Rate Yourself: 1   2   3   4   5

   b. Explanation: _____

   c. Improvement: _____

4. **Empathy**: the ability to listen without judging; the ability to hear and understand the logic of different points of view in a noncritical manner. This is the basic ability to put yourself in the shoes of another. Understanding different approaches in this manner contributes to valuing multiple and diverse perspectives.

   a. Rate Yourself: 1   2   3   4   5

   b. Explanation: _____

   c. Improvement: _____

5. **Creativity**: the skill of being able to generate new ideas, solutions or perspectives. This engages the risk of being different or doing things in a different way and builds upon those competencies that value new and diverse approaches.

   a. Rate Yourself: 1   2   3   4   5

   b. Explanation: _____

   c. Improvement: _____

6. **Adaptive Capacity**: the ability to integrate into a new situation with the capacity to maintain a sense of your own identity. This requires both awareness of the key elements of identity that must be preserved and the ability to adapt behavior to a new setting.

   a. Rate Yourself: 1   2   3   4   5

   b. Explanation: _____

   c. Improvement: _____

7. **Risk Taking**: the willingness and ability to take a risk after a successful change or while struggling to recover from an unsuccessful one. Experience builds the necessary self-confidence to enable this behavior.

   a. Rate Yourself: 1   2   3   4   5

   b. Explanation: _____

   c. Improvement: _____

A Global Perspective

Global Cosmopolitans often describe having a global perspective or mindset as a consequence of living and working with people from different cultures as well as from their personal and family experiences. This gives them an ability to have both a local and a global perspective. They describe how this viewpoint helps them understand new personal or business opportunities, helps them understand people from very different backgrounds or even influences how they read the newspaper.

From your own personal base of experience, how would you define a global mindset?

_____

_____

_____

_____

_____

_____

Are there ways to improve your global mindset and the way you use it?

_____

_____

_____

_____

_____

_____

_____

PARADOXICAL NEEDS

During change and transition, individuals normally feel pulled in opposite directions by conflicting psychological needs. Global Cosmopolitans describe having to satisfy paradoxical needs or find a new balance between them in facing new situations.

For example:

1. Belonging and being different: People want to be part of a new group, and at the same time they want to hold onto what they believe differentiates them.

2. Continuity and change: While seeking change and excitement, people also cling onto a certain sense of stability and continuity. This conflict is particularly strong concerning issues of identity.

3. Independence and dependence: People should feel personally competent and self-sustaining yet also realize their need to depend on others.

Describe a current situation in which you feel conflicting psychological needs. How are you managing the situation?

_____

_____

_____

_____

_____

_____

In reviewing you lifeline or what you know about your personal narrative, are there any recurring themes of paradoxical needs?

_____

_____

_____

_____

_____

_____

TWO-EDGED SWORDS OF MOBILITY: WHEN STRENGTHS CREATE NEW CHALLENGES

How can a strength become a challenge? In the image of a two-edged sword, one edge represents a strength which is well developed and is used in a positive and constructive way. The other edge represents the potential downside of that same strength for the individual.

Here are some representative examples:

- I am an excellent observer, but at times, this leads me to be disengaged from the activities at hand. I need to engage more in the situation that I am in.
- I love the adventure of moving, but I do not know how to stay in one place and find the excitement in that place. It would help if I became more connected to the people or the work that I am doing.
- I am an excellent listener to others, but I do not share my thoughts and ideas enough with other people. I need to be a clear presenter as well as a good listener.
- I have friends all over the world, but I do not allow myself to be close to the people who are in my current context. I need to stay focused on my current social situation rather than working so hard to maintain my past networks.

Describe a two-edged sword that you experience.

_____

_____

_____

_____

_____

_____

_____

What is your plan for developing the other edge?

_____

_____

_____

_____

_____

_____

_____

If you have a number of two-edged swords, repeat this exercise for the others.

II   SAILING THE SEVEN C'S: NAVIGATING PERSONAL CHANGE

While change represents significant turning points for all individuals, it is threaded throughout the lives of Global Cosmopolitans. A key aspect of any self-assessment process is gaining perspective on your own experience of change.

This is an opportunity to apply the Seven C's of Change framework to a change that you recently navigated or other change that was significant in your life. (This may have been identified in your life-line exercise.) This is an opportunity to understand your approach to change, a vehicle for identifying those parts of the journey that you sail through as well as those which are a bit more turbulent. The more that you are able to understand yourself in the process of change, the more you can improve your ability to sail through the next one.

For each stage of the cycle, answer the following three questions:

- Task: What was the nature of the task at this stage?
- What helped: What facilitated accomplishing the task?
- What hindered: What hindered or threatened to derail the change? What interfered with accomplishing the task?

Start with a brief description of the change and what triggered the change cycle. Then answer the checklist questions for each stage of the cycle.

What Changed?

What is the specific change that you want to consider for this exercise?

_____

_____

_____

_____

_____

_____

_____

What Triggered the Change?

What were the factors, the new opportunities or personal dissatisfactions that triggered the change?

_____

_____

_____

_____

_____

_____

_____

THE SEVEN C's OF CHANGE

1. Complexity: What are the complications created by the prospect of this change for myself and others?

Any prospective change raises a variety of issues that greatly increase the complexity of one's life space. These include greater focus on uncertainties about the future, concerns about the impact on others and reassessment of the current situation. This new complexity creates an overload that can be paralyzing or lead to denial of important factors.

Task: What was the nature of the complexity created by this change? How did I manage the life complexity resulting from all of these issues?

_____

_____

_____

_____

_____

_____

What helped: What helped me recognize the many implications of this change and cope with this increased complexity?

_____

_____

_____

_____

_____

_____

What hindered: What kept me from confronting aspects of the complex impact of the change on myself and others? What was difficult for me to look at?

_____

_____

_____

_____

_____

2. Clarity: How could I bring clarity to the complex and seemingly intractable issues?

In the face of complexity, the way forward depends on finding frameworks to organize and prioritize the numerous issues created by a prospective change. Failure to achieve this clarity yields an unwieldy list of issues and little understanding of their interaction.

Task: What were the key confusions raised by the prospect of change? How was I able to frame the prospective change to clarify and prioritize the dilemmas posed by the complex set of issues?

_____

_____

_____

_____

_____

_____

_____

What helped: What helped me gain and maintain clarity? Who were the people and the emotional processes that helped?

_____

_____

_____

_____

_____

_____

What hindered: What kept me from getting clarity initially or along the way? What caused confusion to continue or return as I explored the change opportunity?

_____

_____

_____

_____

_____

_____

3. Confidence: What allowed me to feel that I could be successful?

Realizing that one is sufficiently in control affords the possibility to take the risk of proceeding with a change process. A more general lack of confidence or self-doubt can be an inhibiting factor. Without sufficient self-confidence, there is the trap of constant rethinking or other forms of paralysis.

Task: What did I see as the key risks of the change? How did I mobilize the self-confidence to take the risk and move ahead?

_____

_____

_____

_____

_____

_____

What helped: What helped me have sufficient confidence to proceed?

_____

_____

_____

_____

_____

_____

What hindered: What were the sources of self-doubt that kept me from going forward?

_____

_____

_____

_____

_____

_____

4. Creativity: What allowed me to be creative and find new solutions?

The decision to proceed requires the generation of new and appropriate options for moving forward. These may be creative new approaches or the adaptation of past successful strategies to the new setting. Derailment is possible if one falls back on previously successful approaches that are not suited to the current context or if one is not sufficiently creative to find new solutions for the unique aspects of the current situation. It is important to find the appropriate balance between creativity and realism in generating options.

Task: What were the perceived difficulties that had to be resolved to make the change? How did I generate creative and realistic options to build the path to a successful change?

_____

_____

_____

_____

_____

_____

_____

What helped: What helped me generate new solutions appropriate to the setting? What provided the reality test to ensure that the solutions were workable?

_____

_____

_____

_____

_____

_____

What hindered: What made this task difficult or kept me stuck in previous patterns that did not apply to the current situation?

_____

_____

_____

_____

_____

_____

5. Commitment: Can I commit and take the first steps to implement the change?

This is the time to choose and make it happen. These are often first steps that close options to return to a previous situation. Backing down can happen when there is self-doubt about being able to drive the change, second-guessing or getting blocked when it comes to overcoming obstacles.

Task: How did I choose a plan and take the first steps to move from the idea to a reality that would make this happen?

_____

_____

_____

_____

_____

_____

_____

What helped: What helped me move into action?

_____

_____

_____

_____

_____

_____

_____

What hindered: What slowed me down and kept me from taking the necessary first steps to move from the current state?

_____

_____

_____

_____

_____

_____

_____

6. Consolidation: What was the new identity and the ex-identity that this change represented?

Part of change is ending a past situation and moving on. This is the time to begin seeing oneself in a new role. Derailment can happen if one has difficulty letting go of the old situation or the old role or gets stuck in the change process rather than moving ahead.

Task: What aspects of my identity had to be abandoned to move forward? How did I begin to incorporate this change into my new identity?

_____

_____

_____

_____

_____

_____

_____

What helped: What helped me make this transition? What allowed me to see myself as being in a state of change? What aspects of the new situation was I able to start incorporating as part of identity?

_____

_____

_____

_____

_____

_____

_____

What hindered: What made it difficult to let go of the old and move forward with the new identity? What were the hardest pieces to let go of?

_____

_____

_____

_____

_____

_____

7. Change: What is it like living the change?

The change has happened and one is dealing with it and living the consequences and the new challenges as they occur. While there are still elements of a transition taking place, the change needs to contain the feeling of, and be seen as, a new beginning. Successful change should be an energizing experience and opportunity allowing motivation to further change.

Task: What needed to be resolved to create comfort in the new situation? Did others recognize the change?

_____

_____

_____

_____

_____

_____

What helped: What things helped me stay energized both in the new context and in looking forward to engaging in new issues and changes?

_____

_____

_____

_____

_____

_____

What hindered: How did I cope with elements of regret and loss? What kept me from easily living the new identity rather than looking backward or being mired in regrets?

_____

_____

_____

_____

_____

_____

USING APPROPRIATE HELP AND SUPPORT THROUGH A CHANGE CYCLE

Although changes may not directly concern other people in your life, other people can be actively involved in the change. They can be sources of help, particularly if you are able to articulate the kind of help you need. They can also be active in some aspects of problem solving at each stage of change. In other cases, change is necessarily a solitary process.

Read through the change cycle that you just described, noting the role that people have played in the change process. Look for examples in your own relational behavior.

When did you actively involve people for help and support? Can you cite an example where it was helpful? Were there situations where it caused a problem?

_____

_____

_____

_____

_____

_____

_____

Identify moments when you chose to avoid dialogue? Can you cite an example where this was helpful? Where it caused a problem?

_____

_____

_____

_____

_____

_____

Identify at least one improvement you can make in managing help through a change cycle.

_____

_____

_____

_____

_____

_____

_____

AFTERWORD

It is highly recommended that you talk through this change exercise with another person. The very process of articulating the issues at each stage of the change cycle affords a depth of understanding that is often greater than solitary reflection. The reciprocity created if the other person has also done the same exercise greatly enhances the quality of this exchange.

III WRITING YOUR PERSONAL NARRATIVE

A personal narrative is the story of your life from birth to the present that you tell yourself and recount in various versions to others. While writing your narrative is highly recommended, this is an advanced option that requires significant time and energy.

While writing your life story may appear to be an overwhelming task, almost every individual finds it to be a powerful life experience. Many have told me in similar terms, "This was a gift to myself." You may not see yourself as a writer. You may not even enjoy writing. But the very act of writing provides a focus that triggers memory and forces clarity in telling a personal story. This is the opportunity to tell your life story from your own perspective.

Writing your own narrative is a unique opportunity to reflect on the story about yourself that you have written over time. It is a chance to clarify the key questions of identity: Who am I? What are my dreams and possibilities? While this story is in continuous evolution, this exercise is an attempt to capture your present story at a point in time.

Global Cosmopolitans find this exercise particularly useful because they often feel that their lives are fragmented. Patterns emerge in this process to offer structure which may not be visible in observing individual episodes. The narrative offers the possibility of pulling the pieces together into a coherent, understandable account.

Step One: Write Your Story

People often ask, "How long should the story be?" While I usually suggest a length of about twenty-five double-spaced pages, many react that this seems impossibly long. Often, these same people end up finding it challenging to tell their story in *only* twenty-five pages.

Others ask, "Which language?" Since this is a story for you, use the languages that help you tell the story, in terms of events, people and emotions. You can switch languages as you see fit. If you decide to share the story with another person, you can always work on the translation.

With all your daily pressures, it's hard to step back and reflect on your life in an organized way. Begin by finding time and space to write. Some people need to work alone; others prefer to write in the company of someone else writing their own story. You might need to talk to other people to help fill in the details. Some people find writing easier if they pretend someone is interviewing them or if they are writing this as a letter to a special friend. You might be tempted to stop and analyze, but at this stage just let the story flow. If you need to analyze, put your notes in another document for later.

Start your narrative with your earliest memories and quickly move on to parts of your life that have particular importance for you. Some people find it useful, for example, to focus on significant events in childhood and early adolescence. Others prefer to emphasize life after secondary school or university. Make sure you spend time as well looking at the more recent events in your life. The detailed recounting of significant events will serve well in deriving learning from the narrative.

Certain episodes are easier to recount than others. Yet, sometimes, painful times are what need exploration the most. You might save the detailed development of such issues in your story for later. By at least recognizing these areas, you have taken a first step. Eventually you might feel more comfortable to explore these incidents or find another framing that more easily allows exposition. If you trip on difficult issues, it can be extremely useful to consider what your resources are for exploring these issues with guidance and support.

At first, do not worry about writing a well-constructed story. Just write! This narrative is your chance to concentrate on finding your own voice. Capturing the complexity of your experience might seem impossible, but remember that this is a work in progress, the latest version of your story.

The key action is to sit down for at least two hours at a time and begin writing, typing or, at the very least, taping your story. Faced with this exercise, some people suddenly have a strong need to organize their desk, make a phone call or do anything to avoid the task at hand. Turn off the phone and the television and give yourself the gift of some time with the story of your own personal journey. It will certainly take more than one sitting, so set aside at least two or three times when you can write.

Step Two: What Can You Learn from Reading Your Story?

Once you have finished writing, take an extended break to allow some distance from what you have written. Remember that every re-reading is an opportunity to see your story from a different perspective. The analysis of patterns from the story is best addressed at first by reading it alone. Subsequently, reading the story aloud to a trusted person will often yield additional insights both from the other person's perspective and from the very act of reading aloud.

Looking for Patterns

The reading of stories allows the opportunity to see patterns that emerge over time. First, see what appears to you in simply reading through the story. Remember to keep in mind that some patterns might be in the past and have been put to rest, while other patterns might be emerging. Remember, this is your story and you are in charge of the analysis. The following questions may help you frame other themes and patterns in the narrative.

What Was Included and What Was Left Out

As you read through your story, look at what you have chosen to include as well as what you chose to leave out.

- Did you choose to write about the difficult periods, when you failed or when you encountered considerable loss or upheaval? Did you choose to write about the successful moments or when you were happy and energized? What is the balance?
- Were you able to capture your emotions as you told the story? Have you focused only on the external view of events rather than incorporating your reactions and feelings?
- What part of your life got the most attention and why? Are there time spans that have been completely left out?

Turning Points

Given that you have already completed the lifeline exercise, do you have a better understanding of turning points, their impact and the lessons that you learned? You may choose to revisit that exercise to reflect on any differences between these two representations.

Skill Development

What patterns of skill development can you see in your story?

- Learning Opportunities: When and how do you learn new skills? Are you able to adapt previously developed skills to deal with new situations?
- What were the skills developed over the course of this narrative that allowed recovery from painful incidents or transitions?

Themes That Describe You: Getting Closer to Your Identity Story

While you might feel like there is more than one story you could have written, it can be helpful to look through this story to capture the key themes in how you present yourself. Try to identify eight to ten themes that describe the person you are in this presentation.

Relationship to Change over a Lifetime

What are the patterns that describe your relationship to change?

- Do you feel like change happens to you or that you are the one that make change happen?
- Where do you get stuck in the change process?
- Have you improved in managing change?

IV   CREATING DIALOGUE

As discussed earlier, it is very useful to share your story with others. Friends and family will appreciate the opportunity to hear about you and your perceptions of any shared history. Listening to what surprises them and draws their attention will give you some insight into their assumptions about you and the impact that you might have had on them. In some cases this might create the appropriate setting to discuss important decisions that you have to make together.

If given the opportunity, others will also be able to add stories that you might not remember or might have perceived differently. Sharing your own analysis of the personal narrative can also provide interesting learning. The patterns which others see may vary significantly from those you have drawn in your own assessment. In addition, others may add anecdotes which support their views and provide richness to your own understanding. While it is your story, and it is up to you to pull the threads of your life together, it can be eye opening to see how other people can take the same information and pull it together in a different way. It might help you see what you need to do to complete the telling of your story so that another person can understand what you are trying to communicate.

If you have the opportunity to share your story with another person who is doing the same exercise, it is quite informative even if they have had limited interaction with you previously. This exchange will then be focused more clearly on the personal narrative and allow a chance to test your own understanding of your work. This can provide a very different perspective.

If there are private pieces of your narrative, you do not necessarily have to share them. Some individuals "test" the willingness of others to engage before revealing issues which may feel more sensitive or conflictual. The quality of the discussion is obviously a function of the trust that can be created with another or the group you are engaging.

V THE NEXT CHAPTER

As a final exercise, draft the next chapter in your life story. Though this is a serious exercise, let yourself have fun, thinking about what you would really like your life to look like in five years.

This exercise calls for your imagination and creativity. To get started you might want to draw a picture of what your office or home might look like in five years. This is designed to move you from an analytical mode to a more imaginative and creative approach.

Then take some time to describe in writing your imagined life at this future date. Pay attention to some of the details which will indicate the positive quality of this new existence. In addition, describe some of the key actions and milestones that have brought you to this new life.

Some questions that you might want to consider are:

- Where would you like to be living?
- Who would you like to be living with?
- What are the major elements of your professional life? How are these different from your current situation?
- What has changed in your social context?
- What were the key steps that permitted you to arrive at this new life space?
- Who were some key individuals who helped you make this transition?

While this exercise is playing with imagination, it might result in setting a goal and initiating at least one step, if not multiple steps, in that direction. Imagining the possible is a major motivation for getting there. Make sure you save the story to look at in a couple of years.

AFTERWORD

You have just completed a journey of reflection and discovery. If you have followed through the entire program of exercises and personal narrative, you have invested a substantial amount of time and energy. I hope that, like many others who have already traveled this route, you have found this to be an enlightening and energizing experience. It is quite normal that the process of writing and analyzing your story will trigger strong emotions linked to the insights and discoveries. Should this prove personally disconcerting and you have no one in your personal network with whom you could comfortably discuss your concerns, this might be a time to consider pursuing these issues with professional help.

However, almost all people find that these reflections trigger new and better relations with family and friends as the stories and insights are shared with a broader group. New revelations emerge from people saying, "I didn't know that..." or "I was surprised as I always thought that..."

Hang onto the document. People have told me that they have used it in many ways. Some have used it as a basis to start a therapy or coaching relationship. Many people have used it as a vehicle to start interesting and important family discussions. Many say they take a look at it every few years to add a chapter or two. There was even a group of alumni from INSEAD that revisited their stories at a twenty-year reunion.

With these thoughts, I am concluding this book. Thank you for embarking on this journey with me. Now it is up to you to write the next chapter.

NOTES

CHAPTER 1. INTRODUCING GLOBAL COSMOPOLITANS

1   For more about Carlos Ghosn, see the Encyclopedia of World Biography supplement, from which much of the information presented here was taken: http://www.notablebiographies.com/supp/Supplement-Fl-Ka/Ghosn-Carlos.html.

2   Unless otherwise indicated, all biographical information in this section comes from Barack Obama's autobiography, *Dreams from My Father*.

3   Nobel Peace Prize 2009 press release: http://nobelprize.org/nobel_prizes/peace/laureates/2009/press.html.

4   Ruth E. Van Reken, "Obama's 'Third Culture' Team."

CHAPTER 2. INSIDE THE NEW GLOBAL COSMOPOLITAN GENERATION

1   Barack Obama, *Dreams from My Father*.

2   There are a number of outstanding books on the narrative study of lives, including Mary Catherine Bateson, *Composing a Life*; *Peripheral Visions*; and *Willing to Learn*; Ruthellen Josselson, *Revising Herself*; Dan P. McAdams, *Power, Intimacy, and the Life Story*; *The Stories We Live By*; and *Turns in the Road*.

3   Ruthellen Josselson, *Revising Herself*, p. 27.

4   Robert Brooks and Sam Goldstein, *The Power of Resilience*, p. 3.

CHAPTER 3. LEARNING FROM A GLOBAL LIFE: DEVELOPING THE CREATIVE EDGE OF DIFFERENCE

1   Howard Gardner, *Multiple Intelligences*.

2   The adaptive capacity has been written about in a variety of books, including Carl Folke, Johan Colding and Fikret Berkes, *Navigating Social-Ecological Systems*; Yves Doz and Mikko Kosonen, *The Fast Strategy*; Warren G. Bennis and Robert J. Thomas, *Geeks and Geezers*; Ron Heifetz and Marty Linsky, *Leadership on the Line*.

3   Self-efficacy is described extensively by Albert Bandura in *Self-Efficacy: The Exercise of Control* and *Self-Efficacy in Changing Societies.*

4   Interesting work is being done on cognitive complexity in the literature on biculturalism. See, for example, V. Benet Martinez, F. Lee and J. Leu, "Biculturalism and Cognitive Complexity."

5   Rosabeth Moss Kanter, "Shake Your Kaleidoscope and Find Innovations."

6   Mary Catherine Bateson, *Peripheral Visions.*

7   Paolo Freire, *Pedagogy of the Oppressed.*

8   Works on the Global Mindset include Anil K. Gupta and Vijay Govindarajan, "Cultivating a Global Mindset"; Hal Gregersen, Allen J. Morrison and J. Stewart Black, "Developing Leaders for the Global Frontier"; Orly Levy, Schon Beechler, Sully Talor and Nakiye A. Boyacigiller, "What We Talk About When We Talk About 'Global Mindset'."

CHAPTER 4. LIFE CHALLENGES AND THE ROAD TO IDENTITY

1   William Bridges, *The Way of Transition*, pp. 2–3.

CHAPTER 5. RELATIONSHIP CHALLENGES: INVISIBLE RULES, SILENT VOICES

1   A recent and interesting reference is Shinobu Kitayama, Hyekyung Park, A. Timur Sevincer, Mayumi Karasawa and Ayse K. Uskil, "A Cultural Task Analysis of Implicit Independence."

CHAPTER 6. RELATIONSHIP CHALLENGES: CONNECTION AND DISCONNECTION

1   On the relational perspective, see Judith V. Jordan, *Relational-Cultural Therapy*; Judith V. Jordan, Maureen Walker and Linda M. Hartling, *The Complexity of Connection*; Jean Baker Miller, *The Healing Connection*; Christina Robb, *This Changes Everything.*

CHAPTER 9. MOVING FORWARD: A PORTRAIT OF TWO CRUCIAL DECADES

1   Daniel Levinson, *The Seasons of a Man's Life* and *The Seasons of a Woman's Life.*

2   Gail Sheehy, *Passages.*

NOTES

THE GLOBAL COSMOPOLITAN WORKBOOK

1   See Monica McGoldrick, Randy Gerson and Sylvia Shellenberger, *Genograms*. McGoldrick, Gerson and Shellenberger developed and popularized genograms. Search online for additional resources.

2   See Helen Rose Fuchs Ebaugh, *Becoming an Ex*.

BIBLIOGRAPHY

BOOKS

Appiah, Kwame Anthony, *Cosmopolitanism*, New York: W.W. Norton and Co., 2006.

Appiah, Kwame Anthony, *The Ethics of Identity*, Princeton, NJ: Princeton University Press, 2005.

Bandura, Albert, *Self-Efficacy: The Exercise of Control*, New York: W.H. Freeman, 1997.

Bandura, Albert, *Self-Efficacy in Changing Societies*, Cambridge: Cambridge University Press, 1997.

Bartlett, Christopher and Ghoshal, Sumantra, *Managing across Borders: The Transnational Solution*, Boston, MA: Harvard Business School Press, 1989.

Bateson, Mary Catherine, *Composing a Life*, New York: Plume, 2001.

Bateson, Mary Catherine, *Peripheral Visions*, New York: Harper Collins, 1995.

Bateson, Mary Catherine, *Willing to Learn: Passages of Personal Discovery*, Hanover, NH: Steerforth Press, 2004.

Bennis, Warren G. and Thomas, Robert J., *Geeks and Geezers: How Era, Values and Defining Moments Shape Leaders*, Boston, MA: Harvard Business School Press, 2002.

Bridges, William, *Transitions: Makings Sense of Life's Changes*, Cambridge, MA: Da Capo Press, 2004.

Bridges, William, *The Way of Transition: Embracing Life's Most Difficult Moments*, Cambridge, MA: Perseus Books, 2001.

Brooks, Robert and Goldstein, Sam, *The Power of Resilience*, New York: McGraw-Hill, 2004.

Bruner, Jerome, *Acts of Meaning*, Cambridge, MA: Harvard University Press, 1990.

Bruner, Jerome, *Making Stories*, Cambridge, MA: Harvard University Press, 2002.

Butler, Timothy, *Getting Unstuck: How Dead Ends Become New Paths*, Boston, MA: Harvard Business School Press, 2007.

Doz, Yves and Kosonen, Mikko, *The Fast Strategy: How Strategic Agility Will Help You Stay ahead of the Game*, Philadelphia, PA: Wharton School Publishing, 2008.

Erikson, Erik, *Identity and the Life Cycle*, New York: W.W. Norton and Co., 1980 (originally published 1959).

Evans, Paul, Pucik, Vladimir and Björkman, Ingmar, *The Global Challenge: International Human Resource Management*, 2nd Edition, New York: McGraw-Hill/Irwin, 2010.

Fivush, Robyn and Haden, A. Catherine, *Autobiographical Memory and the Construction of a Narrative Self*, Mahwah, NJ: Lawrence Erlbaum Associates, 2003.

Folke, Carl, Colding, Johan and Berkes, Fikret, *Navigating Social-Ecological Systems: Building Resilience for Complexity and Change*, Cambridge: Cambridge University Press, 2008.

Freeman, Jill and Combs, Gene, *Narrative Therapy*, New York: W.W. Norton and Co., 1996.

Freire, Paolo, *Pedagogy of the Oppressed*, New York: Herder and Herder, 1971.

Fuchs Ebaugh, Helen Rose, *Becoming an Ex: The Process of Role Exit*, Chicago: University of Chicago Press, 1988.

Gardner, Howard, *5 Minds for the Future*, Boston, MA: Harvard Business School Press, 2008.

Gardner, Howard, *Changing Minds: The Art and Science of Changing Our Own and Other People's Minds*, Boston, MA: Harvard Business School Press, 2004.

Gardner, Howard, *Leading Minds*, New York: Basic Books, 1995.

Gardner, Howard, *Multiple Intelligences: The Theory in Practice*, New York: Basic Books, 1993.

Gladwell, Malcolm, *Blink: The Power of Thinking without Thinking*, New York: Little, Brown and Co., 2005.

Gould, Roger L., *Transformations: Growth and Change in Adult Life*, New York: Simon & Schuster, 1978.

Harvey, Mary R. and Tummala-Narra, Pratyusha, *Sources and Expressions of Resiliency in Trauma Survivors: Multicultural Practice*, London: Routledge, 2007.

Heifetz, Ron and Linsky, Marty, *Leadership on the Line*, Boston, MA: Harvard Business School Press, 2002.

Ibarra, Herminia, *Working Identity*, Boston, MA: Harvard Business School Press, 2004.

Jordan, Judith V., *Relational-Cultural Therapy (Theories of Psychotherapy)*, Washington, DC: American Psychological Association, 2010.

Jordon, Judith V., Walker, Maureen and Hartling, Linda M., *The Complexity of Connection*, New York: Guilford Press, 2004.

Josselson, Ruthellen, *Revising Herself: The Story of Women's Identity from College to Midlife*, New York: Oxford University Press, 1996.

Kanter, Rosabeth Moss, *World Class: Thriving Locally in the Global Economy*, New York: Simon & Schuster, 1995.

Kegan, Robert, *The Evolving Self: Problem and Process in Human Development*, Cambridge, MA: Harvard University Press, 1982.

Kotre, John N., *White Gloves: How We Create Ourselves through Memory*, New York: W.W. Norton and Co., 1996.

Langer, Ellen J., *The Power of Mindful Learning*, Reading, MA: Perseus Books, 1997.

Levinson, Daniel J., *The Seasons of a Man's Life*, New York: Knopf, 1978.

Levinson, Daniel J., *The Seasons of a Woman's Life*, New York: Random House, 1997.

Lieblich, Amia, McAdams, Dan P. and Josselson, Ruthellen, *Healing Plots: The Narrative Basis of Psychotherapy*, Wasington, DC: American Psychological Association, 2004.

Maalouf, Amin, *On Identity*, London: Harvill Press, 2000.

Mainiero, Lisa A. and Sullivan, Sherry E., *The Opt-Out Revolt: Why People Are Leaving Companies to Create Kaleidoscope Careers*, Mountain View, CA: Davies-Black Publishing, 2006.

McAdams, Dan P., *Power, Intimacy, and the Life Story*, New York: Guilford Press, 1988.

McAdams, Dan P., *The Stories We Live By: Personal Myths and the Making of the Self*, New York: W. Morrow, 1993.

McAdams, Dan P., *Turns in the Road*, Washington, DC: American Psychological Association, 2001.

McGoldrick, Monica, Gerson, Randy and Shellenberger, Sylvia, *Genograms: Assessment and Intervention*, 2nd Edition, New York: W.W. Norton and Co., 1997.

Miller, Jean Baker, *The Healing Connection: How Women Form Relationships in Therapy and in Life*, Boston, MA: Beacon, 1997.

Mishler, Elliot G., *Storylines*, Cambridge, MA: Harvard University Press, 1999.

Obama, Barack, *Dreams from My Father*, New York: Three Rivers Press, 1995, 2004.

Pollock, David C. and Van Reken, Ruth E., *Third Culture Kids*, Yarmouth, ME: Nicholas Brealey Publishing, 2001.

Riessman, Catherine Kohler, *Narrative Methods for the Human Sciences*, Thousand Oaks, CA: Sage Publications, 2008.

Robb, Christina, *This Changes Everything: The Relational Revolution in Psychology*, New York: Farrar, Strauss & Giroux, 2006.

Rogers, Carl R., *On Becoming a Person*, New York: Houghton Mifflin, 1961.

Sarup, Madan, *Identity, Culture and the Post-Modern World*, Edinburgh: Edinburgh University Press, 1996.

Schein, Edgar H., *Career Anchors: Rediscovering Your Real Values*, Revised Edition, San Diego, CA: University Associates, 1990.

Schein, Edgar H., *Helping*, San Francisco: Berett-Koehler Publishers, 2009.

Schein, Edgar H., *Process Consultation Revisited: Building the Helping Relationship*, New York: Addison Wesley, 1998.

Sheehy, Gail, *Passages: Predictable Crises of Adult Life*, New York: Bantam Books, 1976.

Sternberg, Robert J. (ed.), *Handbook of Creativity*, Cambridge: Cambridge University Press, 1999.

Tichy, Noel M. and Bennis, Warren G., *Judgment: How Winning Leaders Make Great Calls*, New York: Penguin, 2007.

Tichy, Noel M., McGill, Andrew R. and St. Clair, Lynda (eds.), *Corporate Global Citizenship Doing Business in the Public Eye*, San Francisco: New Lexington Press, 1997.

White, Michael and Epston, David, *Narrative Means to Therapeutic Ends*, New York: W.W. Norton and Co., 1990.

Zander, Rosamund Stone and Zander, Benjamin, *The Art of Possibility*, Boston, MA: Harvard Business School Press, 2000.

ARTICLES

Benet Martinez, V., Lee, F. and Leu, J., "Biculturalism and Cognitive Complexity: Expertise in Cultural Representations," *Journal of Cross Cultural Psychology*, 2006, 37, 386–407.

Briley, Donnel, Morris, Michael and Simonson, Itamar, "Cultural Chameleons: Biculturals, Conformity Motives, and Decision Making," *Journal of Consumer Psychology*, 2005, 15 (4), 351–362.

Gregersen, Hal, Morrison, Allen J. and Black, J. Stewart, "Developing Leaders for the Global Frontier," *Sloan Management Review*, 1998, 40 (1), 1998, 21–32.

Gupta, Anil K. and Govindarajan, Vijay, "Cultivating a Global Mindset," *Academy of Management Executive*, 2002, 16 (1), 116–126.

Haas, Martine, "Acquiring and Applying Knowledge in Transnational Teams: The Roles of Cosmopolitans and Locals," *Organizational Science*, 2006, 17 (3), 367–384.

Kanter, Rosabeth Moss, "Shake Your Kaleidoscope and Find Innovations," http://www.reinventingeducation.org/RE3Web/newsletters/20050401/article01.htm.

Kitayama, Shinobu, Park, Hyekyung, Sevincer, A. Timur, Karasawa, Mayumi and Uskil, Ayse K., "A Cultural Task Analysis of Implicit Independence: Comparing North America, Western Europe, and East Asia," *Journal of Personality and Social Psychology*, 2009, 97 (2), 236–255.

Levy, Orly, Beechler, Schon, Taylor, Sully and Boyacigiller, Nakiye A., "What We Talk About When We Talk About 'Global Mindset': Managerial Cognition in Multinational Corporations," *Journal of International Business Studies*, 2007, 38, 231–258.

Markus, Hazel and Kitayama, Shinobu, "Culture and the Self: Implications for Cognition, Emotion, and Motivation," *Psychological Review*, 1991, 98 (2), 224–253.

Markus, Hazel and Nurius, Paula, "Possible Selves," *American Psychologist*, 1986, 41 (9), 954–969.

Van Reken, Ruth E., "Obama's 'Third Culture' Team," http://www.thedailybeast.com/blogs-and-stories/2008-11-26/obamas-third-culture-team.

INDEX

NOTE: Page references in **bold** refer to self-assessment exercises in the Workbook.